The publisher and the University of California Press Foundation gratefully acknowledge the generous support of the Philip E. Lilienthal Imprint in Asian Studies, established by a major gift from Sally Lilienthal.

Silence and Sacrifice

Silence and Sacrifice

FAMILY STORIES OF CARE AND THE
LIMITS OF LOVE IN VIETNAM

Merav Shohet

UNIVERSITY OF CALIFORNIA PRESS

University of California Press
Oakland, California

© 2021 by Merav Shohet

Library of Congress Cataloging-in-Publication Data

Names: Shohet, Merav, 1976- author.
Title: Silence and sacrifice : family stories of care and the limits of love in
    Vietnam / Merav Shohet.
Description: Oakland, California : University of California Press, [2021] |
    Includes bibliographical references and index.
Identifiers: LCCN 2020039780 (print) | LCCN 2020039781 (ebook) |
    ISBN 9780520379374 (cloth) | ISBN 9780520379381 (paperback) |
    ISBN 9780520976702 (ebook)
Subjects: LCSH: Families—Moral and ethical aspects—Vietnam. |
    Sacrifice—Vietnam. | Love—Vietnam.
Classification: LCC HQ674.5 .S56 2021 (print) | LCC HQ674.5 (ebook) |
    DDC 306.8509597—dc23
LC record available at https://lccn.loc.gov/2020039780
LC ebook record available at https://lccn.loc.gov/2020039781

Manufactured in the United States of America

30 29 28 27 26 25 24 23 22 21
10 9 8 7 6 5 4 3 2 1

For Etan, and for all your grandparents and ancestors

Contents

Illustrations

Acknowledgments

"It takes a village" is the phrase that best characterizes the writing of this book. Long ago conceived as an attempt to understand family, virtue, sacrifice, and loss in Vietnam, it took many people across countries and continents to bring to fruition. I am most grateful to all the families and my many friends and interlocutors in Vietnam. From the minute I set foot in their homes, and long after, when our contacts were sometimes only intermittent Facebook chats, they treated me with warmth, patience, and kindness that I never felt I fully deserved. Giving their consent and trust to an inquisitive foreigner to enter their lives and intimately observe and participate in their cares was an act of courage, faith, and generosity that I can never repay. To protect everyone's confidentiality, I use pseudonyms throughout and refrain from naming anyone in Vietnam, but I hope that everyone—whether in Đà Nẵng, Quảng Nam, Huế, Hanoi, or Saigon—knows who they are and how I continue to cherish them. I am also deeply grateful to the directors and staff of the College of Foreign Languages in Đà Nẵng and the Institute for Family and Gender Studies and the Vietnamese Language Center in Hanoi for facilitating and vouching for the success of my research projects in the mid-2000s. I continue to carry my *ơn* to all of you in Vietnam with humility, hoping that the present volume justly represents even a fraction of all that I learned from you.

Fieldwork was supported by the Social Science Research Council and Andrew W. Mellon International Dissertation Research Fellowship Program (SSRC-IDRF), the Fulbright-Hays Dissertation Research Abroad (DDRA) program, the Pacific Rim Research Program, the UC Pacific Rim Mini-Grant program; the UCLA Asia Institute Hiroshi Wagatsuma fellowship program, the US Department of Education–UCLA Center for Southeast Asian Studies academic year and summer FLAS fellowships, and the Sloan Center on the Everyday Lives of Families Graduate Research fellowships. Writeup, starting with the dissertation and ending in a book that shares little with it, was supported by UCLA Department of Anthropology and Graduate Division Cota Robles grants, the Centre for Ethnography at the University of Toronto, and Boston University College of Arts and Sciences startup funds and UROP mentorships that allowed me to work with fabulous student research assistants Chau (Lisa) Vu and Katharine Draisen. *Silence and Sacrifice* would not have been possible without these institutional supports or the able Vietnamese language instruction that I received from thầy Bình, thầy Tín, thầy Bắc, thầy Hoà, and cô Thuý Anh at Harvard, UCLA, SEASSI, and VASI and the enduring friendship and help of cô Thuý Anh, Huy, An, and Leo Nguyễn.

My mentors, teachers, colleagues, and friends at UCLA left an indelible mark, as did many others throughout this journey. Ellie Ochs, who became my academic mother and dissertation cochair, nurtured me and the project out of which this book grew long before it was even a seedling and through to the final draft. I am exceptionally fortunate to have entered her orbit during my first year in graduate school; her boundless generosity, tenderness, and wisdom as a mentor, coauthor, and friend are qualities that I can only strive to emulate. Linda Garro, Doug Hollan, Alessandro Duranti, Carole Browner, Jason Throop, Candy and Chuck Goodwin, Thu-hương Nguyễn-võ, Paul Kroskrity, Yunxiang Yan, and George Dutton served as official or unofficial committee members, teachers, and/or inspirational figures whose modes of thinking and questioning course throughout the present book. I appreciate to no end their diverse ways of modeling academic rigor, mentorship, and friendship. The same goes for the many graduate students or postdocs with whom I overlapped, some only for a semester. Justin, Jason, Kevin, Keith, Kathy, Lesley, Laura, Amy, Tami, Olga, Carolina, Eileen, Sarah W., Anthony, Anjali, Angela, and Anja all served as sage elder siblings whom I looked up to and admired. Likewise, Heather, Katie, Brent, Steve, Michael, Cre, Mara, Hanna, Anna, Kristin, Inma, Robin, Netta, Sonya, and Ann Walters, Paul Connor, Harry, and Tracy Humbert: thank you for being there at key junctures along the way. Keith, Jason, Justin, Maggie, Mara, and Heather: your brilliance and encouragement sustained me many times over many years.

At the University of Toronto, where I was a postdoctoral fellow at the Centre for Ethnography and later a lecturer, Michael Lambek and Donna Young, together with Sam Bamford, Katie Kilroy-Marac, Bianca Dahl, Alejandro Paz, Dan Bender, Jo Sharma, Mary Silcox, Andrea Muehlebach, Sarah Hillewaert, and Jack Sidnell, engendered belonging despite academic precarity. I am especially grateful to the women's writing group, intellectual stimulation from all the faculty and students of UTSC and St. George, and the delights and warmth of the Culinaria Research Centre. If I am a better thinker, writer, and teacher, it is thanks to the many experiences and resources encountered here. Equally nourishing were Jerry and Amee, An and Leo, Saul, Tessa, Naomi, Sonya, Laura, Sarit, Carole, Ari, Audrey, Francesca, Steve Cooper, David Gale, and Rabbi Micah.

I am also exceedingly grateful for the vibrant and growing community of Vietnam scholars who pushed me, directly through supportive dialogue or indirectly through their writing, to hone my ideas and deepen the ethnography. At different stages, I especially appreciated comments from Hy Van Luong, Hue Tam Ho Tai, Ann Marie Leshkowich, Christina Schwenkel, and Erik Harms, and there are many others to thank besides. Similarly for too many colleagues, mentors, and friends in psychological, medical, and linguistic anthropology: I hope you all know who you are! Finally, transitioning to Boston University has been a most fortuitous event in my life, and I am deeply grateful to all my colleagues in the Department of Anthropology, to chairs Tom Barfield and Nancy Smith-Hefner, mentor Rob Weller, the wonderous Veronica Little, and deans Nancy Ammerman, Anne Cudd, Nazli Kibria, and Stan Sclaroff for supporting my work.

Many colleagues and students at BU and beyond helped make the writing process both rewarding and pleasurable. I am especially indebted to

Annemarie Samuels, who since our coffee in Brookline in 2017, following Yael Assor's introduction in New Orleans, became a cherished and generous friend and a constant source of inspiration, insight, and support. She read each chapter multiple times, tirelessly commenting on successive drafts and giving me the courage to go on when I felt like giving up. Kimberly Arkin and Allen Tran also have been treasured friends whose wry humor and critical comments on multiple chapter drafts pushed me to hone and restructure certain arguments, while Rob Weller helped allay my fears and live with prose that was just good enough. Ellie Ochs performed magical editing work on several of the chapters and Sharon Abramowitz on an early iteration of the introduction. A number of other mentors, friends, students, and relatives, including Anu Ahmed, Ekaterina Anderson, Barry Cohen, Katie Draisen, Lisa Friedland, Adam Kuper, Chuck Lindholm, Keith Murphy, Dat Nguyen, Harriet Phinney, Cat Scaramelli, Annika Schmeding, Insa Schmidt, Orna Shohet, Revital Shohet, Jessica Simes, and Elanah Uretsky, commented on at least one of the book chapters. Writing boot camp partnerships with Annemarie Samuels, April Hughes, Saida Grundy, Ben Siegel, Cat Scaramelli, Jessica Simes, Cati Connell, Paula Austin, Dana Moss, and Sultan Doughan kept me on track during key writing spurts, as did the friendship of Insa Schmidt, Heather Loyd, and Maggie and Ned Blackhawk. Thank you all for countless conversations, company, and more.

I also greatly benefited from the questions and input of audiences at the University of Sydney Anthropology of Language in Mainland Southeast Asia Workshop; Leiden University's International Institute for Asian Studies Lunch Lecture Series; UCLA's Mind, Medicine, and Culture Seminar and the Experiencing (In)Competence Symposium in Honor of Elinor Ochs; UCSD's Psychological and Medical Anthropology Lunch Seminar group; Hebrew University of Jerusalem's Matter for Change working group; Boston University's Tertulia dinner talks and anthropology department Lunch Series; the University of Michigan at Ann Arbor Center for Southeast Asia Studies Lecture Series; the University of Toronto Centre for Ethnography and Sociocultural and Linguistic Anthropology working group; and the American Anthropology Association, Association for Asian Studies, European Association for Southeast Asian Studies, and Society for Psychological Anthropology meetings where I presented earlier iterations of my work. Each engagement prompted me to rethink the ethnographic snippets presented and reformulate how they fit in the present kaleidoscope. My work also profited from host or discussant comments by Laura Ahearn, Nir Avieli, Jennifer Cole, Tom Csordas, Ayala Fader, Janis Jenkins, John Lucy, Sarah Pinto, and Saiba Varma, in addition to those already named earlier.

I might never have had the courage to let go were it not for gentle or strident prodding by many of the people named (or not) above and the encouragement of my editor, Kate Marshall, and production manager, Julie Van Pelt. I am especially grateful to Ayala Fader and an anonymous University of California Press reviewer for providing generous and insightful reviews of my manuscript and to Enrique Ochoa-Kaup for stepping in when Kate was away. I am also grateful to my brother Gil and friend Ben Siegel, who helped format the figures and create the map, and I acknowledge with gratitude the permission of Penguin Random House LLC to use the epigraph in chapter 1 from Bảo Ninh, *The Sorrow of War: A Novel of North Vietnam* (1995), published by Pantheon Books, an imprint of Knopf Doubleday Publishing Group; the University of Chicago Press's permission to use the epigraph in chapter 2 from Paul Ricoeur *Time and Narrative*, vol. 3 (1990); and Wiley's permission to revise, borrow from, or build on selected materials I previously published in *American Anthropologist* 115, no. 2 (2013): 203–17; *American Ethnologist* 45, no. 1 (2018): 60–73; and *Ethos* 45, no. 4 (2017): 555–76.

My parents, Orna and Yuval Shohet, have been unfailingly supportive throughout, as have my siblings, Keren, Revital, and Gil, and many relatives in Israel, especially my grandmother Eliza and late grandmother Eta, and Huy's extended family in Boston and Vietnam, especially Vi, Phuong, Alan, and Anna. When I say it takes a village, I also directly thank Etan's teachers, friends, and their parents, especially Priya and Vikas, Chitra and Karthik, Dascha and Dru, Jaime and Ken, Katya and Daniel, Elizabeth and Rob, Claire and Steve, Karine and Jules, Maggie, Mei, Tanya Paris, and many others who helped along the way. Huy, thank you for sparking my interest in the project and for caring. I dedicate the book to Etan: I learned *tình cảm* last but not least from you, and I hope that this book may help you understand one day the many silences and sacrifices you have already learned to undertake.

Notes on Vietnamese and Transcription Conventions

Vietnamese is a tonal language consisting of six tones, with three main regional dialects (northern, southern, and central) and numerous local dialects, some of which do not always distinguish clearly between two of the tones or alternatively transpose different vowel clusters and/or consonant sounds. Vietnam's official script *(quốc ngữ)* is a Romanized (Latin) alphabet with additional diacritical marks to signify particular vowel qualities and all but the midlevel tone (which has no diacritics). Writing Vietnamese without these diacritics is similar to writing English without vowels, which would make reading many words ambiguous or difficult at best. I therefore use the diacritics in all but the most well known place-names: Vietnam, Saigon, Ho Chi Minh City, and Hanoi. Throughout the monograph, I italicize Vietnamese terms and, in an effort to maximize readability while affording readers some sense of the features of particular utterances, I adopt the conventions of many linguistic anthropological texts in using the following symbols to represent recorded speech.

Transcription Conventions

. . .	pause or trail-off by speaker
:	phonological elongation
–	speaker's self-interruption
=	no interval between turns
italics	speaker's emphasized utterance
bold	point of analytic interest
((comment))	nonverbal action and other comments by transcriber
[. . .]	omitted text
[word]	clarification by transcriber (e.g., elided pronouns, dialect vs. standard Vietnamese)

Prologue

LANDING

It was midnight, February 12, 2007, when my fiancé Huy and I lifted our bags off the X-ray conveyer belt, counted them once more, and wheeled the load through automatic glass doors, past security guards. A throng of people surged around the wide pathway, greeting the newcomers, searching for relatives, friends, or taxicab clients. We proceeded forward, gingerly, tired, suddenly very hot. It was 77°F (25°C) outside, the sky dark but clear. I had arrived by taxi at Boston's Logan airport forty-six hours earlier, the crisp air there a bone-chilling 15°F (-9°C).

From the corner of his eye Huy spotted his stepmother's nephew, Huân.[1] The skeletal youth in baggy jeans and pink-striped button-down shirt waved at us, his face beaming. We greeted, shook hands, and were soon aboard a six-seat taxi, the suitcases piled on at odd angles as we headed to Huân's home in a narrow alleyway in Saigon. He led the way on his scooter, the taxi driver following close behind. I felt guilty imposing on Huân's mother this late at night, but no argument could be made. Family is family, no matter how distant. *Especially* when their family was so very distant. We were their connection to "out there" *(bên kìa)*.

All of Huân's paternal aunts and uncles immigrated to the United States in the early 1990s, after Huân's grandfather, who had fought alongside the

1

Americans for the Republic of Vietnam (commonly known as the South), returned home a broken man in the 1980s. For years following the victory of the Democratic Republic of Vietnam (DRV, known as the North) over the South, which resulted in the country's reunification in 1975, Huân's grandfather languished in a Communist "reeducation camp" in the North. Unlike many of Vietnam's "boat people"—refugees largely from central and southern Vietnam who tried to flee the country in the years after the South's defeat—Huân's grandfather was able to leave, together with his wife and unmarried children, under the auspices of Vietnam's Humanitarian Operation (H.O.) agreement with the United States, which allowed former reeducation inmates to depart legally. Throughout the late 1970s and 1980s, refugees risked drowning at sea, pursued by Vietnam's navy or, once far enough offshore, being attacked by pirates before finally reaching resettlement camps in Malaysia, Thailand, or the Philippines. From there, they might gain entry to the United States, Canada, Australia, or one of several European countries that accepted them.[2] As part of Vietnam's warming relations with its former foe, the H.O. agreement was meant to reduce the number of boat people refugees.

Since he was already married and had a child, Huân's father was not granted a visa to leave Vietnam. He had since died of cancer, but Huân, his mother Su, and sister Xuân kept in intermittent contact with their relatives abroad. Now, fifteen years after these relatives' departure, we visited their home in Saigon before Huy would deposit me in Đà Nẵng to begin my research. There, too, I would encounter many families whose relatives had resettled in the United States, whether as boat people or as H.O. beneficiaries. Like Huân's family, they counted on or yearned for relatives abroad to send remittances that helped with daily life and larger aspirations. Most of the time, they made do with the resources they had at hand at home, forging a life together.

Huân's widowed mother greeted us warmly, all smiles, a rapid stream of Saigonese talk engulfing my ears, my eyelids fighting to stay open, my brain pumping with concentration. We piled our luggage against the wall, alongside the two motor scooters, on the cool, gleaming tiled floor of their newly rebuilt house, and were invited to sit down. Huy's friendly cô (Auntie) affectionately punched him again and again while he updated her on her brothers- and sisters-in-law. He assured her of their health and gently admitted to the deterioration of her father- and mother-in-law, who were now senile and weak and still living with their children and grandchildren in a comfortable house north of Boston. We took out of our bags the laptop computer and digital camera that Huân's uncle sent him. His mother and he both cooed with pleasure at these gifts from abroad, brought in along with my research equipment.[3]

It was well past one in the morning, and still the honking of horns outside was incessant, muted only slightly by the dark. My hosts insisted that we feast on greasy yellow noodles with beef and vegetables that Huân fetched from a street corner vendor before we could all finally retire to bed. Five hours later, I awoke from the sun's hot rays and the same blaring of horns, now compounded by hammers and drills working on the house next door. I was anxious to thank my hosts and move on to purchase tickets to my fieldwork destination, Đà Nẵng, a smaller, more provincial, coastal city in central Vietnam.

Since Huân felt more comfortable chauffeuring and talking with Huy on the back of his scooter, the two of them went to search for airplane tickets while I stayed at home to chat with Su.[4] I watched as she efficiently unfolded a metal table and placed it in front of the door, then laid it out with a vase of yellow flowers, fake paper money, an urn for incense sticks, rice bowls, chopsticks, a bowl of meat-stuffed bitter melon soup, and plates of fruit, greens, fried tofu, and fresh and fried spring rolls. It would be almost a full calendar year later before suddenly, as if slapped by déjà vu, I understood the significance of the end-of-year ritual that Su had so nonchalantly prepared. For me, this was just an ordinary Monday in early February. And though I knew that in a few days, the Lunar New Year (Tết), reputed to be the biggest, happiest, most anticipated and fondly remembered holiday in Vietnam, was to be celebrated, I wasn't yet feeling any sort of holiday spirit or reckoning time in the same way as my hosts.

In previous trips to Vietnam and in Vietnamese homes in the United States, I had seen tables laid out in a similar manner, prepared for one or another person's death anniversary. Invariably, there would be a large feast organized for the deceased's kin group and friends. Before lighting the incense and completing the ritual by murmuring an inaudible prayer, Su paused to fetch her granddaughter from the daycare facility nearby and then waited for her son and guest to return home. Mistakenly thinking that Su was preparing to quietly memorialize her dead husband, and more interested in child development, I diverted my attention to her adorable three-and-a-half-year-old granddaughter, Hạ, who was more talkative than the children I encountered during previous research trips. We played together in the living room (the motor scooter now parked in the 5-foot by 2-foot gated yard in front, to make room for the worship table) while Su busied herself in the kitchen.

After three hours of scouring the ticket agencies, Huân and Huy returned home, empty-handed and frustrated. They could secure neither plane nor train tickets to Đà Nẵng. Previous field trips had led me to believe that hardly anybody ever flies to Đà Nẵng. But I had never been in the country for *Tết*, the one time in Vietnam when all families reunite to worship their ancestors together, nor had I considered how real income had increased over the past five years. The economy was booming now that the United States and its allies had lifted the embargo and allowed Vietnam to enter the World Trade Organization (WTO) a few months earlier. A rapidly expanding middle class could now afford and was eager to fly, leaving us ticketless. Vietnam was no longer a poor country. And at *Tết*, especially, families united in their natal provinces.

Little Hạ clung to her uncle and his guest. She addressed them with the correct kinship terms unprompted, tacitly displaying her knowledge of and embeddedness in this hierarchical yet intimate system. Huân was *cậu* (maternal uncle), Huy was *chú* (literally, "paternal uncle," but more broadly used for any adult man slightly younger than one's own father), and I was *cô Mỹ* (American Auntie), which marked my foreignness. Showing off the beanie baby that I gave her, Hạ sat on her potty in the corner by the stairs and flashed her bright smile, squealing with delight at having her picture taken with Huân's new digital camera from Boston.

The next day, still without transportation to Đà Nẵng, I continued to learn the ways to a little girl's heart: photograph and video-record her as she plays.[5] As we ascended the three-story house's roof, where Huân showed off their new solar-heated water tank (another sign of the family's rising prosperity and attention to environmental sustainability), Hạ kept running to the railing, as though ready to jump, sending my heart lurching to my stomach. My worry was misplaced. Hạ's grandmother Su was always nearby, holding a bowl and spoon to feed her whenever Hạ deigned to take a bite and always ready to protect her from harms posed by the perilous roof or the scissors that moments earlier Hạ had used to cut out pictures from a magazine. As I would repeatedly observe throughout fieldwork, in contrast to the middle-class American homes I had previously studied,[6] there was no material evidence of child-proofing in this household: childrearing relied on cooperative and attentive orchestration rather than environmental design.

Unable to secure either plane or train tickets, we at last boarded a bus later that night, and three days after our initial arrival in Vietnam finally found ourselves in Đà Nẵng, a coastal city on the Hàn River, about 800 kilometers north of Ho Chi Minh City. Connecting the two cities is the long, winding Route 1A Highway, which snakes across mountains and along the coast, amid rice fields and fruit tree groves. All types of vehicles, from the long-distance bus we boarded to private taxis and cars to transport trucks, local buses, motor scooters, bicycles, carts and even cows and water buffalo, raced one another along the one- to two-lane road.

Groggy and wobbly from the twenty-four-hour bumpy bus ride, we checked into a small motel near the city's market by the river, then took a stroll through the darkened city center. It was not yet 11 p.m., but the streets seemed deserted, eerily quiet after the bustle of Saigon, Vietnam's unofficial southern capital. A faint stench rose from the fruits, flowers, banana leaf food wrappers, noodles, and other crumbs discarded along the road and alleyways, remnants of a busy trading day just two days short of Vietnamese New Year's Eve, which doubled, that year, as *ngày lễ Va-len-tin* (Valentine's Day). The holidays were a boon for florists and pastry shop owners and guaranteed to burn a small hole in upwardly mobile urbanite men's pockets.

A reminder of the newly celebrated Western holiday came earlier that day, when an unusually cuddly couple sitting on the bus bench to our left offered us a taste of their Dove chocolate bar. In return, all we could offer were answers to their questions, including how people celebrate love in the United States, where we were going, and why I—a freckled, olive-skinned, curly haired brunette—could converse with them in their language. The sun was still shining when they disembarked at a stop in

Quảng Ngãi province. They were returning, like millions of other non-Saigonese, to their families' homes in Vietnam's countryside. This province had been made infamous by the Americans' brutal massacres of civilians, as in the village of Sơn Mỹ (known to Americans as Mỹ Lai).[7] Weeks later, I made a pilgrimage to this village with my host mother and her colleagues, who solemnly commemorated their lost compatriots. As the couple departed, I was left contemplating a million questions about them and the new families I had come to study in postwar, late-socialist Vietnam. Anxious, filled with wonder and excitement, I let myself fall asleep, first on the bumpy bus and later that night in our chilled motel room.

Map 1. Map of Vietnam

Introduction

VIETNAM IS A COUNTRY, NOT A WAR

SACRIFICE IS MUTE AND SECRETIVE

This book is concerned with a basic human question: How do families hold together when turbulent forces threaten to tear them apart? In Vietnam, many families were split during years of civil war and anticolonial and anti-imperial struggles with the French and Americans. They reunited only after the wars ended with the Democratic Republic of Vietnam's victory and the collectivization of the economy under one-party Communist rule in 1975. Subsequently, liberalizing reforms initiated under the *đổi mới* (Renovation) policy of 1986 led Vietnam to embrace a "market economy with a socialist orientation" (*kinh tế thị trường định hướng xã hội chủ nghĩa,* or market socialism for short). The reforms culminated in Vietnam's admission to the World Trade Organization in 2007. Yet the nation's booming economy tested family unity once again, as opportunities differentially benefited members across generational and political strata, straining their ties.

In the face of such radical change, we might expect families to be irreparably fractured and public Confucian values—already challenged by the egalitarian ideals brought by the Communist Revolution—to be abandoned. I argue, however, that practices of "sacrifice" *(hy sinh)* and "love" *(tình cảm)* keep families knotted together. Any cohesion or continuity that families achieve, however, is precarious: it involves suffering and hard work to sustain and sometimes runs up against the limits of love.

Family members often repeat the refrain, "Respect those above, yield to those below" *(kính trên nhường dưới).* They suture this bidirectional notion of hierarchy to ideas of everyday acts of sacrifice, in which suffering is ideally shrouded in silence. Indeed, only silent sacrifice counts as moral care. The importance of ordinary, silent sacrifice was made explicit to me on an overcast day in June 2007, when I sat across from fifty-eight-year-old Loan in her spacious living room in Ho Chi Minh City (HCMC), sipping fresh-squeezed watermelon juice. Loan was a retired political cadre sent to the People's Republic of China for revolutionary Communist indoctrination at the age of seven. Her son now worked for a banking firm abroad, while she and her husband, Đan, made their new home in Saigon (as locals call HCMC), where Đan could continue working until sixty, the mandatory retirement age for men (women are required by law to retire at fifty-five).

A longtime colleague and close friend of my host mother in Đà Nẵng, where I was conducting ethnographic research, Loan had declared me to be "family" during our last outing in April and insisted that I visit her in Saigon. She reminded me of lessons I had learned from others living along Vietnam's central coast about sacrifice *(hy sinh).* It involves suffering in silence for the sake of intimate kin and it binds families together:

> Sacrifice refers to difficulties that [one] directs toward oneself, whereas when there's something advantageous [one] secures it for [one's] father, for [one's] mother, for [one's] husband and children ... Sacrifice doesn't just mean fighting in wars; the term includes a lot of meanings, so when you talk of sacrifice it means accepting suffering for oneself ... hoping that [the beneficiaries] don't know about your sacrifice, right? For example [if] you sacrifice but you have to say that you sacrifice that's really ugly ... Sacrifice is mute and secretive.

Loan's experience of separation from her family—both in her childhood and now as a parent watching her son advance a capitalist regime at odds with the socialist one she had spent her life defending—was not unique. From the minute that I landed in Vietnam (first in 2002 and during subsequent trips in 2004, 2005, and 2007–8), I encountered families whose members had fought on opposing sides of the war. Their seeming ease at reuniting puzzled and intrigued me, as did their constant invocation of the term *tình cảm,* which I learned refers to sentiments and acts of love and concern that motivate material aid and affective intimacy and care.[1] The research set out to understand what these terms mean and what work they perform in practice.

Vietnamese literary and national (public) discourses abidingly invoke the term *hy sinh* (sacrifice) to extol both patriotic (and masculinist) death in war and more muted everyday acts of care usually associated with women's devotion to their families.[2] In interviews, family members linked *hy sinh* to patriotic death in war, as elaborated in chapter 1. Yet, they hastened to add, "not only those who fought on the battlefront, but those who remained behind, they also were sacrificing." Even more frequently, they associated sacrifice with family roles that entail silence and moral care, as Loan had explained.

Everyday sacrifice, then, is both similar and dissimilar to ritual slaughter and patriotic devotion to the point of death. Like the canonical, publicly oriented forms of sacrifice that enact communion, quotidian sacrifice involves the moral modification or sacralization of the participants involved.[3] Yet quotidian sacrifice is also a continual, gendered practice, experience, and ethical orientation rooted in idealizations of love rather than primarily or only a discrete, irreversible, paradigmatically violent act. And in Vietnam, sacrifice is embedded in a social structure grounded in what I term "asymmetrical reciprocity": a set of bidirectional but asymmetrical relations that, in emphasizing both respect and yielding, steer family members to struggle to prove their *tình cảm* (loving sentiments premised on material relations of care) for one another. This (re)conceptualization of sacrifice beyond the ceremonial or heroic reframes one of anthropology's most hallowed concepts, to advance the "ethical turn" in anthropology,[4] by attending to a so far overlooked insight that emerges from the ethnography: gender and kinship are key dimensions of ethics. I use the tools of cultural, linguistic, and psychological anthropology to show how virtuous personhood is gendered and engendering and how hierarchical relations pervade and centrally organize webs of reciprocity.

The chapters that follow feature family members' accounts of love and loss, conflict and control in the ongoing rhythms of domestic life to tease out the contours of silent suffering in forging intergenerational continuity. Bridging the quotidian and the historical, *Silence and Sacrifice* considers fleeting instantiations of familial sacrifice within Vietnam's broader economic and biopolitical mission to improve the "quality" and well-being of the population.[5] Specifically, I consider how relatives navigate moral binds and entangled love relationships that arise against the backdrop of scars and long shadows cast by war, and from the daily challenges of maintaining ties within stratified households. Drawing on extensive participant observation and audio- and video-recorded interactions, the ethnography illuminates how quotidian sacrifices are embedded in mundane greeting practices; narrative accounts of personal experiences; the labor of taking care of children, spouses, the old, and the sick; efforts to discipline one's emotions to promote others' well-being; and enactments of elaborate ancestor worship. These practices flood families' daily rituals and form the heart of stories they recount about others to one another, (re)affirming love in life together. Though ostensibly banal, these interactional rituals constitute mechanisms through which kin achieve seeming equanimity and continuity in understandings and enactments of ethical personhood and (dis)affiliation with dominant Vietnamese state discourses about "social evils," "cultured happy families," and "modern love."

If I originally wanted to study the traumas and memories of war, time spent in Vietnam during the first decade of the twenty-first century indicated that what people were most concerned with was how to live morally in the present while orienting to a future where they would have to grapple with—and benefit from—a rapidly changing economy. This new economy was spearheaded by state bureaucrats as well as entrepreneurs envisioning new pathways for Vietnam to paradoxically embrace and abandon its collectivist (Confucian and then socialist) past. The prologue to this book, which describes my landing in Saigon and journey to Đà Nẵng in February 2007, as well as initial observations of love in a family's life, illustrates the exuberant rate of development and the ways that the past and future hung over families raising children in Vietnam at the time of this study.

Unlike other Vietnam ethnographies, *Silence and Sacrifice* is neither a Foucauldian story of the emerging, atomized neoliberal self in Vietnam nor an archival document of haunted yearnings for a past that may never have been.[6] I seek to understand the subjective lives of people inhabiting new marketizing conditions, especially how they forge a sense of continuity in these transforming circumstances.[7] The project builds on Helle Rydstrøm's (2003a) study of gendered moral socialization within families in Vietnam's northern rural region, Tine Gammeltoft's (2014) rendition of contemporary modes of belonging within families and clinics in Hanoi, Ann Marie Leshkowich's (2014a) account of women traders in HCMC, and Kimberly Hoang's (2015) account of bar girls' modes of mobilizing gender to question as well as reinforce global and state discourses of development and modernization in the south.

Like Rydstrøm, I studied moral socialization within families. Focusing on family units in Đà Nẵng's sprawling metropolis and its neighboring rural province, Quảng Nam, I attend to a gender regime that is less strictly "Confucian" than in Rydstrøm's (2003a) rural and Gammeltoft's rural (1999) and urban (2014) north Vietnamese studies. Here, women take on multiple roles that cannot be easily subsumed in a passive victim versus agent dichotomy. Like Leshkowich (2014a) and Hoang (2015), who follow Saba Mahmood (2005), I do not take women's "oppression" as a given but rather delineate how women in Vietnam use gendered discourses of *tình cảm* (love-care), *hy sinh* (sacrifice), and asymmetrical reciprocity to constitute themselves as moral beings within their specific familial configurations. This lens enriches understandings of women's subjectivities and theorization of intergenerational relations of continuity and change. Focusing on the material and narrative labor and oft-silenced suffering involved in sustaining life together, the ethnography reveals how in this Buddhist-Confucian, late-socialist context, modern romantic love can converge with rather than oppose intergenerational love, as members expect and strive to enact sacrifice and show *tình cảm* (love and material care) for (would-be) spouses, children, ancestors, and other relatives and friends. Gossip, directives, silences, and other forms of talk discipline family members as they face the demands and dilemmas of moral personhood in ordinary, traditional, yet also modern life.

SCALES OF SILENCE AND SACRIFICE

Huy's father died following his immigration to the United States after languishing in a reeducation camp as retribution for serving the South's American-collaborating Army of the Republic of Vietnam (ARVN), just like Huân's grandfather, mentioned in the prologue. Their and other tragic stories of displacement and death led me to study Vietnam's postwar history and society. These stories are commonplace. Many families during and after the war had been split up and later reunited. They suffered losses, absences, and delayed gratifications. Some put off marriage, never consummated their loves or raised children; others were unable to tend sick family members and missed funerals. War had taken its toll. As an immigrant to the United States from the often-turbulent Middle East, I was attuned to Vietnamese senses of ambivalence about leaving or returning, reuniting or staying away from what had been a homeland that ensnared family members on either or both sides of the war.[8] And as I began to read Vietnamese history and literature, I became interested in trauma and "memory work."[9] At the same time, Vietnamese acquaintances in the United States and Vietnam seemed profoundly *un*interested in trauma, memory, or history. Why dwell on a painful past, they would ask?

Their questions and seeming indifference to a painful past challenged me. As the Israeli-born granddaughter of Holocaust survivors on one side and Kurdish Jewish Singaporean refugees fleeing the Japanese invasion of Southeast Asia during World War II on the other side, I had always assumed that sufferers and their descendants never forget history. Memorializing trauma and war seemed essential to one's identity. Instead, Vietnam taught me that there are other ways of carrying on life and acknowledging and maintaining familial continuity.

As the slogan goes, "Vietnam is a country, not a war." Teachers and friends who introduced me to Vietnam's literature, proverbs, and history consistently highlighted *not* trauma and victimhood but a quiet resilience. Vietnamese people, they emphasized, valorize bearing suffering with equanimity through sacrifice *(hy sinh)* and the moral sentiment of *tình cảm:* love, care, and concern that motivates material action and support.

This study enlarges the domain of sacrifice beyond ritual, religion, and patriotic death to include ordinary moral behaviors that transpire almost unnoticed in daily life, except when violated. Sacrifice here is conceptualized not just as a discrete and irreversible act, but as a continual practice, experience, and moral orientation.[10] The Vietnamese whom I came to know did not habitually distinguish "sacrifice" from "self-sacrifice," unlike speakers of English and other Indo-European languages or those with monotheistic traditions. For them, sacrifice (whether quotidian or dramatic) was always a multiparty affair that entailed, as in classic anthropological theory, the modification of the moral persons involved.[11] It could but did not need to and often did not involve death, material violence, or destruction. Instead, they insisted that sacrifice (*hy sinh*) is etymologically derived from the word *sinh* (life, birth, biology).

In contrast to dominant anthropological and other humanistic formulations, where the overwhelming focus is on the sacred quality of sacrifice, which is paradigmatically achieved through holy death,[12] sacrifice (*hy sinh*) in Vietnamese does not typically refer to the ritual slaughter of life.[13] It represents what speakers of English might consider self-sacrifice: everyday family-based or patriotic and nationally oriented renunciations for the sake and benefit of others. This book's approach to sacrifice refocuses attention on what it means to sustain life as a set of ordinary ethical practices and moral orientations socialized in families' daily lives and maintained through community- and state-level discourses. Given Vietnam's seismic political and economic shifts over the course of the twentieth century, sacrifice provides a means of bridging what might otherwise become irreconcilable or, at least, conflict-generating differences, for example, between generations, genders, and political-economic regimes. I argue, then, that practices of sacrifice enacted on a small and larger scale engender and sustain amicable relations between factions that could alternatively be prone to rift and rupture.

The focus on family-based sacrifice rather than on religious or state institutions builds on yet also contradicts key scholarship on postwar Vietnam. For example, in his sensitive ethnography, *Culture, Ritual and Revolution in Vietnam*, Shawn Malarney (2002) suggests that, despite a traditional lack of association between sacrifice and death in Vietnam,[14] the tropes of patriotism and revolutionary martyrdom proved so powerful as to effectively trump previous meanings associated with the term *hy sinh*. State efforts to ennoble war death, Malarney recounts, ultimately met with approval and gratitude, not resistance. By casting the war as a "sacred obligation," a struggle for "national salvation," the state linked the struggle against the French and against the Americans and their South Vietnamese allies to previous struggles against foreign invaders, particularly the Chinese, who had occupied Vietnam for over a thousand years (111 BCE–938 CE). Drawing on a number of memorialization practices of acknowledgment and celebration, as well as by bequeathing material benefits to "sacrifice families," the state was able to narrow the meaning of "sacrifice." It rendered *hy sinh* synonymous with revolutionary ardor to give up one's life "in a just cause to protect and improve the collectivity."[15]

State containment of the notion of sacrifice, however, seems questionable, particularly in central and southern Vietnam, where consensus regarding the Communists' vision of unity was not achieved. Indeed, as Ashley Pettus (2003) demonstrates in her ethnography, *Between Sacrifice and Desire*, the semantic entailments of sacrifice constituted contested territory, even in the North's public discourses disseminated in newspapers and journals published by the Women's Union (an official organ of the Communist state). On one hand, throughout the war and postwar collectivization years, as well as during the early marketization period when Pettus's study ends, sacrifice has been an effective discursive mode by which the state is able to discipline women. On the other hand, the ways in which women were to display virtue (by embodying sacrifice) were changing in these state representations. No longer called on to embody socialist asceticism and collective struggle, women now sacrifice by facilitating more individualistic and materialistic urban middle-class aspirations to become "civilized happy families" made up of disciplined, beauty-conscious consumers.[16] Contra Malarney's argument of a unified and purified vision of sacrifice in Vietnam as relating only to patriotic death, sacrifice manifests multiple sides.[17] Even beyond Vietnam, sacrifice extends beyond public state discourses into mundane ethical orientations and practices.

Examining sacrifice as a quotidian practice, experience, and moral orientation entails focusing on the interactional *work* involved in sustaining stability and the so-called ordinary. It means considering routine life-worlds along with crisis situations as worthy of study and attending to how families manage life together and living in community rather than assuming these. Like many others, I regard communities and the culturescapes and individuals who populate them as characterized by dynamism, indeterminacy, ambivalence, relationality, multiplicity, partiality, and rupture at times. Cauldrons of conflict rather than harmonious halcyons make for interesting studies of the human dramas of existence.

While Joel Robbins (2007b) has disparaged anthropology's obsession with continuity to the neglect of change, I counter that continuity is not a hoary Durkheimian construct that relies on the faulty assumption of societal coherence and stasis. Instead, this book details the ways in which continuity is a precarious and often evanescent achievement, both in situations of crisis, when people subsequently have to remake their worlds, and in mundane life itself.[18] The ordinary and the expected are not foregone conclusions within a rigid and predictable totality. The routine, as conversation analysts like Emanuel Schegloff (1986) have taught, is an achievement in its own right. It requires intricate, emergent efforts to initiate and sustain, even in fleeting minute-to-minute interactions.[19]

To study the ethical labor entailed in routines and seeming continuities, I ethnographically account for what matters to whom, in which way, and under what conditions. This perspective is applied to both micro social encounters and larger-scale societal transformations framed as state-sanctioned teleologies.[20] Accordingly, *Silence and Sacrifice* draws on thick descriptions to analyze discourses and practices of *hy sinh*, the Vietnamese (but arguably more generalizable) form of sacrifice that anthropologists have largely minimized.[21] On a broader level, it reflects upon ethics, affects, and the ordinary itself. Indeed, in countries like Vietnam, in which "the ordinary" has been a rapidly transforming target, spanning dramatically different political and economic regimes, what does ordinary mean? From whose point of view and in what social circumstances? I draw on the methods of linguistic anthropology, including narrative, language socialization, and interactional analysis, to get at these questions.

Narrative as a Model for Life

Questions of scale, perspective, and continuity surrounding sacrifice, I believe, benefit from close attention to narrative practice and other modes of representation through which lives are made and multiple truths—sometimes compatible, at other times colliding—are reckoned. Narrating life experiences often leads narrators to engage in *sideshadowing*.[22] That is, narrators entertain a multiplicity of perspectives, possibilities, and temporalities regarding life events to keep at bay or, alternatively, underscore (in)commensurabilities among these sideshadowed versions of events.[23] The term comes from literary critics Michael André Bernstein (1994) and Gary Saul Morson (1994), who have sought to confront the epistemological problems implicit in teleological tales that pervade novelistic and historical accounts. Such narratives typically are strongly ideological and project inevitable futures, for example, by *foreshadowing* progress and modernity (e.g., the US westward expansion as manifest destiny) or *backshadowing* disaster. In the backshadowing case, linearity haunts narratives of collective trauma when narrators use their present-time hindsight to visualize a clear, logical progression of events and/or morally assess protagonists (e.g., Holocaust victims) in the past for "failing to see the writing on the wall."

Sideshadowing, by contrast, emphasizes moral and causal uncertainty and contingency and foregrounds the subjunctive, open-ended qualities that lend narratives their capacity to imagine alternative possible worlds, for example, by deploying hypotheticals and the *irrealis* mood.[24] This way of analyzing experience in relation to narratives, I think, is especially sympathetic to the idea of ordinary and virtue ethics as developed in Michael Lambek's (2010b) edited volume and Cheryl Mattingly's (2010, 2014a) ethnographies, where morality is conceived as *more* than reproducing orderly societal norms and conventions and ethics is a continual, existential struggle for what may be incommensurable goods. Like them and other ethics and morality scholars,[25] I insist that ethics and morality involve relationships and the mediation of the body, and also the mediation of discourse, as I elaborate in the rest of this book. Introducing the concept of *family*-centered ethnography to enrich person-centered ethnographies,[26] the book also explicitly examines the role of gender in enacting moral personhood. It advances the "ethical turn" in anthropology by showing how kinship and gender are central to studies of ethics and morality. The "self," I demonstrate in the ensuing narrative-based chapters, is gendered and always tethered to and entangled in a web of dynamic family relations.

Language Socialization and Interaction Mold and Model Culture

In foregrounding kinship and gender in the study of everyday ethics in Đà Nẵng, I analyze sometimes fleeting but often routine communicative practices, including both direct instructions to children and others and subtler exchanges that involve the body and spatial, symbolic, and material resources that interlocutors use to take meaningful action in their local moral worlds. As language socialization theorists have shown, it is in the process of learning and using language that people acquire, exhibit, and entrench (or contest) their community's cultural values, affects, and practices; and it is through participation in cultural practices that people learn and adopt (or negotiate and at times question) the preferred linguistic and other communicative habits of their communities.[27] In the following chapters, I therefore attend closely to communicative practices and nuances to examine the ways in which normative femininity and masculinity are engendered in the course of family members' interactions with one another.

Ethics, I insist, are both gendered and engendering; and as subjects speak with and about one another, they reify local constructions of masculinity and femininity by disciplining and assessing one another's ability and commitment to abide by the norms of asymmetrical reciprocity and *tình cảm*. These norms are not universal across class, gender, or political or familial positioning. Rather, they vary across the life course, permitting or foreclosing different forms of agency depending on who is involved in the relation and context-specific interaction.

The present linguistic anthropological study of discourse, narrative, interaction, and socialization allows me to highlight the tensions between Levinasian approaches to ethics that emphasize interpersonal community dynamics[28] and Foucauldian approaches that focus on power, subjectivation, and biopolitics.[29] As I show particularly in chapters 2, 4, and 5, every interaction, including the most micro, is pervaded by relations of power and hierarchy that affirm care as both nurturing and potentially disciplining and hurtful. Ethics and moral frameworks then are exposed as dynamically enacted rather than static precepts that subjects—as complexly related family and community members—either abide by or reject. They are asymmetrically gendered and imbricated within family dynamics that challenge, and indeed render impossible, any reduction to simplified, universal principles.

Yet, despite the variability and nuance that characterizes moral judgments in each of the following chapters, families in Đà Nẵng and Quảng Nam nonetheless exhibited similar configurations and practices and articulated similar value patterns as those of Loan and Huân in Ho Chi Minh City in the south and of friends and informants in Hanoi, Vietnam's capital. Rural, urban, or urbanizing, they mixed "traditional" and "modern" ways of being and engaged in devotional practices that brought into question labels like "sacred" and "secular." Their accounts and practices also problematize the narrative linearities assumed by theories of modernization and secularization that accompany these terms. Nonlinearity, however, does not imply lack of patterns: household configurations, relationships, interactions, and ethics in fact proved remarkably consistent despite members' diversity across political, class, generational, and gendered lines. This is *not* to say that families were uniform or that individuals within families all shared the same values and motivations. I claim no homogeneity within Vietnam. What I interrogate is how, despite differences, participants engage in similar practices with similar results, whether with shared, different, or contradictory motives. Together, these reinforce what I came to see as three interrelated organizational principles that help sustain seeming continuity within a dynamic field of change, achieved, in part, through the living and telling of sideshadowing narratives that embrace contradictory positions and articulate the contingencies and indeterminacies of life.[30] The three principles are sacrifice, asymmetrical reciprocity, and *tình cảm* (love and care manifested through material provisioning).

Sacrifice, Asymmetrical Reciprocity, and Tình Cảm

Sacrifice *(hy sinh)*, as we heard from Loan, ideally entails silently and *willingly* suffering and taking on hardships for the sake of others. It is a disposition learned from infancy through embodied practice and undergirds structures of filial piety traditionally characteristic of East Asian families who share China's Confucian and Buddhist legacies.[31] And as discussed earlier and will be elaborated throughout the book, quotidian sacrifice is inseparable from Vietnam's mode of social organization, wherein hierarchy and inequality pervade.

The second principle, asymmetrical reciprocity, is summarized in the mantra, *kính trên nhường dưới* (Respect those above, yield to those below). It structures relationships in such a way that sacrifice not only initiates but also perpetuates and sustains exchange relationships. Despite the Communist Revolution and its reforms, both the state and laypeople in early twenty-first-century Vietnam continue to valorize inequality, particularly along age, gender, and class lines. In contrast to liberal assumptions regarding personhood, moral personhood here is presumed to be entangled in multiple layers of reciprocity with the dead as well as the living. Further, hierarchy is not constituted along a single directionality, for example, the oppressed succumbing to those who exploit them. Rather, relationships are conceptualized as ideally asymmetrical but bidirectional. This perspective resembles Maussian-inspired models of "generalized reciprocity"[32] or "communism,"[33] as well as the Sinitic gifting system of *guanxi*,[34] which are characterized by kinship and social relations in which there is no strict accounting of what is given or owed to whom and when it is to be returned. It contrasts with "direct" or "balanced reciprocity"—the mode of exchange characteristic of commodity-based economies, where presumably all "gifts" are strictly accounted for in terms of their (economic) value and where they must be returned or otherwise compensated within a more or less strictly delimited time frame.[35]

Practices and relations of exchange initiate, maintain, and perpetuate sociality itself, as proposed by Marcel Mauss ([1925] 1990), building on Bronislaw Malinowski's ([1922] 2014) discussion of the *kula*. As with the *kula*, so with sacrifice: it is less important to understand *what* is sacrificed than *how* sacrifice operates and what are its effects. In Vietnam's current regime of market socialism, relations of sacrifice rooted in asymmetrical reciprocity sustain the tamping down of conflict and the valuation of seeming harmony between different generational, political, and class strata. These rely, in part, on evocations of home, as the term for nation (*quốc gia*) is derived from the term for family (*gia đình*), and both enjoin and idealize relations of sacrifice based on unequal but mutually obligatory and beneficial filiality.

Yet relations of relative harmony and seeming stability do not sponta-
neously or "naturally" materialize. They rely on the continual affirmation
of the value of *tình cảm*, the third principle that I highlight. Unlike *hy
sinh*, which readily translates to its English analogue, *sacrifice*, *tình cảm*
eludes simple translation. It refers to a moral sentiment of love, care, and
concern among persons, which Vietnamese say arises naturally between
kin as well as friends.

Tình cảm, I was invariably told, is a type of feeling that motivates
action: rather than an emotion internal to a bounded individual, it inspires
and is manifested through the provisioning of material goods, including
money, to those with whom that feeling is shared. It circulates and reverberates, affirming the bonds presumed to exist between individuals, or
bringing those bonds into question when material manifestations of *tình
cảm* are said to be absent. A person's rejection of an invitation to stay for a
meal, or of a friend's or family member's pleas for aid, for example, is
indicative of their lack of *tình cảm* and potential slide toward immorality.
In these ways, *tình cảm* resembles the *hau*, Mauss's ([1925] 1990) theorization of the spirit of a gift, as well as the Chinese system of *guanxi*: it
motivates the continuation of reciprocity and, thus, sociality.

Yet while Mauss and his successors conceptualized social relations as
fundamentally agonistic,[36] I propose, along with more recent interpreters
interested in the issue of "care,"[37] that this form of sociality that is constituted through asymmetrical reciprocity need not necessarily be agonistic
(though *tình cảm*-based relations certainly can be and often are). Rather,
tình cảm motivates the labor and circulation of care involved in sustaining
sacrifice, which in turn sustains a kind of stability and continuity in
conditions of constant flux. Morality here is fundamentally contextual,
immanent, and emergent. It is habituated through practices attuned to
the particularities of each social situation and the residues of historical
relationships, and it engenders, as well as reflects, the gendered dynamics
of kinship relations.

Moral practice in this ethnographic context involves continuous as well
as periodic and more eventful devotional performances.[38] Importantly,
morality here cannot be equated with the teachings of a single book (e.g.,
the Bible or the Quran, in some monotheistic traditions) or a singular,
overarching, and hermetic set of rules. Vietnamese family members,

whether calling themselves atheist, Buddhist, Cao Đài, or Catholic,[39] draw
on their plural heritage for ethics in everyday life. They reduce ethics to
neither utilitarian nor Kantian (or even Levinasian) absolutist principles.
Instead, they allow for fragmentary, ambivalent, contingent, and at times
incommensurate desires to guide their actions. This is constitutive of what
I call sideshadowing logics, where people suspend or bury judgment and
privilege ambiguity. Reason and sentiment, mind and body, secular and
religious, traditional and modern become intertwined, even entangled
pairs as we consider sacrifice as a relatively undramatic and routinized
everyday moral practice that is embedded in the logic of *tình cảm* and
asymmetrical reciprocity. The chapters that follow elaborate these claims
through personal, at times sideshadowing, stories recounted primarily by
women that I documented during fieldwork. Before delving into these
accounts, I provide a brief overview of Vietnam's history, followed by an
account of my ethnographic enmeshment in familial webs of sacrifice,
tình cảm, and asymmetrical reciprocity.

A LONG-SUFFERING COUNTRY

Huân's family members, like Loan's and millions of others, were deeply
affected by the series of wars and regime transformations that gripped
Vietnam in earlier decades of the twentieth century. If Americans tend to
think of the 1960s and 1970s as the era of "the Vietnam War," Vietnamese
are quick to counter that this "American War" was but one of the many
fights and sources of loss that extend both before and after the Americans
came and left. Most recently, there had been the invasion of Cambodia to
rout out the encroaching Khmer Rouge in Vietnam's southwest (1978–
87) and the consequent costly border war with China in 1979, which
together took thousands of lives. Vietnamese at the time were still grappling with reunification following the civil, anticolonial, and anti-imperial
wars waged against the French and against the Americans, as well as
among one another. Frequently, interlocutors pointed to their country's
very long, war-filled history.

Vietnamese civilization (*văn minh Việt*) itself is said to have originated
in the Red River valley in the north in the third century BCE.[40] Repeated

Chinese invasions and roughly a thousand years of Chinese occupation (111 BCE–938 CE) substantially shaped this civilization, which appropriated the literacy and Confucian, Buddhist, and Daoist traditions brought to it by the invaders. In the centuries that followed, the Chinese repeatedly tried to reestablish their rule and were repeatedly rebuffed, despite intermittent success, giving rise to many of Vietnam's stories and legends of heroism by both male and female figures.[41] A series of dynasties succeeded one another and continued to resist shorter-term Chinese invasions and occupations during this period, which continued into the fifteenth century. At the same time and continuing into the eighteenth century, these successive Vietnamese kingdoms gradually began to spread southward, conquering other peoples, including the Cham and Khmer in present-day central and southern Vietnam.[42] By the eighteenth century, two ruling houses, the Trịnh and the Nguyễn, ruled present-day northern and southern Vietnam, respectively. A populist rebellion led by three brothers known as the Tây Sơn overthrew the Nguyễn lords in 1788 and subsequently tried, unsuccessfully, to spread and also overcome the Trịnh in the north.[43]

European presence in Vietnam, meanwhile, remained limited. Trade contacts and religious conversion missions were led by the Portuguese in the sixteenth century. But it was not until after the Tây Sơn rebellion that Europeans established lasting colonial presence in Vietnam. First using the pretext that it was helping restore (successfully in 1802) Nguyễn Ánh to the throne, France now began to enter Vietnam.[44] In subsequent decades, the French used the repression of Catholics at the hands of emperors whose power they had helped restore as a further excuse to exert military power and forcefully occupy Vietnam. France formed the colony of Cochinchina (which also included the territories today known as Laos and Cambodia) in the south in 1858 and the protectorates of Annam and Tonkin in central and north Vietnam in 1864 and 1881, respectively. During World War II, Nazi-collaborating Vichy France invited Japan, then allied with the Axis powers, to rule Vietnam. When that war concluded in 1945, the French (now under President Charles de Gaulle) attempted to reassert their colonial rule in Vietnam, despite nearly a century of Vietnamese agitation against their occupation.[45] France formally ended its rule in Vietnam only in 1954, after suffering a humiliating defeat at Điện Biên Phủ in Vietnam's northwest.[46] In Vietnam, this period of French colonization, followed by brief Japanese and then American occupation, is recounted as but the latest in a long history of foreign powers attempting to wield control.

It is beyond the scope of this book to recount the history of relations between Vietnam and its Chinese, French, Japanese, and American occupiers, who succeeded each other in exerting influence over the Vietnamese—themselves a nation whom the government describes as containing at least fifty-four ethnic minorities, among whom the Kinh (normally equated simply with unmarked "Vietnamese") form the vast majority, about 85 percent. Generations of Vietnamese people have survived many wars, betrayals, and divided allegiances. They often take pride in asserting the syncretic traditions of their language, religions, and cuisines and describe *tình cảm* (loving sentiment that motivates material care) and syncretism, not purity, as what makes them uniquely Vietnamese. Pairing the two, participants in this study would say, unsolicited, "We take the best from each stream," and then repeat the common phrase, "Vietnamese are poor but rich in *tình cảm*" (*Việt Nam nghèo, mà giàu tình cảm*).[47]

Back in 1945, war with the Americans hardly seemed inevitable, since after Vichy France's collaboration with the Japanese, who occupied Vietnam during World War II, it was American Green Berets who helped Hồ Chí Minh, Vietnam's first premier, declare independence in Hanoi on September 2. Yet, as the Cold War escalated, the Americans became increasingly committed to restoring French rule in Vietnam to fend off Hồ Chí Minh's Communists. When the French suffered their final defeat at Điện Biên Phủ in northwestern Vietnam in 1954, leading to what was supposed to be a temporary split into North and South Vietnam, the alliance of the Americans with the Republic of Vietnam (the South) was cemented. And while this alliance, too, would suffer setbacks and betrayals, these political maneuvers are not the subject of this book. I note simply that it was this alliance that allowed the Americans to first land troops and establish a base in Đà Nẵng in 1965, having already launched reconnaissance missions there in earlier years. The Americans' presence in Đà Nẵng led many families to splinter at least until after March 29, 1975, when the Democratic Republic of Vietnam (the North) definitively conquered this part of Vietnam and continued its march south, with the takeover of Saigon (renamed Ho Chi Minh City) officially ending the war a month later, on April 30, 1975.[48]

Pertinent to this study is how families came to reunite after getting split during the war, with some members moving to the North to join the Communist Revolution while others stayed behind to guard their lands or simply to live as neutral subjects but were taken over by the conflict raging in their lands. How did they come to forge a sense of continuity, first of all, after the North won the war and nationalized the economy, sending many of its former enemies to punitive reeducation camps, which led many more to attempt to flee the country on rickety boats? And also, how was unity achieved in the ensuing *đổi mới* (Renovation) period of privatization and liberalization, culminating in Vietnam's entry into the WTO and increasing adoption of a market economy that we might see as abandoning socialist ideals?

Heonik Kwon (2006, 2008), working just to the south of Đà Nẵng, has written eloquently about the struggles of Vietnamese villagers to make sense of their war losses. His ethnographies address the ways in which villagers mobilize widespread beliefs in ghosts to attempt to make peace both with former enemies and with the hauntings of those who were never buried and cannot be properly worshipped and appeased. Such struggles continued as I began my research, with families and news organizations intermittently attempting to recover the remains of a lost loved one believed to have perished in the region. Yet this ethnography takes as its departure point less the memory work involved in making peace with the past than the ethical work undertaken to make sense of the present and anticipate the future in Đà Nẵng and its neighboring rural Quảng Nam province.[49] During the wartime decades, this region saw heavy fighting and bombardment, but by the early twenty-first century it was rapidly (re)developing. Đà Nẵng has celebrated its independence yearly on March 29 and currently enjoys the boons of foreign investments by South Korea, China, Japan, the United States, Australia, France, Germany, Sweden, Denmark, and other nations who have promised to bring prosperity to the roughly half a million residents of this once-again bustling if now more provincial and shrunken metropolis.

The centrally planned, collectivized economy where only some were eligible to become cadre servants of the state and enjoy attendant privileges as a result was transformed. Liberalizing and privatizing reforms, known as *đổi mới*, spawned an urban middle class composed of often-overlapping state cadres and entrepreneurs with access to foreign and domestic material, social, and symbolic capital.[50] Between February 2007 and February 2008, land prices in Đà Nẵng doubled, tripled, and even quadrupled, as laws were liberalized to allow foreigners to purchase property there.

I had witnessed the escalating pace of infrastructure development since my second trip to the region in 2004 and was surprised by 2005 and 2007 to see that many of the tree-surrounded modest mud houses that I had visited were now razed to the ground and replaced with two- and three-story concrete homes. Beaches, too, were taken over by land developers who replaced formerly pristine public lands with luxury resorts for the newly wealthy and established megastores and malls now frequented by the region's rising middle class. Everyone, it seemed, was building a new house for themselves, having sold off farmland or taken out loans that I feared they would be hard-pressed to repay and might lose in years to come. But my friends and acquaintances did not share my pessimism and skepticism. Unlike the disillusioned figures in contemporary Vietnamese novels that I had mistakenly assumed expressed the general mood of the people, in Đà Nẵng citizens expressed optimism and excitement about their country's booming market economy. The research undertaken in this study examines this apparent optimism and ready compliance with state narratives about development and discerns axes of difference, particularly gender and political affiliation inflected by class and age, that at times become points of tension and even contention.

METHODOLOGY: THE ETHNOGRAPHER AS KIN

Silence and Sacrifice draws on eighteen months of ethnographic research among a snowball sample of urban, periurban, and rural multihousehold and multigenerational extended family units in the city of Đà Nẵng and the province of Quảng Nam on the coastline of central Vietnam.[51] I focused on five core family groups that included eight matriarchs and three patriarchs over age 60; thirty-six women and twenty-seven men ages 20 to 60 who were the elders' children; and twenty girls and thirteen boys under age 20 who were their grandchildren. Including the focal sample and others in their social networks, I visited and interviewed a total of eighty households (all in Vietnamese) and collected eight hours of video recordings during pilot studies in 2004 and 2005 and ninety-four hours of video recordings from February 2007 through February 2008.

Audio-recorded interviews focused on sacrifice, *tình cảm*, and participants' routines and life trajectories. Video recordings of household interactions included routine chores and activities (e.g., cooking, washing, and playing) and major life course events (e.g., weddings, birth celebrations, and mortuary and ancestor worship rituals). I logged, transcribed, and translated portions of these recordings with the aid of research consultants in Vietnam and, later, with Vietnamese-educated consultants in North America. These data allow me to attend to linguistic nuances and moral stances articulated or enacted in the course of interactions in families' homes, to unravel the range of narrative and other practices that make life together possible.

My status as the future bride of a man who had spent half his life in Vietnam before emigrating to the United States with his family facilitated my rapport with families in the field. They saw me not just as a researcher but also as a person who would have to embody the role of a Vietnamese wife and mother one day. And because I had not had a lifetime learning what this role would entail, many saw themselves as giving me a crash course, by involving me in their activities and sharing intimate details of their lives. When speaking of sacrifice, many would sometimes use my fieldwork as an exemplar. They said that I was "sacrificing," since I was putting off my love life and future motherhood and instead pursuing my studies, an ocean away from my fiancé. Whereas I saw myself as blithely or selfishly pursuing my academic goals, even to the chagrin and against the advice of my own grandmothers in Israel, my Vietnamese interlocutors explained that my attention to them and their cares, instead of creating my own family, was a form of *hy sinh* (sacrifice).

Using a circular logic, they explained that it was my *tình cảm* (love and care) for Huy that engendered my *tình cảm*, or affinity and resonance, with them. My readiness to speak their language, use their kinship forms of reference and address, eat and drink with them just as they ate and drank, without fussiness, accompany those so inclined to the pagodas and/or worship at home, and share in their joys and sorrows, they added, was proof of my *tình cảm* with them. This *tình cảm* was reinforced by my habit and continual desire to just hang out with them instead of focusing on my books all the time. Never mind that hanging out in these ways is simply the bread and butter of ethnographic methods, as I repeatedly explained in gaining their consent: I was "doing research" by hanging out. As is often the case for anthropologists,[52] the lines between friendship and research were blurred, since it was precisely this "hanging out" that legitimated me as a person with *tình cảm* (intimate feelings of care): someone worthy of entering their homes, and, more important according to them, producing a family down the road. My ability to learn from them and recount it to others, they added, boded well for my future as the wife of a Vietnamese man and mother of his children. Hearing about my life through their eyes afforded me another lens through which to begin to understand how sacrifice and *tình cảm* (love and concern rooted in material care) were key to producing families and kinship in the everyday.

Focusing on intimate relations in pursuit of a family-centered ethnography, I have sought to understand how ethical lives are enacted predominantly in the "ordinary" domestic sphere. The research thus responds to Adam Kuper's (2018) call to return to the study of kinship as lived rather than conceptualized. Its centerpiece is the realm of mundane sacrifice for and by family members who are not necessarily devout, as I was specifically *not* seeking to study a movement but rather to understand how sacrifice—and as I discovered, asymmetrical reciprocity and *tình cảm*—pervades the lives of people from all walks of life and with all sorts of religious, political, or economic affiliations.[53] Such sacrifices and acts of "love" illuminate the crucial role of gender hierarchies in the study of ethics and call into question the notion of gender-neutral moral personhood. This does not mean, of course, that sacrifice—whether in its "masculinized" patriotic or ritual forms or in its "feminized" quotidian manifestations—should either be condemned as inevitably exploitative or romanticized as a domain of agency and recognition for women (or men). It means, rather, that attending to this domain of the communicative micro practices of the everyday invites a reexamination of the role of cultural ideologies and practices of love and devotion in constituting gender and sacrifice. The following chapters trace this argument in more detail.

WHAT LIES AHEAD

In kaleidoscope-like fashion, each of the chapters touch on all the book's themes but from somewhat different angles. Part I, "Sustaining National and Family Sacrifice," examines in depth the concepts of sacrifice, asymmetrical reciprocity, and *tình cảm* in chapters 1, 2, and 3, respectively. First, to illuminate the relation between love, everyday family sacrifice, and national sacrifice, chapter 1, "'Not only those on the battlefield': (Extra)Ordinary Sacrifice," recounts the story of Tan, a patriotic former war prisoner and combatant whose biography was embroiled in his nation's history. Weaving together the ordinary and extraordinary, and gesturing at the visceral as ethical, Tan's account of his life exemplifies the ways in which individual, familial, and national sacrifices are mutually entangled. Tan illustrates how "ordinary sacrifice" is at once an essential and encompassing component of the "extraordinary" (religious or patriotic) sacrifices more typically theorized in anthropology. His narrative demonstrates the relative silence of sacrifice and of love as pain-filled, personal and patriotic. By attending to the linguistic and temporal nuances of Tan's story as it unfolds, this chapter indicates how the extraordinary is lived as unexceptional and how muted suffering over years has come to be understood as sacrifice rooted in *tình cảm*.

Chapter 2, "Rituals and Routines of Sacrifice: Respect Those Above, Yield to those Below," relates ritual ancestor worship feasts to toddlers' socialization into respect through mundane greeting routines. It analyzes how sacrifice and asymmetrical reciprocity are enacted and learned early in life, cultivating the new generation's ethical subjectivity. Using language socialization as a primary lens, the analysis focuses on the multiple temporalities and constructions of personhood involved in honoring the ancestors in Nga's family and on routine interactions with Em, one of the toddlers whom I followed over the course of a year. I show how young family members develop moral subjectivities that undergird sacrifice and, like the worship feasts, regenerate the socio-moral order, even in the face of Vietnam's rapid changes. As well, the chapter continues the argument about the import of kinship and gender for theorizing ethics.

Chapter 3, "Troubling Love: Models for Gender (In)equality," then considers how love and a sense of duty to sacrifice entwine multiple allegiances, including state patriotism, workplace expectations, intergenerational aspirations, and spousal desires. The chapter recounts the story of Hảo, a young woman who struggled to experience passion typically associated with love. Over the course of a year fraught with her grandmother's illness, Hảo disciplined herself to fall in love with and marry a persistent suitor. Success in her efforts was not a foregone conclusion, yet it was buttressed by her privileged position: she was fortunate to have been born to parents and grandparents who fought on the winning side of the war. Unlike the characters in chapters 4 and 5, Hảo became a model middle-class woman. She benefited from Vietnam's unification in 1975, the present marketization reforms, and mandatory social policies that facilitate the transition of single daughters to working middle-class wives and mothers. Hảo's story complicates developmentalist accounts that pit romantic marriage against intergenerational familial love while showing that for some women, success across domains is not only desirable, but possible and mutually reinforcing.

Part II, "Care Narratives and the Limits of Love," further complicates the connections developed in the first three chapters, by attending more explicitly to silenced family conflicts. Having focused on characters who align with public narratives and state discourses of sacrifice, asymmetrical reciprocity, and tình cảm, and some of the surmountable difficulties that they face in doing so in part I, in part II I more closely examine those characters whose relations with normative discourses are even more fraught. These protagonists embrace Vietnam's public ethics, yet disagree among each other about who best embodies the ideals to which they all claim to aspire. While affirming the insights drawn in part I about the importance of sacrifice, asymmetrical reciprocity, and tình cảm in structuring kin dynamics, part II continues to add nuance to formulations of subjectivity, love, and care. As in part I, I focus on specific characters' stories and the linguistic nuances of their daily interactions but here to show how the ethics of care and love are often nonlinear projects that are tension-filled due both to internal contradictions inherent to the cultural tropes that proclaim them, and to the ambivalences experienced by the characters enmeshed within a dynamic field of kin and communal relations.

Chapter 4, "Waiting as Care? Sacrifice and Tình Cảm in Troubled Times," examines how ordinary sacrifice and tình cảm figure in family members' lives during critical periods of serious illness and imminent loss. The chapter recounts how close family members of an elderly woman named Bà Bảy reacted to a series of hypertension-related strokes that left her comatose and waiting to die. Bà's relatives altered their routines to assume responsibility for her care in the hospital and later at home. Their acts of caregiving and response to her illness underscore the import of silence in sacrifice and highlight the difficult gendered work involved in care. Bà's circumstances also underscore how waiting is not just a waiting *for* but also a waiting *on* and dwelling *with:* a liminal state where the usual order of things is in disarray, temporality is backgrounded, and care is achieved by reformulating norms and routines. Here, waiting opened a narrative space for recollecting family rifts that otherwise remained unspoken. These narratives reframed my understanding of how family members perceived Bà Bảy's illness. Bà's condition was framed not simply as the consequence of virtuous enduring and suffering in silence and waiting *for* care but also as karmic retribution for earlier wrongs she inflicted on others by waiting *to* care for them.

Chapter 5, "Children and Lovers: Marriage, Morality, and Motherhood," extends the discussion of moral personhood, sacrifice, and love to examine the pragmatic work performed by gossip in delimiting possible relations between happiness, feminine virtue, motherly love, and foiled romantic desire. The chapter underlines the moral, affective, and material labor involved in enacting and ethically reasoning about sacrifice, *tình cảm,* and asymmetrical reciprocity and shows how difficult it can be to "care," particularly for women, who are subjected to, and engage in, gossip as a form of social control. The stories of Hiệp (an outsider to Đà Nẵng who found herself in muted conflict with her husband's family), Lộc (a happily married man still pining for an old flame), Thu (a former widow and prostitute whose son had just succumbed to AIDS), and An (a forty-year-old mother who had unsuccessfully tried to resist marriage) illustrate how ordinary life is entangled in Vietnam's wider history, embroiling protagonists in perilous and morally ambivalent situations that afford them unequal opportunities to enact ethical personhood, moral femininity (or masculinity), and belonging in Vietnam's rapidly changing state.

The conclusion, "Mourning in Silent Sacrifice," considers how grief is (mis)managed when a family is faced with a member's untimely death.

Unspoken forms of sacrifice that family members and friends expect to manifest as acts of caregiving, showing respect, and yielding to misbehaving intimate relatives illuminate how kinship comes to matter, precariously unifying the extended family. The chapter reflects on the ways that gender and other hierarchies inflect realizations of virtuous personhood and relations of love and loss. I close by suggesting that attention to the temporality of mourning is key to understanding ethical life. In contrast to canonical narratives that impose coherence on lived experience, personal sideshadowing accounts afford ethical confrontation with incommensurable conditions and highlight why family-centered ethnography is essential to formulations of ethics.

PART I Sustaining National and Family Sacrifice

The following three chapters introduce the concepts of sacrifice *(hy sinh)*, asymmetrical reciprocity, and *tình cảm* through the characters of Tan, Nga, Em, and Hảo. Though unrelated and ignorant of the existence of one another, as they belong to different generations and households and occupy somewhat different class positions, they share more than a common national heritage. Their stories and interactions with others in their social worlds illustrate patterned ways in which to understand the various meanings and workings of the principles of sacrifice, asymmetrical reciprocity, and *tình cảm*.

Like the grammar of a language, these principles structure the life experiences and ethical subjectivities of all my interlocutors, albeit in nonuniform ways. Close attention to narrative form as well as content, to ritual as event and as ordinary practice, and to discourses and experiences of love in these three chapters begin to illuminate the significance of language and communicative practices, as well as of gender and kinship, in constituting moral experience and the ethical lives of family members in postwar, late-socialist, marketizing early twenty-first-century Vietnam.

1 "Not only those on the battlefield"

(EXTRA)ORDINARY SACRIFICE

The sorrow of war inside a soldier's heart was in a strange way similar to the sorrow of love. It was a kind of nostalgia, like the immense sadness of a world at dusk. It was a sadness, a missing, a pain which could send one soaring back into the past.

– Bảo Ninh, *The Sorrow of War* (1995, 94)

In December 2005, I sat in the upstairs living room in Tan's house, ready to interview him. At the time, Tan's four-story house was one of the tallest structures in Đà Nẵng City. The house's two living rooms; four bedrooms; four flushing toilets, three shower heads, and one bath; spacious kitchen with running water, refrigerator, stovetop, rice cooker, microwave oven, dishwasher, and washing machine; and roof deck on which to hang drying laundry marked it as a place of luxury or at least financial success beyond the means of most of the area's dwellers. Tan's daughter Khanh and her European husband, Hans, had sponsored the erection of this structure. As Tan's wife, Hoa, had proudly told me, the house was built both to secure for Khanh and Hans a comfortable place in which to reside on their biennial visits and to assure Tan and her a restful retirement after years of toiling and suffering. The benefits of *đổi mới*, or Vietnam's project of economic liberalization and privatization, had come earlier for Tan and Hoa than for most of the other families I would come to know.

Tan and Hoa's second daughter, Oanh, along with her husband, Sơn, and their infant daughter, Bảo, had recently moved in as well. Their combined incomes allowed them further to support a cousin from Sơn's village, who had come to live with them and help with cooking, childcare, and other household chores. Oanh had completed her tertiary education in Hanoi the previous year and started working for a private company in Đà Nẵng; her husband—a military career man like Tan—had successfully arranged a transfer to central Vietnam to live with his wife and her parents. As Tan later told me, Sơn's family in the North could spare him since they had three other sons, whereas Tan and Hoa had no sons of their own. They only had Oanh and Khanh to take care of them in their old age. With his daughter, son-in-law, grandchild, and their helper living there, Tan's household was at once "modern" and "traditional," exemplifying the comforts enjoyed by Vietnam's rising middle classes.[1]

At seventy years old, Tan barely betrayed his age. His erect posture with only a slight rounding of the shoulders, slim, muscular build, and shock of still-dark hair made him look at least two inches taller than his 5 feet 7 inches (170 cm; taller than most of my acquaintances in the area). These belied his professed frailty. In reality, he suffered from high blood pressure and consequently restricted his travel only to local, short rides away from home. He spent most of each day lying on his bed on the third floor of their house, reading newspapers or listening to the radio. His room, like most of the house, did not have air-conditioning, and he only sometimes turned on the fan, even in summer.

At home, Tan helped by carrying the family's laundry all five flights of stairs to hang atop the roof (or stairs in wet weather) and then bring it back down when it was dry. Year-round, he and his wife, Hoa, rose daily before 5 a.m. to play badminton at the local club for an hour or two. They would then eat a bowl of noodle soup together (usually *bún*, sometimes *phở*) before returning home and then each would retire to their separate rooms. Like most of the older couples I would come to know, they had chosen each other as life-mates decades earlier, but they did not sleep together, nor did they appear to enjoy the same friends. Hoa would spend her days talking and visiting with her friends from the local club that she and her husband belonged to; sometimes, she prepared lunch and dinner, though her daughter and the helper did most of the cooking, shopping, and tending to baby Bảo. Tan regularly attended his extended family's various worship occasions, usually without Hoa. He also often fixed things around the house and spent time playing with his infant granddaughter in the upstairs living room or read in his own room.

From our conversations, it was apparent that he was well educated, as well as interested in and knowledgeable about world affairs. At lunch, he would assert his opinions about American politics, Israeli-Palestinian relations, and his version of international history, which I at first understood as synonymous with Marxist theory about mankind's stages of human development and class conflict. He regularly quoted Hồ Chí Minh's famous slogans, declaring, "There is nothing more precious than independence and freedom." It always made me think of the American revolutionary Patrick Henry and the New Hampshire state motto, "Give me liberty or give me death." Tan himself would often draw parallels between Vietnam's and the Americans' common history, lamenting that the United States could "skip stages" that had been overcome in Europe, whereas Vietnam was late in marching toward a now-capitalist destiny.

Tan's declamation was more than mere propaganda. In contrast to the American slogan—a personal declaration that foregrounds the personal pronoun *me*—Hồ Chí Minh's is grammatically framed as a general truth. Tan uses the quote to connect his life experience to the suffering of his nation and its aspiration for collective rather than individual freedom.

Having spent several days at his house at the invitation of his daughter Oanh and having spoken at length with his wife, I was eager to hear his story. But Tan was unsure if he wanted to recount it. "You have to give me time, so I can prepare and think," he said.

I wanted to learn about being a family under Vietnam's changing conditions, from war against or for the French and Americans to the collectivization period after Vietnam's reunification in 1975 with the Communist North's victory to the current *đổi mới* era of market reforms, and about the various meanings of *hy sinh* (sacrifice) in Vietnam. I had begun this research in both Đà Nẵng and Huế, since both were cities in the former Republic of Vietnam and both had been under the control of American as well as Việt Minh and later Việt Cộng and North Vietnamese military forces. What did it feel like to be fighting on opposing sides, and what was the reunion like, if it took place?[2]

I had already heard from Tan's wife that he had left his home at eighteen and was imprisoned by the French before making his way to the North, where they married in 1960. What might Vietnam's tumultuous history look like from his perspective? Would "trauma," which I tended to associate with political imprisonment, war, and family separation, figure in his story? Or would it be minimized, or even go unrecognized, as suggested by the dearth of literature on Vietnamese veterans' afflictions (in contrast to that of Americans')?[3]

In the pages that follow, I retell Tan's story, as it unfolds. His story lends insight into Vietnam's tumultuous twentieth-century conflicts and early twenty-first-century rapid development. It illuminates the meanings that sacrifice (*hy sinh*) encompasses in Vietnam, where individual, familial, and national sacrifices are mutually entangled in this personal account. Tan's story begins and ends with family and nation at center stage, rendering the two and his own life in each as inseparable. This experience-near account indicates how tropes linked to Vietnam's national master narrative become deeply sedimented technologies of self-formation in the life of one man.[4] As Tan narrates, he sometimes wanders nonlinearly into related events. His pacing is jagged; he stutters, self-corrects, and repeats certain phrases and themes. This suggests that his is not a well-rehearsed story but one recalled and formulated in the process of its telling. As the story progresses, we sense the ethical conflict between the present telling and the instilled silence of sacrifice and how love is pain-filled, personal, and patriotic. As well, Tan's story illustrates how the extraordinary is lived as ordinary and how muted suffering over years connotes sacrifice.

"SHE THREW ME THE SANDALS OVER THE FENCE AND SAID TO GO UP THE MOUNTAINS"

"You have to tell me a topic," Tan continued to demur, either not knowing where or how to start or not understanding that I was not asking him to act as an expert on war or Vietnam's recent reforms. In the spirit of person-centered ethnography, I was interested in him as a "respondent" and wanted to learn about *his* phenomenological, subjective experience of events.[5]

> I echoed him, "A topic?"
> Yes, some topic. . . . What-what-what to talk about?
> "For example, what if you talk about when you were eighteen, when . . . when you left the house," I suggested.

Very poor.
"Very poor," I echoed.
Yeah, [I was] very poor back then.

Suddenly, stories came streaming from Tan. His parents had nothing. No fields, no orchards, nothing. They lived with his mother's parents on the rural outskirts of Đà Nẵng and relied on them to eke out a living. By age ten, Tan was laboring as a peasant. He was able to study only at night. The French colonizers drafted him to serve in their army. He went into hiding in 1952 and joined the revolution (gia nhập vào cách mạng).

Journalists and historians debate the extent to which Vietnamese peasants joined the revolution as Việt Minh and, later, as Việt Cộng recruits, on *ideological* grounds to support Communism or radical or nationalist grounds in light of the French colonial administration's oppression of and disdain for the Vietnamese people.[6] Tan did not directly address this debate but emphasized his opposition to French force. He did not mention any political ideology or leader by name, other than Hồ Chí Minh, whom he later affectionately called, as do many Vietnamese, "Uncle Hồ" (Bác Hồ). He simply recounted that he joined the revolution (Bác đi hoạt động cách mạng) and spent over a year with the Resistance before the French captured him and sent him to jail. Torture followed. It included terrible beatings and what sounded like waterboarding:

> They tied me down, face up,
> then they poured water into my nose,
> [and] poured water into my mouth.
> And they . . . kicked.
> At night, they tied [my] hands behind [my] back.
> Tied [me] to a column.
> And mosquitoes . . . mosquitoes bit constantly, it was unbearable.
> Tied to a post for several nights on end.

Hearing these horrors, I listened with barely a sound.

> When that was done then they cooped [me] in a cell.
> The cell was small, around . . . not even a meter squared.

Tan had to sleep and eat in that confined space, barely breathing through a small hole in the airtight space. This lasted for two months, until a verdict was finally rendered. The French sentenced him to eight years in jail for having joined the Resistance. "Eight years?," I repeated.

> Yeah. Eight years in jail.
> That was the sentence.
> But they didn't enforce it.

Tan spoke in a matter-of-fact voice. He recounted being deprived of water, food, and sanitation at the military prison, crowded with so many others. Sweat from those on the upper floors dripped down on those below. Fleas tormented them all. Seven or eight prisoners died each day, many unable to bear the hardships and brutal beatings.

But then the French lost at Điện Biên Phủ (in early May 1954).[7] Their defeat concluded the "First Indochina War" against Hồ Chí Minh's nationalist communist troops and ended France's official claims to rule Vietnam's north, center, and south (as the protectorates of Tonkin and Annam, respectively, and the colony of Cochinchina in the south, all occupied since the mid- to late nineteenth century). A prisoner exchange would follow after the conclusion in July 1954 of the Geneva Convention. Tan did not explicate the specifics. Perhaps he trusted me to know already that it was here that the international community negotiated to temporarily divide Vietnam at the 17th parallel, with Hồ Chí Minh and his Communist Party ruling the North as the Democratic Republic of Vietnam (DRV).

The DRV had been originally declared independent with the support of US Green Berets on September 2, 1945, weeks after Japan (and the Axis Powers in Europe earlier) had surrendered to the Allies (including the Americans, British, and Soviets). The Japanese had occupied Vietnam at the invitation of Nazi-collaborating Vichy France since 1940 and toppled the French in 1945 only after Vichy fell to the Allies in Europe. Later in 1945, just as Hồ Chí Minh declared Vietnam's independence, France reasserted its claims to Vietnam, now under the leadership of President Charles de Gaulle. Following the Geneva Convention of 1954, the French were to help administer the southern half of Vietnam under Emperor Bảo Đại. He was soon thereafter replaced, with American support, by Prime Minister Ngô Đình Diệm, who opposed the scheduled elections that were to decide Vietnam's unified fate in 1956. This in turn led to the prolonged civil and anti-imperial war between the North and the American-allied South. The war concluded in 1975 with the North's victory, more than a decade after Diệm's assassination in 1963 and the series of military coups that followed his death.

Tan's mother, along with his youngest brother, Xin, came to visit him in prison. This was before the prisoner exchange, which finally took place in August 1954. Conditions had finally improved slightly, in preparation for the announced exchange. Having heard the news and rumors of the upcoming exchange, Tan's mother came to tell her son that he would need to go up the mountains upon being set free. She was not allowed to enter and could not converse with him directly on this visit. But she had brought him a pair of rubber sandals ("Uncle Hồ sandals made of rubber from car tires," he explained as an aside). She threw the sandals in over the barrier toward Tan and instructed him to go up the mountains. This would be the last time Tan ever saw his mother, though he did not yet tell me this.

As an imprisoned Resistance fighter, Tan was released up North in Cửa Hội, a coastal town where the DRV government provided special treatment for their newly released exchanged prisoners. Torture had ended, and now Tan and fellow fighters were fed and given time to heal for two months, while reporting on the hardships they had endured in prison. After being mobilized to rebuild Hưng Nguyên Dam in Nghệ An, Tan recounts, the army was disbanded. Peace had come (to the North), after all, he reminded me.

Still a foreigner in this land, and unwilling (or unable) to return home to the South (the Republic of Vietnam), which officially opposed the DRV, Tan was recruited to become a railroad worker and learned to fix trains and other machines. After a year and a half of study and apprenticeship, in 1959 he became a laborer at a factory and continued working there for several years. In 1963, as fighting was heating up in the South, Tan and fellow southerners were encouraged to join the military again. They were told it was their duty to liberate the people in the South, he explained.

In recounting his story, Tan did not mention any political figures other than "Uncle Hồ." For example, Lê Duẩn, to whom recent historians have come to attribute an increasingly important role in the way that the wars were conducted and the North achieved its goals, was left unnamed.[8] Tan also did not clarify that his poor background, as a farmer and later a worker, likely worked to his advantage. A privileged background, as a landlord, large landholder, or part of the intelligentsia, for example, might have marked him as a suspect bourgeois. His nonprivilege and pedigree as a resistance fighter imprisoned by the French, on the other hand, likely served as political capital throughout the 1950s and 1960s and beyond.

Tan told much of his story in an orderly chronological sequence, following the structure of socialist autobiographical statements (lý lịch). These were used for decades to legitimate individuals' class status and commitment to the revolution,[9] and since I was used to reading about these events in history books and memoirs, his account at first seemed canned and almost trite.[10] At the same time, however, Tan's account also exemplified one warrior's lived experience of Vietnam's broader, conflict-filled history. It only partially overlapped with the accounts of political or social historians, not surprisingly, since events often are remembered in terms of their affective and moral force. They take on a narrative structure and are more than simply a formless reflection of a world out there.

Indeed, life itself takes on a narrative structure, complete with its moral reckonings of events and experiences.[11] As tellers piece together events into a story, they imbue them with moral and affective connections, temporal and causal trajectories, and render certain protagonists significant (or not). These endeavors often have the effect of recruiting listeners (and the tellers themselves) to their version of events. Significantly, it is through the performance[12] of *telling* that moral moods, emotions, and versions of the self take shape and become ephemeral or potentially more enduring lived realities.[13] The ways in which Tan selects key events to recount and the order in which he recounts them, repeating certain themes or events while skipping over others, construe how sacrifice (hy sinh) figures in his life. In his story, as in others that I would hear, sacrifice appears as a pervasive and relatively silent yet embodied suffering. Attending to Tan's story as it continues to unfold, I trace in this chapter the various, entangled resonances of sacrifice and war losses that pervaded the memories of families from central Vietnam. Though usually silenced in ordinary conversation, they are key to understanding family dynamics of silence, sacrifice, and care in subsequent chapters.

SUFFERING HUNGER TO RESCUE THE SOUTH

Continuing in chronological sequence, Tan recounted how he was assigned to both combat and logistics and transportation units. He was sent through the winding Hồ Chí Minh Trail (which he simply describes as "the mountains") to Military Area Five, otherwise known as central Vietnam. This large swath of land included his native Đà Nẵng–Quảng Nam. But Tan was not able to return home throughout the war.

At this juncture, he began to depart from the template genre of the *lý lịch* (government-mandated autobiographical statement), though the changes were subtle and barely perceptible at first. Military service, for him, was not exactly a heroic period of great achievement, nor did he remember it (in what would have been backshadowing fashion emphasizing hindsight) as strictly a victorious inevitability. It was rather a time of starvation and hardship. The force of his story lay not in a teleological truncation of a painful process that led to a fortuitous and desired result. Rather, his personal affects of fear and loss experienced during this critical period in his and the nascent nation's life deepened the plot line by slowing it down and troubling its chronology.

Accordingly, Tan skipped to the middle of the war to describe at length the period from 1967 to 1971, when those in his regiment all suffered terrible hunger. For three whole months, they had not even a grain of rice. "No rice to eat at all," he repeated. They had to forage in the jungles, eating anything from papaya, taro, and pineapple tree bark to taro leaves, flowers, ferns, and roots. They would strip tree bark to get to the inside, cut it up in cubes, then dip it in salt.

I had never heard Tan talk in such detail about food, but here he recounted at length what he consumed when there was nothing provided to eat. Two years later, my host father, also a North Vietnam Army combatant whose family had migrated north from Đà Nẵng, dwelled on the same period of starvation. Like Tan he described in vivid detail how they had to hunt field mice and grab at any leaves or roots to quell their hunger pangs.

And then, for a period of three or four months, Tan continued, they even lacked salt. The Americans were blocking the delta and there was no way to transport salt from the coastal lands to the highlands. Men in his unit swelled up from this prolonged salt deprivation. Some died of malnutrition. And from malaria. Malaria ran rampant, he recounts, the mosquitoes biting everyone everywhere all the time. For each hundred men in a camp, there was enough to feed perhaps three people. They survived on gruel made from cassava or potatoes occasionally dug up from the tribal people's farms. They prioritized feeding the sick, while the healthier foraged.

Having spent several minutes dwelling on the hunger and malaria, Tan reverted to a more patriotic tone and waxed poetic about "the united determination of the Vietnamese people." Quoting Uncle Hồ, he declaimed, "There is nothing more precious than freedom and independence." Tan explained the necessity and inevitability of their cause, in line with the nationalist dogma of the time:

> That was the determination,
> the most encouraging spirit,
> to [allow us to] survive the hardship.
> And second of all . . . the country-the land of Vietnam is one,
> no one can divide it.
> Vietnam is one country and the people of Vietnam are one.
> The rivers and mountains are all connected.
> No one can divide it.
> That was the spirit.
> But the-the . . . most valuable ideal was . . .
> the one that we all kept in our hearts was . . .
> "Nothing is more valuable than independence."
> So . . . even with all the hardships,
> even though many had to sacrifice . . .
> we had to gain independence.
> That was the spirit.

For a brief instance, in a somewhat halting manner, Tan touched on the emotional labor involved in keeping up this "spirit":

> So, at night . . . I . . . well . . . even if I cried,
> I truly understood the spirit.
> But [we] had to be patient,
> because the hardship . . . lasted for twenty years.
> It lasted for twenty years . . . the war.

Tan's point was that suffering had to be endured and even embraced with patience. Sacrifice had to be silent—crying only under cover of night. Sacrifice and suffering were remarkable, perhaps, only in their pervasiveness and in their being taken for granted, as ordinary.

Hunger and malaria were not the only dangers. How fortunate he feels, Tan recounted, to have survived the chemical warfare inflicted on Vietnam by the Americans, particularly with the use of the herbicide Agent Orange. Consistent with others' accounts, whether anthropological, historical, or literary, Tan averred that at the time they did not know the extent of risk and harm to which his unit was exposed:[14]

> Back then I knew nothing . . .
> The spray wet the whole area.
> It wet the whole body.
> But luckily I did not get too infected.
> The cassava and fish all died.
> We couldn't stand seeing food go to waste
> so we cooked and ate them.
> Only later after [the war] did we realize it was so toxic.
> At the time we knew nothing.

Not stopping, Tan continued to describe the scene in a way that suggests ambivalence about his initial assertion that they did not know anything:

> Every time they scattered it they used three C-47 airplanes.
> It was like rain, wetting the whole area.
> Like . . . every living tree or plant, after the spraying . . . in the morning.
> By evening they all withered.
> And it stank.
> It was a kind of chemical.
> So pungent [we] couldn't breathe.
> Couldn't breathe!
> But . . . well they sprayed it in bags and bags . . . along all the trails.

This visceral memory of stench and hunger triggered further memories of the horrors of war. Tan specified the weapons used against his unit. Using short sentences that seemed lyrical in their symmetry, Tan explained:

> That toxic chemical agent was the second thing.
> Another aspect in addition was the problem of the struggle.

The hardship was unbearable.
I am talking about the . . . the battlefront.
They gathered fifty pieces of artillery.
And they shot,
they shot on average . . .
forty cannons per meter square.
Forty exploding cannons.
105mm cannons.
155mm cannons.
And there were bombs.
Bombs from planes . . . they dropped.
Worst were the phosphorous bombs.
Phosphorous bombs and gasoline bombs.
They had a lot of different types.
Phosphorous bombs where the phosphorous was flammable,
it burned everywhere it touched.
And there were . . . gasoline bombs.
They dropped them.
And the bombs burned everything.
Whenever they dropped them on my regiment, several died.
Burned, completely charred their bodies.
And . . . after the gasoline the-the-the gasoline bombs dropped . . .
there were . . . the . . . the bomblets.

I listened, riveted, fascinated also by the details of horror amplified through repetitions and expansions of the quantities and kinds of bombs and ravages the Americans wreaked. I could not help but envision the patriotic displays and dioramas in the War Museum in Ho Chi Minh City and at the Củ Chi tunnels. Dug to evade the Americans' superior firepower by allowing fighters to travel underground, this network of tunnels in the southwestern part of Vietnam had since turned into a tourist attraction. I recalled the plaques that proudly commemorate the revolutionaries' courage and hardship overcoming their Goliath enemies.

I echoed Tan, "bomblets?," to encourage him to continue. He did.

Tan explained the mechanics of bomblets—the cruelty of a large bomb that housed five hundred mini-bombs inside it, all of them exploding to inflict yet more damage:

The big bomb . . . when it exploded, it released bomblets.
Weapons like those.

And there was another type . . . DK . . .
DK was another type of cannon that used nails.
When it exploded, it released nails.
And mines too!
Steel ball mines.
Mines that used steel balls [otherwise known as M18A1 Claymore mines].
And the type of mine . . .
Nail mines.
Steel ball mines, nail mines.
In the North they called them mines.

Having rattled off the numerous dangers threatening his unit, Tan reached another of his points: the political and ethical differences between his underdog, morally justified side and the imperial enemy. He explained that it was all part of US president Richard Nixon's strategy to "use all the most modern weapons" to win the war, to rule Vietnam, and to divide it. The Americans' intention, he continued, was to take over the South and then the North and ultimately China:

The ideology [was to] dominate the entire Southeast.
To become the ruler.
The hegemon.
It was a greedy ideology.

Consistent with fellow Vietnamese accounts of the war, the "domino effect" doctrine of the United States that framed the conflict as an attempt to stymie the spread of Communism appeared through Tan's eyes not simply as an effort at "containment," but far more aggressive and sinister.[15] As a countermove, Tan now went on to extol Hồ Chí Minh again:

So therefore Vietnam was . . .
the spirit was like . . .
the leader of Vietnam, Uncle Hồ.
He said, "Nothing is more precious than independence and freedom.
Mountains to mountains.
Rivers to rivers.
The country of Vietnam is one.
Nothing can divide it."
That was the . . . the-the-the- my determination.

I admit, I was getting a bit bored with the patriotic declamations. Coupled with the detailed description of the weapons, it seemed that Tan was copying verbatim from Party propagandists. But more likely it was the other way around. The history books are written on the basis of accounts such as Tan's. When Tan repeatedly declaimed Uncle Hồ's inspiring words, he was evincing the power of this oratory for common combatants such as himself.

Amid the horrors of war, what allowed men (and women) to go on with the struggle? How could Tan stand the danger? And what of the separation from his loved ones?

Tan's detailed rendition of the weapons, hunger, and disease threatening to rob him and fellow Vietnamese of life and limb during so much of the war was a harrowing account. Yet I yearned to hear about the personal dimension, of feelings of separation and loss that Tan had experienced. Perhaps like Renato Rosaldo (1989), who missed the force of rage expressed in Ilongots' narratives of headhunting, I inexplicably missed the force of sheer terror that Tan, in his lilting, lyrical narrative of war, was experiencing even in the recollection years later. I underheard the fear and anguish that attunement to these auditory details evoked at the time. Instead, I tuned in only to when, twenty minutes into his monologue, Tan at last recalled his wife.

Upon relistening, transcribing, and translating the recording, however, I have been struck by the pathos Tan expressed. He took care both not to demonize the enemy while recounting the horrors they inflicted, and to evince the sense of *collective* suffering involved. While admitting his own dire discomfort, he largely deflected attention from his own deeds and feelings, other than his affiliation with the nationalist slogans preached by the country's paterfamilias, Uncle Hồ. Danger and fear, he at first implicitly and later explicitly repeated, could not be overcome without a collective spirit of unity that saw Vietnam not as multiple or divided, but as ineluctably "one."[16]

"NOT ONLY ON THE BATTLEFRONT BUT ALSO ON THE HOME FRONT PEOPLE SACRIFICED EVERYWHERE"

Feminist historians have documented the contributions and sufferings of Vietnamese women throughout years of war and struggle against foreign invaders, drawing some lines of continuity between the twentieth century and earlier periods.[17] During the time of my fieldwork, the diary of Đặng Thuỳ Trâm, a military doctor who perished in battle against the Americans in 1968, had just been published after its return to her family, becoming an instant best-seller. Tan, however, did not reference this personal diary. Indeed, he does not even explicitly refer to his own pain of separation from family, but draws his listener in by describing the separation largely as simple, understated facts, with long pauses:

As for my family situation,
I . . . had just got married to my wife . . . for several months.
And she was pregnant.
She was one month pregnant when I left.
When I left . . .
I left . . .
I left for eleven or twelve years.
Until I came back.
She gave birth to Khanh in the meantime.
Gave birth to Khanh.
She was twelve when . . . I came back [in late 1975].

Recounted at first as a long-lost memory that he is at pains to recall, as belied by the pauses, trailing utterances, and direct reported speech, Tan's timeline now began to slow down and become vivid as he recollected his initial meeting with his daughter:

I got back . . .
when I got back . . .
my wife gave me directions to find home.
I got to the right place.
When I got to the-the-the thatching . . .
where she was staying,
Khanh, she was only fourteen,
no . . . twelve or thirteen years old.
She ran to the yard, seeing me enter.
She was outside when she saw me,
and she called out, "There's a soldier uncle,"
"There's a soldier uncle, a soldier uncle!"
Silly girl!

After stopping to chuckle, Tan now stepped back to comment on the significance of these details:

> I have another . . . well, admiration . . . for the problem of . . . my wife.
> The situation back then was dire.
> War destroyed everything.
> It was really harsh.
> Very harsh.
> She had the responsibility . . . of raising a child.
> She had to take her everywhere, and go into hiding [during bombings].
> And also, she joined the war effort . . . for the country.
> And . . . to sustain that love *(Rồi là . . . một phần đó chịu đựng cái tình cảm đó)*.
> Sentiments of love missing her husband *(Cái tình cảm đó xa chồng)*.
> Not knowing whether . . . I was alive or dead.
> [We] couldn't send any letters.
> For ten years, there was no contact.
> Only after the war was there contact.

Tan's wife, Hoa, had told me at length about how difficult it had been, not knowing whether her husband was alive or dead, and how hard it was to encourage their daughter to believe she still had a father whom she had never met. In contrast, Tan had not mentioned missing his wife and yet-to-be-born child at the time. He attributed all these feelings to Hoa, praising her ability to endure living through this prolonged ordeal of separation and uncertainty. Implicitly, he framed the affective dimension of sacrifice as women's domain.

He went on to explain her—or his—feelings of "frustration" with the war. He used the pronoun *bác*, which stands for either "Uncle" or "Aunt" in this context, and I did not interrupt him to verify. Then, he modified the term *bác* with *gái* (female) to indicate that now he was definitively talking about his wife. But he next dropped the pronoun and gender marker, leaving it unclear whether he was reporting his or her experience:

> That was why . . . **she/I** was also-also-also-also-also-also . . . frustrated
>   *(bức xúc)* about some aspects.
> **My wife** . . . **she** was frustrated with being so far from her husband . . .
> being separated from him for ten years,
> not knowing if he was alive or dead.
> Yes.

That was . . . again . . .
She/I was just one in millions of Vietnamese.
Uhm. So it was a form of sacrifice.
That not only those who fought on the battlefront,
but those who remained behind,
they also were sacrificing.

Referring to a question that I had posed to his wife ("Had there ever been a time when you wanted to sacrifice but could not?"), Tan explained that sacrifice involves a variety of deeds and is not restricted to giving up one's life in war:

The other day you asked about sacrifice . . .
That was also sacrifice.
Sacrifice including feelings,
Sacrificing all this and all that in order that . . .
husbands and children could have the peace of mind
to go-go-go . . . rescue the country.

One of Tan's points, which I had already heard from his wife and others in Đà Nẵng, Huế, and Hanoi, was that patriotic death in battle was only one exalted and state-sanctioned form of sacrifice. Sacrifice, he stressed, was more expansive. For patriotic sacrifice to be sustainable, there had to be a multitude of seemingly smaller sacrifices, often involving the recurring sentiment and love, as well as material acts of caretaking. If I were to understand "sacrifice," I had to understand what *tình cảm* meant as well, for it was always invoked alongside *hy sinh* and signified something less masculinized than patriotic death.[18]

Patriotic sacrifice relied on an ethos of suffering and bearing hardship in relative silence. Like its broader counterpart of everyday "homefront" sacrifice, battlefront sacrifice involved minimizing certain feelings while not entirely foreswearing them. Patriotic-dramatic and quotidian sacrifice are intimately connected, even as one entails bloodshed in its paradigmatic form whereas the other is deliberately understated. Tan's story links suffering and sacrifice to motherhood, nationalism, and progress. In the narration to follow, Tan aligns with wider cultural and political tropes that frame Vietnam's victory over the Americans as morally preordained and just. In an assured but non-self-aggrandizing manner, he ties his personal acts and circumstances to those of the nation that he had helped "rescue" and "liberate" (in Vietnamese, *cứu nước*). Tan does not privilege his own experiential difficulties and suffering but alludes to them through the women in his life: they are the real carriers of burdens and hardships.

"BUT THE ONE WHO SUFFERED MOST WAS MY MOTHER"

Tan concluded, "So . . . the-the-the situation . . . that was the family situation." But he was not done recounting the sense of suffering and separation that his family experienced. Even after the war's conclusion, he could not immediately return home, because there was still the problem of securing Vietnam from another revolt by supporters of the southern regime. Combatants like him had to continue to defer their own individual, family-oriented desires and instead first assure the collective security of their newly unified nation. He narrates this period as a sequence of logical steps, using a number of temporal and causal connectors:

> **After** reunification,
> **after** winning the war,
> **when** the Americans retreated,
> the army of the Puppet Government surrendered.
> **But** ah, . . . I had to stay here [in the South].
> **Because** there were still 1.2 million disbanded enemy soldiers.
> **So therefore** everyone in the military,
> all the regiments had to be ready to fight.
> We couldn't just go back home.
> **So after** Independence, everyone wanted to go back to their wives and kids.
> **But** at the time [we] still could not . . . could **not yet** go back.
> Only **a year later** could [we] go.
> **A year later after** everything had settled down [we] could finally go.
> **So the next year** I went back north to meet my wife . . . and we had Oanh.
> **And** that was it.
> No more children.
> [We] had no more energy left,
> no energy.

I thought Tan might end his story then and there, but he continued, again without prompting other than my echoing him, "No more energy. Exhausted."

Tan explained that to have had only two daughters was an anomaly for his generation. His peers kept encouraging him to "try for a boy," articulating the common Confucian gender ideology that boys are preferable to girls.[19] But he had "no more energy." By late 1976, when his second daughter was born, Tan was already over forty years old. In telling his story, however, Tan did not mention his age, or the family planning policy that would come a full decade later.[20] If he seemed apologetic about failing to produce a boy at this juncture, Tan also sounded resigned to his fate. Later, he would return to assert with more confidence that those who teased him are "just conservative" and that "boys and girls are the same."

Tan chose at this point to resume the relatively chronologically linear account of his life that conforms to the genre of the *lý lịch*. He minimizes personal emotion and frames himself as simply a token of a type: a Vietnamese patriot loyally serving his nation. Matter-of-factly, he recounted that after Reunification he had to join the fight against China, which invaded Vietnam after the Americans had left, taking advantage of his nation's war exhaustion:[21]

China thought that Vietnam was exhausted from fighting the US,
and that Vietnam would be easy to beat.
But beating it was not easy,
they did not win.

Although these wars continued for over a decade, Tan's service was moved to Đà Nẵng in 1980. At long last, after over twenty-five years away, he was able to return to his natal lands.

Circumstances here, he says tersely, were "difficult." His salary was not sufficient to feed his family, and so he had to rely on his "brothers in the regiment." His wife, Hoa, had also joined the military, yet together they were hard-pressed to make a decent living and support their two daughters throughout the 1980s. Hoa settled with him and their daughters in Đà Nẵng after so many years apart. She was an outsider, a Northerner. Tan did not say so, but his siblings later intimated that she never really integrated well into his clan because she lacked *tình cảm*.[22] In 1988, Tan finally retired. Soon after, he used some of his connections to send his elder daughter, Khanh, to Eastern Europe, where she would be able to earn more as a foreign worker and support her parents back home in Vietnam.

Tan reflected for a few seconds, then circled back to the suffering of his mother, the separation from whom he had originally begun his tale. Again, his reverie is filled with parallel structures and expansions through which he conveys admiration and longing for his mother:

> But . . . in this process of going . . .
> I think that . . . the one who suffered most was my mother.
> She . . . my father died young.
> And she had to do everything to raise . . . six, seven children.
> We were little then, but we all grew up.
> Joining this, joining that.
> Poor her.
> That's . . . I love my mother the most.
> Um . . . my father died when he was forty-five.
> The children were all young.
> And she had no farm,
> no garden,
> nothing,
> relying only on her parents' help.
> My grandfather and my grandmother, and . . . my uncles.
> They helped each other out. . . .
> By herself, she took care of . . . seven children.
> Each one grew up.
> Everyone got a job.
> And was well educated.
> Look at the youngest, Uncle Xin.
> He was the youngest.
> She loved him so much.
> She took him everywhere she went.
> Yes, when he was young.
> That was the situation like that.
> But then . . . I left.
> When I left she was still alive,
> but when I returned she had passed away.
> So I never saw her.

Although Tan's loss sounded understated to me, he repeated the details of his mother's life to subtly communicate his thoughts and feelings about her. A sense of a muted, ongoing loss was amplified when he recounted yet again her short prison visit to him in 1954, when she threw a pair of sandals in and instructed him to go up the mountains.

Tan did not say explicitly that he suffered, but the subtext rang loudly for me in this seeming silence. He described how his journey back to central Vietnam in the 1960s took nearly four months to trek on foot, marching around and around, each man carrying a weight of 42 kilograms (approximately 92 pounds) of guns, bullets, and equipment on his back. "Nothing is more precious than independence and freedom," they kept telling themselves, he told me now. He recounted again how difficult it was, starving and caving under the weight, surviving on three cans of corn a day. Rain drenched them. As they kept going, marching into his home province of Quảng Nam, they also were provisioned with dried cassava and even canned ribs. His attention to the visceral details of survival underscored how existence seemed barely sustainable, as though the soldiers were reduced almost to "bare life."[23] Once again, he told me how lucky he feels to be alive at all, having witnessed so many others perish from the hardships of war.

Repeatedly, Tan expressed pity for all the youth, "whole classes of students, classes of intellectuals" who could not survive the unbearable conditions or who "sacrificed" in battle. On both the enemy's side and on "our" (winning) side, many died, many sacrificed. Unlike the Vietnamese state's rhetoric that only those who died in patriotic battle sacrificed,[24] Tan did not make that distinction: "The fighting was horrible. No words could describe it." Adding what bordered on further unpatriotic discourse, he explained, highlighting the idiom of lack:

That was the story of the revolution back then.
It was very **weak**,
didn't . . .
lacked weapons.
No food,
no rice.
Even **lacked** salt.
The bullets that it took over a year to carry from North to South
through the mountains and forests,
were **all used up** in just one battle.

But then Tan retracted the sentiment, saying in wonder, "But we still won." With this simple statement of fact, the seemingly impossible or improbable turned into an inevitable, a kind of preordained, foreshadowed miracle.

In this way, Tan ended his brief foray into a type of sideshadowing account that dared to consider, indirectly, the what-might-have-been, when at the time, experientially, it seemed that everyone was on the verge of loss, with carnage on every side. His preferred narrative style and stance is not that of entertaining sideshadowed alternate possibilities (which we will see in later chapters in stories recounted by others). In line with teleological state narratives, Tan preferred linearly structured stories of success against all odds, achieved through determination and common purpose. Loss and doubt are relegated to the margins. Yet still, Tan admits reluctantly, heroic success was intertwined with suffering and did not feel particularly heroic at all. Reflecting on and recalling his ambivalence-filled past, Tan added:

> Just this morning I sat here thinking about it, pondering.
> I think we were good.
> I think we were very good.
> High spirited, in good spirits.
> It was because of the Party leaders, the Communist Party.
> The Communist Party had to have been an excellent leader.
> And it was.
> Only after sitting and thinking, I saw that,
> I would say that . . .
> if I had been the leader . . . I would have given up.
> Yes.
> But that determination in common,
> it was . . . even though everything was so difficult.
> And . . . no one expected to survive.
> But . . . we won.

Tan's narrative turns heroic at this point, yet he does not attribute the heroism to himself. He admits feeling fear and exhaustion, which might have led him to give up. But, he reiterates, he was buttressed by his brothers in arms and the spirits of the times, buoyed by the Party. One could not say the same of Nixon and Johnson, he continues. He contrasts them with the leaders on his side, for the United States did not want to fight, he concludes. They retreated in failure. A huge failure.

Like many American veterans, Tan attributes this failure to the American people, who he explains aided his side by protesting and going on hunger strikes and demanding that their government retreat. "The American soldiers in the South," he adds, also helped, since "they-they-they disobeyed orders. They dropped their guns and refused to fight." Protests against the war in the United States, in Vietnam, and all over the world, he repeated and continued, forced the Americans to retreat, leading to their miserable defeat.

Tan was not gloating. He had had years to contemplate the sorrows of war and had recounted to me not feats of honor but the visceral pain of hunger and fear, witnessing death and destruction. The slogans of the Communist Party were not mere propaganda for him. In his account, they served as foreshadowing signs that helped him survive and overcome the unbearable. The story of Vietnam as a weak and poor nation standing up to the giant, seemingly all-powerful United States was not an overblown myth but a patriotic point of pride. Unlike other Southeast Asian nations, such as Thailand or the Philippines, who received aid from the Americans, he now elaborated, Vietnam had improved in leaps and bounds despite the superpower's destructive force. For Tan, the teleology of Vietnam's "progress" was a hard-won one, gained not through individual acts of merit but the collective force of leadership and vision that had inspired many like him to sign on and fight despite the odds.

ASSESSING PROGRESS

Tan continually merged his own personal circumstances with those of the broader nation: Vietnam, like his family, had progressed from precarious poverty through war and on to a time of freedom and plenitude. These experiences were captured through a life story that strives for "coherence."[25] Such accounts feature a clearly delineated beginning, the introduction of trouble, and its resolution through the intervention of protagonists who act in morally constant ways to restore or institute a new order.[26] The story is "tellable" in virtue of its linear plot line and dramatic events.

Tan's story of national success that facilitated his and his compatriots' progress mirrored propagandistic state accounts that applaud Vietnam's accomplishments. Conditions after the war were quite dire, he explained: infrastructure in the North was on the verge of collapse, the economy was about to crumble, and invalids abounded on both sides. Over a million released soldiers and others who had helped the Americans were now unemployed. And yet the government was able to build factories and feed the hungry, eliminating starvation, he recounted. In just a dozen years, after a ten-year war against the French and another twenty years of war against the Americans, he elaborated with pride, Vietnam was able to recover. Vietnam now was on par with the other countries of Southeast Asia who had not suffered such setbacks.

And yet Tan's personal story contains hints of less certain plot lines. His account intermittently veers nonlinearly away from battlefield and national virtues toward ongoing family suffering, which challenges the patriotic master narrative that relegates hunger and loss to the completed past. Despite improvements, changes were slow. Unemployment was high. Vietnam had only just gotten rid of feudalism, he elaborated:

> There are some traditions that are out of date.
> But they still remain.
> For example, corruption.
> Corruption is the remnant of the old system.

But Tan does not dwell on challenges to the state; his account quickly reverts to a teleological quest for improvement, wherein he declares that "the new system does not have the concept of corruption."

Despite *đổi mới*'s departure from the socialist state's command economy, in Tan's account the reforms formed a continuous line of progress away from feudalism. Feudalism, he explained, echoing perhaps the teachings of Marx and Engels (1978a), was a patriarchal, monarchical system wherein boys were worth more than girls:

> Nothing was based in science,
> everything happened because the gods let it.
> That was feudalism.
> Girls had to serve boys.
> They were treated as slaves.
> That was the custom.
> Girls had to play the role of servants,
> slaves for boys.

Familiar with this trope that narrates girls and women of the past as hopelessly oppressed, saved by the progress brought on by communism, I was eager to return Tan to a person-centered, experientially based mode of narration. I asked if in his house his sister had had to serve the boys in this way. "No, my family didn't have it. We didn't have that custom," he immediately retorted.

His own father and mother, Tan explained, were well educated. They both "had a lot of knowledge" and knew both the Traditional Chinese script (*chữ Nho*, literally, "Confucian script") and the Romanized script (*chữ quốc ngữ*, literally, "nationalized script").[27] His family, unlike other families, was "not as feudal." His parents did not beat their children. "They taught us using education, not by violence," Tan explained, repeating again, to emphasize the contrast, that "feudal men used violence."[28]

His own family, he continued, also did not engage in arranged marriages and instead allowed him and all his siblings to find their own partners based on love, and to choose freely. He named his older and younger brothers and older sister in turn. Using repetition and parallel structure, he recounted first how his brothers Văn and Xin and their wives "went to school together and fell in love and got married" (*là cũng đi học rồi yêu đương nhau rồi lấy nhau*) or "simply loved on their own" (*cũng tự yêu nhau thôi*); likewise, his sister Bi and her husband, who "on their own loved each other," and himself and his wife. Each one, he repeated, found his or her own partner on their own, with no matchmaking and no force, each on their own fell in love with their spouse and had both sides agree to the marriage. Tan next went on to qualify that with regard to the spirits, his family did "still pray to them" and relied on prayer when someone was sick rather than "go to the doctors to kill the bacteria." As though this needed clarification, he added, with a hint of embarrassment in his chuckle, "Meaning we gave offerings . . . to the ancestors. For protection. That was feudal, these old customs."

Tan contrasted his loving family and devoted mother who was able to raise her children to be such "modern," well-educated, progressive—even if still spiritually devoted—successful citizens with others in his village. It was other villagers who still led lives benighted by feudalism. He said he had witnessed at the time how if a woman got pregnant out of wedlock, people beat and tortured her. They beat her to a pulp. That's another reason why the present government was so much better, Tan concluded: "Fortunately the revolution brought it down. The revolution brought the feudal system down. Otherwise, it would have continued to last." The French supported the feudal system, he now added. "But our revolution destroyed feudalism," he said with pride. "If feudalism was here, it would rule the wrong way. It's against science."

In these ways, Tan seamlessly linked the circumstances of his own family to those of the nation of which he was a part and which he had helped build and liberate. In his account, French colonial rule and feudal rule merged, both of them regimes in which common, poor Vietnamese had no freedom to flourish and enjoy the fruits of "science." Citizens did not have freedom under feudalism, he repeated. "It was a form of monarchy. And in the village . . . everyone had to listen to the rulers. The head of the village . . . the head of the town . . . whatever he said, [people] had to follow. Or else, [you'd] get beaten. If [you] couldn't do it, they'd put [you] in jail. Another point was . . . the taxation." He harped on this point, again and again: "Heavy taxation. Taxation. The tax we had to pay. Whatever was in the house got taxed. But . . . but-but if [you] didn't pay taxes, they'd force [you] into jail." With these words, Tan narrated Vietnam's feudal and colonial past as mutually reinforcing morally corrupt regimes, to be contrasted with the morally superior ideals of the revolution. He was constructing a morally linear account of progress and improvement that he linked to the progression of time itself, narratively mirroring Marx and Engels's (1978b) evolutionist account of history but without framing it as a dialectic.

Continuing in this materialist and teleological vein, he next even more explicitly tied the inequities to the material conditions experienced under the old political economic order. "Back then," he began, "there were only 25 million Vietnamese. There was a lot of space. There was so much land [to cultivate]. But the people were starving." The Japanese, during their short rule of Vietnam (1940–45), he said, "forced the people to rid their rice paddies and grow jute *(trồng cây đay)* to make bags . . . to weave heavy-duty bags. And . . . they made gunpowder. Rid the rice, grow jute. There was ... a lot of land. Land. So spacious. Yet people were starving."

Returning yet again to the theme of hunger and starvation, Tan went on to describe how during the great famine of 1945 in the North, people in the South also starved, surviving on papaya and pineapple tree bark and buds. How could it be, he asked, that there was so much land and far fewer people, yet people were starving? By contrast, he said triumphantly, "now there are 80 million people, 85 million people. Many times more than before. Yet we have a surplus of rice to export. [I] must say that's good. From having so much land and few people, all starving. Two and half million died of famine in the North, two and a half million died. Two and a half million died of famine," he repeated yet again. "And in the South, even if [people] didn't die, they also languished. Eating parts of the banana and pineapple trees ... the papaya trees too."

I could not help but marvel at how often Tan returned to the theme of hunger and food shortages. It was his way to contrast the bounty that he enjoyed under current conditions with lack and suffering of past decades. Yet again, he repeated the statistics: "Now ... there are 85 million people. We still have the same amount of land. But we enjoy a surplus of food. That's an improvement. [We've] done well (đó giỏi ác)." Speaking with more animation as he framed the issue of development in politicized terms, he contrasted the present period, where he claims there was no more hunger or homelessness, with the dire straits suffered under colonialism:

> There are no more beggars.
> Under feudalism, there were a lot of beggars.
> Especially during the French occupation.
> When the French came here, there were a lot of beggars, so many!
> A well-off family would meet ...
> more than ten beggars a day in front of the house.
> Homeless beggars.
> And then when they were starving,
> they lay down hopelessly in the street, so many of them.
> Back then, under feudalism, whoever died, it didn't matter.
> There was no help, no aid.
> But now ... now that doesn't happen anymore.
> There's none of it.

"No beggars at all?," I asked him, a bit suspicious of this totalizing framing that sounded more propagandistic than experience-near.

Tan spoke somewhat defensively, saying, "Now, if there is . . . anyone . . . without a mother or father . . . who wanders around . . . we gather them all." Dismissing naysayers as those who just spread rumors and do not understand Vietnam, he returned to his own personal experience. His own family, he said, had witnessed several different eras and therefore could attest to the improvement of the Vietnamese people. Considering the conditions, he repeated, "[one] must say [we've] done well." Unlike in the past, when people lived in thatch huts and had to subsist on roots and straw, the cooking smoke filling up their abodes as they cooked, he went on, "now everyone has clothes to wear, has a home or shelter. It's certainly good." He went on to equate the past with medieval times and then proclaimed that in a matter of mere decades Vietnam had done quite well for itself.

Clearly aligning with the Vietnamese state's master narrative of development and improvement on the heels of victory against colonial plunderers, Tan explained that capitalism had come early to Vietnam but only to exploit its resources. "The capitalists kept the feudal system in place. And they did not open a new era . . . a new age of democracy. For-for-for Vietnam to improve." Echoing classic history book explanations, he added that because Vietnam was rich in natural resources, foreigners had always wanted to invade and get the populace to extract these resources for them. It is for these reasons, he concluded, that the Vietnamese people had had to suffer for so long and did not have the opportunity to improve. But now that Vietnam is independent, it is fully able to develop and improve. It is only the losers, he added, just a smattering of Vietnamese Americans, who hate the regime and bear a grudge for having lost so badly; they speak badly about Vietnam, not knowing how it has changed and improved.

MAKING SENSE OF STATED SACRIFICIAL GENRES

As we neared the end of the hour, Tan, who was not a cadre but was a Communist Party member and bona fide combatant who for the majority of his life had championed his state's cause, had come to declaim a familiar trope. I had heard it again and again in Vietnamese language classes taught by Hanoi-trained teachers and other cadres or academics. I understood well and empathized with his and their long struggle against colonial and imperial domination and plunder. What continued to puzzle me, however, was how people like him sounded so certain about Vietnam's future, as though there could be no other trajectory than constant positive progress, development, and improvement. Anticolonial and anti-imperial struggles would end, in this narrative, with Communism as a necessary and just but ultimately mere bump in the road to triumphalist, and no longer colonial, capitalist progress.

Throughout his monologue, Tan did not refer to the collectivization period that followed the war,[29] except indirectly by noting that they were all poor and barely able to make ends meet, even on his military salary and, later, pension. Nor did he draw an explicit distinction between the pre- and post-1986 reforms. Instead, he framed Vietnam as having climbed a linear upward slope. From miserable hunger and the shackles of colonialism, when he had himself suffered grievously both emotionally and physically, to triumphant victory but temporary hard times attributed to the war, its aftermath, and new conflicts with China, and on to the present optimistic development.

Sacrifice, in this account, took center stage under conditions of suffering. But it receded to the background as times improved. Tan had been quite clear that *hy sinh* did not just involve bloodshed: it also encompassed the many acts of suffering for another during times of trouble, when men, women, and even children endured hardship and withheld their desires so that others could benefit. It was ordinary sacrifices, during extraordinary times, that had made victory possible and, in this account, seemed to have ended suffering altogether. And yet a sense of loss repeatedly surfaced in Tan's story, even as he declared that there was no more hunger or homelessness and no shortage of freedom and democracy in contemporary Vietnam. It was this loss that rendered Tan's experience a form of "sacrifice." This sacrifice consists in relatively silent suffering, which Tan largely attributes to others and to the completed past as he recounts his own trajectory, where he intimately twines his autobiography with the victorious collective biography of his nation.

Tan had begun with the story of his mother throwing sandals to him and returned to it again about halfway through our interview. She, he explicitly said, had suffered the most. She had passed away in 1972, twenty years after he had left home and eight years before he could permanently return. She was, in his recounting, a classic paragon of virtue: the long-suffering, loving, and beloved caretaker who from her children's infancy forward bestowed on them the ability to do good in the world. While Tan also acknowledged his wife's suffering and his own starvation— a theme to which he also returned repeatedly—he dwelled most on Hoa's role as their daughter's guardian. He did not explicitly claim for himself feelings of loss and mourning, nor did he describe himself as someone who sacrificed. Rather, what he emphasized was his affiliation and sense of unity with patriotic others, from whom he drew strength.

The repeated refrain, "There is nothing more precious than independence and freedom," had been a collective call that became for him a lived reality. It had allowed him to survive the battlefront and the many hardships beyond combat, of simply and barely living in war. Vietnam's victory was what had brought about the slogan's successful realization for Tan. As he said toward the end of our interview, "I see us as free, no one does any harm to us. We can live however we like, say whatever we want, there's nothing wrong."

If I at first mistakenly remembered Tan's account as harrowing and yet clouded by propagandistic, almost empty claims, I have come to see it as one exemplar of how the extraordinary is rendered ordinary. Suffering had been all-pervasive and entirely unremarkable. It was not particularly endowed with spiritual or transcendent qualities. Loss and sacrifice, which entail suffering, likewise are silent, ordinary and extraordinary at once. In beginning with and circling back to the last encounter with his mother, Tan's loss reverberates through his story's structure rather than verbalized content. It is silent, like sacrifice, opaque and yet redolent in the ways that it is largely spoken around rather than about, a pervasive, "fully social and communicative" presence in the everyday.[30]

Two days earlier, Tan's wife, Hoa, had told much the same tale as he had but from her perspective. She, too, had not claimed sacrifice for herself but spoke of the long separation from her husband and the difficulties of raising a child alone, not knowing if her partner would ever return. She, too, had pointed to the community as sustaining her and giving her courage and extolled the virtues of leaving the injustices and difficulties of feudalism and colonialism behind. For both Tan and Hoa, the Communist

Party had provided a meaningful trope through which to understand their world and the changing tides that had engulfed Vietnam. They saw these changes less as a break with the past than its logical continuation. In these accounts, the comforts they now enjoyed were just rewards for the pervasive suffering that led loved ones and other fellow compatriots on both sides of the war to perish in sacrifice, or just barely manage to endure, buoyed by the promise of national liberation. Arising in response to my request that they reflect on their past (moral) experience, their narratives also were a means to craft and articulate a particular, ethical version of experience. In their accounts, we see how narrative (and some forms of interaction) positions suffering, loss, and sacrifice, alongside love and devotion, as relatively silent, yet centrally social, interpersonal, moral experiences.

Subsequent chapters continue to develop these themes. Specifically, I show first how the readiness to "sacrifice" on an ordinary basis might be learned through extraordinary and yet mundane rituals of devotion, as well as quotidian language socialization routines that, as in Tan's account, but in a less dramatic fashion, involve shaping and disciplining one's corporeal body to cultivate a particular ethical subjectivity. This is followed by accounts that complicate and problematize the linearities with which Tan tried to conclude. Sacrificing, taking care, and loving, as well as family pressures and state policies that enjoin members or citizens to sacrifice, care, and love, I show in the final three chapters, are often dual-edged, sometimes rewarding, sometimes more troubled affairs.

2 Rituals and Routines of Sacrifice

RESPECT THOSE ABOVE, YIELD TO THOSE BELOW

Repetition ... opens potentialities that went unnoticed, were
aborted, or were repressed in the past. It opens up the past
again in the direction of coming-towards.... [T]he concept
of repetition succeeds at once in preserving the primacy of
the future and in making the shift toward having-been.

– Paul Ricoeur, *Time and Narrative* (1990, 3:76)

FILIAL PIETY AND ASYMMETRICAL RECIPROCITY

It was early on a Wednesday afternoon in April 2007 when fifty-three-year-old Nga brought me to her long-deceased father's natal home, where family members were gathering to celebrate her grandfather's death anniversary *(đám giỗ)*. The death had occurred more than a half century earlier. Every year families celebrate this occasion on the same lunar calendar day as the eve prior to the death.

A lavish feast is prepared, with offerings made first to the deceased ancestor, male or female, extending back three to four generations. The household head and his or her relatives place a sampling of each of the feast's dishes, as well as rice wine, tea, and incense, on a table laid out in front of the deceased's altar. Prayers are whispered or mouthed by each relative and friend in turn as they address the deceased directly, then light the incense sticks, bow or prostrate themselves in front of the altar, and, finally, place the sticks in the urn on the altar. For many (and for me, too, as I became habituated to the practice), this is a fulfilling way to commune with and sacralize the departed.

Once the incense sticks have burned at least a quarter of the way down, family and friends partake of the multicourse feast. They sit usually ten to twelve around each table, organized by gender and age, with the oldest men sitting closest to the deceased's altar, older women around another table, and so forth down to the young children, who sit at a mixed-gender table farthest from the altar. While the tables are already laid out with the first course, young to middle-aged adult women and some men make sure to continually supply the tables with more food and drinks (usually beer for the men and some women and sodas such as Coca-Cola and Fanta for the rest). These practices enact and spatially map out kinship, age, and gender hierarchies, which are also indexed through language, particularly the use of kinship honorifics to address and refer to kin and nonkin in one's social world.[1]

When Nga and I arrived, the household's daughter-in-law as well as Nga's younger sisters and Nga's helper—who cleaned and cooked for the family twice weekly—were already busy in the kitchen, finalizing preparations for the feast. Five women, all chopping, rolling, frying, and arranging delicacies soon to be consumed. They were preparing a small celebration of just three tables: one for elderly men and women in their seventies and eighties who had a living memory of Nga's grandfather, and two for Nga's age-mates and their children.

Nga's grandfather's eldest son, who worked as a journalist for the DRV (Communist North Vietnam) during the war years, inherited the house. Nga never met her grandfather. Her family left the area when she was an infant, at the outset of the country's partition in 1954. The grandfather died at home in Đà Nẵng later during the war, while Nga's family was still up North. The grandfather's youngest sister, who had also remained in Đà Nẵng during the war, proudly told me that her son, who years earlier fled to the United States as a "boatperson refugee," was now working to sponsor her to come to the United States. Family members at one time had stood opposed to one another. Yet here we were, together worshipping the dead, Nga and her aunt no longer enemies. Participation in the *đám giỗ* was part and parcel of displaying filial piety *(hiếu)* and good relations of *tình cảm* (intimacy, care, and empathy) with one another.[2]

Akiko Hashimoto (2004, 182) describes filial piety as "at once a family practice, an ideology, and a system of regulating power relations" among kin and between rulers and their subjects. Filial piety pervades most aspects of life in contemporary East Asia, including Vietnam, where it is linked to related systems of hierarchy and patriarchy.[3] Premised on the idea that parents have sacrificed for their children, filial piety mandates that the young act solicitously toward their elders. That even bad parents must be treated with piety means that this is not a transactional relationship but rather a morally compulsory one. Continually emphasized is the boundless, essentially unrepayable debt of gratitude (*on* in Vietnamese, like Japanaese *on* and Chinese *en*) that children owe their parents.

Scholarship on filial piety in East Asia focuses on obedience and authoritarianism within families and regards the contemporary erosion of such relations as a sign of filial piety's possible decline.[4] In examining relations of sacrifice *(hy sinh)*, which parallel and complement filial piety within Vietnam's hierarchical social matrix, this chapter deepens understandings of both phenomena. Filial piety typically emphasizes *upward-directed* respect and solicitousness by subordinates to their social superiors; sacrifice, on the other hand, involves *bidirectional (though asymmetrical)* reciprocity. That is, subjects across different generations learn to value and aspire to participate in *mutual* relations of moral debt and obligation, articulated in the idiom of *tình cảm* (feelings of care and love that motivate material provisioning). As in filial piety, these relations cannot be reduced to tit-for-tat accountings.

The scope of a person's duties to others is contingent on the social hierarchies between them, and expectations (e.g., of care) are often implicit and deferred far into the future.[5] Bidirectional but asymmetrical reciprocity is to be distinguished from symmetrical relations of equal reciprocal obligations between participants and from symmetrically nonreciprocal and asymmetrically nonreciprocal relations (see figure 1 for a diagram of Weberian ideal types of these configurations). *Symmetrically reciprocal* relations of mutual equality in rights and obligations typically are imagined to characterize democracies, where all persons are ideally equal. In reality, however, age and other hierarchies intervene, rendering social relationships *asymmetrically nonreciprocal*, as one's gender, age, or class group, for example, owes more to the other. Research suggests that in contemporary postindustrial (so-called western) societies, the flow of obligations in middle-class families is often unidirectional, from parents to children.[6]

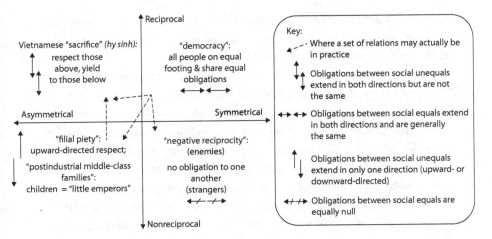

Figure 1. Schema of (a)symmetrical (non)reciprocal relations

This contrasts with sociohistorical conditions in which familial obligations flowed unidirectionally from the younger to the older generation.[7] Alternatively, we can imagine *symmetrically nonreciprocal* relationships, when carried to an extreme, as approximating Marshall Sahlins's (1974) "negative reciprocity," where enemies feel no mutual obligation other than to harm one another.

As an asymmetrically reciprocal relationship, *hy sinh* (sacrifice) is conceptually and semantically broader than filial piety, since friends also sacrifice for one another and citizens sacrifice for their nation. If on its face filial piety invokes asymmetrical *nonreciprocity* by emphasizing respect toward superiors, implicitly it entails long-term asymmetrical *reciprocity:* social subordinates feel *ơn* (boundless gratitude) and strive to honor their superiors for the life and care they have received. In this sense, sacrifice provides the raison d'être for acting toward parents in a filial manner, for it is parents' sacrifices for their children which normatively engender children's debts and obligations to their parents. Parents do not tell their children, "I invested a hundred thousand dollars in your upbringing; now that you're grown up, pay up!"[8] Instead, multiple generations come to view one another as bound in relations of debt, including to one's deceased ancestors and not yet born descendants.[9] In short, whereas filial piety highlights upward-directed obligations, from children to parents (even though ideally these debts are incurred for the care elders provide to their descendants), sacrifice makes explicit these ties in which social superiors yield to their inferiors and social inferiors honor their superiors.

The previous chapter introduced the multivalent meanings of sacrifice (*hy sinh*) as personal and collective, individual and national, daily and silent, as well as eventful, patriotic, and publicly recognized; this chapter illustrates how asymmetrical reciprocity operates in practice to constitute quotidian sacrifice. To be clear, sacrifice is not simply an ethical orientation: it is also a corporeal experience cultivated through myriad enactments of asymmetrical reciprocity that form young and old community members' moral subjectivities. I illuminate this process of adults' and children's ethical subjectivation in several steps.[10] First, I relate the anthropological literature on sacrifice as bloodshed to quotidian sacrifice at home. I then juxtapose two types of interactions: how descendants interact with their ancestors and contemporaries and how children are socialized to interact with their elders. Both ritual ancestor worship events and quotidian ritualized greeting routines engender sacrificing, relational moral subjects who continually engage in asymmetrical reciprocity.

To this end, I adapt the lens of language socialization.[11] Focusing on Nga and other elders and on toddler Em and her relations, I consider how children's curtsy bows conjure displays of respect in ancestral veneration events. The former are inchoate, communicative forms of sacrifice that caregivers teach children to embody and embrace through language socialization routines, for example, quotidian mini-rituals like saying good-bye that teach children how to communicate appropriately. Such routines do more than teach words (or bows): they cultivate novices' ethical subjectivities even before they can explicitly reflect on or articulate them.[12]

Both corporeal acts—of bowing to the ancestors and greeting respectfully—exemplify the ways in which quotidian sacrifice is valued and experienced as natural and essential for being a moral person in Vietnam. We glimpse how people develop the disposition to sacrifice across generations by attending in this chapter to the worship ritual's hierarchical gendered kin dynamics and participation frameworks, and to the pragmatic dimensions of an extended error-correction sequence with a child. Like Nga, family members routinely engaged in these practices, instantiating belonging in the community by performing quotidian sacrifice, which affirms bidirectional hierarchy and generational continuity.

SACRIFICE IN ORDINARY (RITUAL) LIFE

When family members heard that I was interested in "sacrifice" *(sự hy sinh)*, they would immediately smile and say that in that case it was good that I was focusing on families. As we began to see from Tan's story in chapter 1, sacrifice and family life were intimately related for them, even as sacrifice surpassed the immediate concerns of the family.

Anthropological interest in sacrifice dates at least to the late nineteenth century. Edward Tylor ([1871] 2009), William Robertson Smith ([1889] 1969), and James Frazer ([1890] 1948) theorized sacrifice as a gift by which a community ingratiates itself to its gods, or as a communal feast organized to establish a group's unity or to rejuvenate positive relations among members and expiate broken covenants between the human and spirit worlds. Henri Hubert and Marcel Mauss ([1913] 1964) and their followers complicated these lines of thought by emphasizing how sacrifice—through the offering of a victim by a sacrificer to a deity—mediates sacred and profane modes of existence.[13] These and more recent works examine how sacrifice constitutes social bonds and reinforces social order.[14] They cast sacrifice as a religious ritual or nationalist act that is inevitably tinged with, or outright marred by, tangible violence. As Michael Lambek writes, "Sacrifice is one of the most literal acts possible, both as an action and in terms of its end product, that is, a dead body. . . . In this sense, killing is like ritual. . . . Cutting throats and spilling blood are literal acts. The object can be metaphorically displaced—from royal self to human subject, from animal to vegetable—but the act of sacrifice is no metaphor."[15]

Yet slaughter and death are not the only means to constitute sacrifice as ethical action. Sacrifice has other sides that are not so violent but belong under the same analytic umbrella.[16] As Thúy, a Hanoi-based language tutor explained, sacrifice has a variety of meanings. She linked sacrifice, first, to withholding time from oneself and even one's close friends to take care of others (lines 4–6). She suggested that women in particular sacrifice a lot (lines 9–13):

1 Sacrifice depends.
2 It depends on the situation or on,
3 for example, if I/we[17] don't have,
4 don't have a lot of time for oneself,
5 for one's close friends,
6 but [devote it] for others,
7 then that's also sacrifice.
8 Umm, *I* think that Vietnamese people,
9 Vietnamese women sacrifice a lot.
10 For example, in the family
11 it's usually women who take care of the family a lot.
12 [They] do a lot of housework.
13 Women in the family sacrifice more.

Throughout the research, others reinforced this understanding of sacrifice as related to women and the home. It is within the family that one first learns to anticipate and fulfill the needs and wants of others "intuitively" by sanguinely forgoing certain comforts and freedoms.

As well, sacrifice is frequently associated with the *giving of life*, as when a mother conceives, gives birth, and raises her child, or when a person gives up his or her life for the nation at war.[18] This double meaning—of giving one's life in war *and* of enduring pregnancy, giving birth, and raising a child—suggests that sacrifice encompasses more than highly dramatic acts. In its mundane instantiations, sacrifice instead points to little acts of suffering and forbearance from oneself for the sake of others, whether by devoting one's free time to taking care of others or by leaving work in the middle of the day, as Nga had done to briefly bow and pay respect to her elders and ancestors. In addition, sacrifice encompasses forgoing romantic love, food, health, or education for someone else's benefit. And sacrifice necessitates managing one's affective expressions, for example, by restraining one's tears upon the conclusion of a loved one's funeral to allow their spirit to ascend to the next world in peace.[19]

In short, bloodshed renders acts of sacrifice in the traditional sense irreversible and distills a triangular relation of "sacrificer," "victim," and "deity."[20] In contrast, mundane acts of sacrifice in the Vietnamese sense are premised on infinite, cross-cutting relations of hierarchy rooted in asymmetrical reciprocity. Further, to avoid debasing the act, a person who sacrifices should *not* draw attention to their act of self-denial or refer to that act as an instance of sacrifice, as Loan explained (see introduction). Quotidian sacrifice thus is quite different from ritual slaughter events. Despite these significant differences, however, quotidian, religious, and patriotic sacrifices are not entirely disparate and can be productively related. As in quotidian sacrifice, canonical forms of sacrifice, too, can cast hardship as the lot not only of the "victim" (who must shed blood) but also of the "sacrificer" who identifies and suffers with the victim.[21]

In what follows, I describe instantiations of quotidian sacrifice in two home domains: ancestor worship events and child socialization routines. Both types of (ordinary) rituals cultivate, in neo-Aristotelian virtue ethical terms,[22] the moral disposition to sacrifice, for in their intergenerational exchanges with the dead and the living, adults and children learn to act with deference, obedience, and respect toward social superiors and to yield willingly and benevolently to social inferiors. These practices generate moral continuities, as successive generations respond to the expectations of watchful—and implicitly judgmental—related others.

STRUCTURING TIME TO SACRIFICE

I was used to Nga speaking with kind and nonchalant but unmistakably confident authority. She was, after all, a cadre who had climbed to the upper echelons of the city's government bureaucracy, and she commanded the respect of all her peers as well as relatives. As eldest daughter (her older brother lived in Hanoi and rarely came to visit), she was a leader among her close kin as well as at her office. At the death anniversary celebration, however, I glimpsed her in a different role. Her father had been his father's third son, which meant that there were others whose kinship status was senior to hers.

As we entered the smartly renovated parlor where several elderly men were sitting and chatting, Nga assumed the posture of a child, folding her hands on her chest and slightly bowing to greet them with respect. I followed suit. In the kitchen, Nga again resumed her posture of authority and then excused herself to rush back to work to supervise an official meeting. She had interrupted her work commitments just long enough to nominally participate in her paternal grandfather's commemoration feast by respect-fully greeting her elders and lighting incense at his altar. Her husband would join the ritual feast in her stead, allowing them both to treat the event honoring her grandfather as sacred if not particularly eventful.

Nga's eighty-year-old mother, the deceased's daughter-in-law, arrived with her own daughter-in-law shortly after Nga left. She came just in time to sit with the elderly men in the parlor and greet the adults who contin-ued to arrive with a cursory nod and words of welcome. Each guest (men and women alike) in turn curtsied just like Nga had done, folding the right hand over the left and addressing the elders with the appropriate kinship term. After briefly chatting with the elders, each younger adult in turn lit incense for the ancestor at his altar and then went to greet or help those in the kitchen.

Having attended numerous commemorative feasts, I felt a pinch of guilt at not being awed by the occasion. I had become used to these ordi-nary, yet effortful, affairs and caused one set of hosts to roar in laughter when I remarked that there were so many dead people around. Others, such as my friends Tuấn, Mai, and Hảo, apparently shared my ennui, sometimes muttering under their breath, rolling their eyes, or cracking a joke. And yet invariably, they and other family members set aside the time to attend and contribute to these feasts, ensuring that at least one (and usually more) of their household members would honor the dead.

No less important was the work of maintaining relationships with the deceased's living relatives. In suspending work commitments associated with the "solar" (Western) calendar (*dương lịch*), feast participants dis-played their continuing commitment to abide by the lunar calendar (*âm lịch*) and its numerous significant days of devotion to the ancestors and, thereby, also to the living and to kinship itself. Vietnam's two calendars are not esoteric, decontextualized constructs removed from people's daily practice.[23] They contour family members' experience of time in daily life and over the life cycle. Ritual feasts are similar in scale to large Thanksgiving, Christmas, or Passover dinners in North America, but they are not once-or-twice-a-year affairs. They are repeated in variations throughout the year, as people feel obliged to participate in paternal and maternal relatives' death anniversaries going back three generations, as well as in other devotional days honoring the ancestors and gods.

Attending at least ten such occasions a year, family members strive to ensure their own well-being and prosperity and affirm their connections by contributing to them. Failing to do so could result in a "headache" (đau đầu) or worse, Nga and other friends explained, since the ancestors would be "sad" (buồn). Their "sadness" could lead to misfortune for the living. And the living would risk becoming the subject of gossip, since no-shows could be accused of lacking tình cảm with the feast's hosts.[24]

As discussed in the prologue, some occasions, such as the Lunar New Year (Tết), mandate that people return home to worship their ancestors and unite with their natal families. These often occasion significant costs and require traversing great distances. Death anniversary (đám giỗ) and collective ancestor worship ritual feasts (chạp mã), as well as devotional occasions such as Ancestors and Spirits Day (lễ Vu Lan), though smaller in scale than Tết, similarly require the interruption or even suspension of income-related activities and sometimes several hours of travel to one's ancestral village to participate.

Worship events structure time for different generations and sets of kin relations in asymmetrical ways. Whereas everyone celebrates holidays like Tết and lễ Vu Lan, feasts for specific ancestors or a collective group of long-forgotten ancestors depend on the efforts of the kin group organizing the commemoration. The feasts for an ancestor still in most relatives' living memory are quite large affairs anticipated year-round by his or her children and grandchildren. Others, such as the ritual feast for Nga's long-deceased grandfather, are more subdued. Eventually, long-forgotten ancestors are no longer celebrated individually but only as part of a large once-yearly collective ancestor worship feast (chạp mã).

The tangled web of relations among one's parents' brothers and sisters and their affines (relatives by marriage) is on these occasions continually renewed, as descendants have to address each of their relatives with the appropriate kinship honorific and contribute appropriate amounts of cash and other material resources and labor, or else suffer ridicule and shame.[25] These events also reinforce gender hierarchies. Regardless of their individual professional status relative to men, women shoulder the burden of cooking and cleaning, missing work for a day or more to arrange the preparations, while men enjoy the heavy drinking and merriment that characterize these events. Only very rarely, and at risk of offending (and attracting the gossip of) other family members, is a woman even in a position such as Nga's able to hire help in the kitchen and recruit her husband to sit devotionally in her stead.

Class, age, and kinship hierarchies further intersect here, as those on the lower end—particularly young women—provide more physical labor, whereas very old women can sit and be treated more like the men.[26] Yet relations are not unidirectionally extractive. Those with more seniority, especially if they possess material means, bear the financial costs. In these ways, asymmetrical reciprocity is continually affirmed as integral to seem-ingly natural hierarchies of gender, age, kinship relation, and class that my friends and acquaintances repeatedly summarized in one phrase: respect those above, yield to those below *(kính trên nhường dưới)*.

Finally, asymmetries in how the sacred is realized and personhood is reckoned also become evident on these occasions, as ritual participants comport themselves differently in relation to the deceased and to the liv-ing. Whereas some dress up and adopt a solemn demeanor that helps establish the sacred nature of the occasion, younger kin such as elementary school–aged children are not expected to adopt this comportment. More familiar with Israel's Orthodox-dominated temple spaces that are sup-posed to be treated as "sacred" by all those who enter them, I was surprised at first to see four- to ten-year-old children horsing around in the same space and at the very same time that elaborately dressed elders prayed and sacralized the home space, genuflecting in front of the ancestors' altar. Intuitively assuming a Durkheimian (1995) understanding, where the sacred and the profane are categorically opposed and mutually exclusive, I mistakenly thought at first that the children's quite unsolemn behavior was rendering the sacred space profane. Yet, as I would continually observe, home spaces were simultaneously both sacred and profane, depending on the activity at hand and the relative centrality of the participant.

EMBODIED HIERARCHY ENACTS CONTINUITY

Erving Goffman and his followers analyze the different "participation frameworks," or ways in which interaction partners use their communica-tive repertoire, including body posture, gaze, movement, and speech, to orient to their material environment and to one another.[27] At some moments, participants coordinate with one another, while at other times they diverge. These shifting participation frameworks reveal much about participants' cognition, affective stances, and understandings of person-hood and morality, including who is a ratified participant.[28] Goffmanian analyses are usually applied to face-to-face interactions among the living. But in death anniversaries, ancestors are also participants. While not co-present in the conventional flesh-and-blood sense, ancestors are central interlocutors.[29]

In combination with Goffman's (1981) framework, Alfred Schutz's (1967) typology of the social world—which distinguishes "consociates" from "contemporaries," "predecessors," and "successors"—is helpful in teasing out who is relevant in the subjunctive "as-if" world that ritual cre-ates.[30] According to Schutz, consociates are those who share the same temporal and spatial frame with oneself, contemporaries are those who share the same temporal but not spatial frame as oneself, and predeces-sors and successors are those who share neither the same temporal nor the same spatial frame as oneself, and as a result of this lack of unmediated, shared access, one has less intimate understanding and knowledge of them. In the worship ritual, ancestors (predecessors) are treated by wor-shippers not just as predecessors but as contemporaries: they are persons who share a temporal but not a spatial horizon with oneself. For Nga and people of the younger generation, ancestors are beings who constitute typifications of social roles and offices: the long-deceased grandfather rep-resents a generic ancestor, a status-senior to whom Nga simply owes respect. As an interactional partner, he is treated as a personage rather than a person—in Schutz's words, "Someone who I know coexists with me in time but whom I do not know immediately."[31]

Nga has no living memory of her grandfather. She leaves work in the middle of her day and bows and pays respect (to the elders and to the ancestor, at his altar) solemnly but generically, for she performs the action as much for the living as for the dead. Her presence and actions (e.g., lighting incense) help constitute the occasion as sacred and sacrificial for them, as well as for the ancestor. Yet for Nga's elders, a different relation-ship holds. As they pray, the grandchildren horsing around in their midst become peripheral contemporaries. They are momentarily absent, ignored, and excluded from the intimate relation between the elders as

Figure 2. Elderly Bà Hai bows at a house-blessing ceremony (Photo taken by the author, September 8, 2007)

supplicants and the ancestor as a sacred, venerated being. As bystanders[32] and (only somewhat interested) witnesses,[33] the children do not share a focal participant role within the supplicant-ancestor framework. It does not matter that their demeanor is not solemn, tense, or respectful, for their "profane" frame does not violate the sacred one established by the elders. In contrast, the deceased becomes more than a "contemporary" of the supplicant. As a "consociate," the ancestor is someone with whom the supplicant "grows older together."[34] The ritual thus allows worshippers to share an intersubjective social interaction that approximates a face-to-face "we-relationship" with the deceased ancestor,[35] effecting generational continuity and affirming past and ongoing relations of *tình cảm* (as well as gender, class, and age hierarchies) through this performance.

Though sidelined at worship feasts, young children are not entirely oblivious to the sacred import of the occasion: they quite regularly observe their elders' prayers to the ancestors in a variety of everyday life

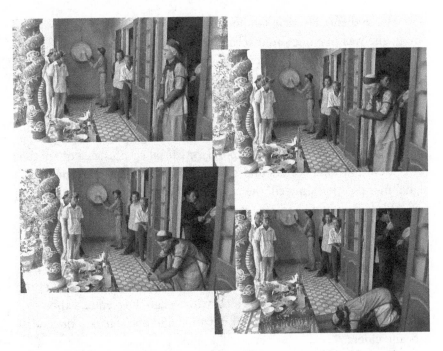

Figure 3. Elderly lineage head bows at a collective ancestor-worship *(chạp mã)* ceremony (Frame-grabs from video recorded by the author, April 27, 2007)

contexts that render them an ordinary aspect of social life. For example, from infancy, children routinely witness ceremonial kowtows such as those shown in figures 2 and 3. Figure 2 depicts an eighty-five-year-old grandmother (Bà Hai) bowing in front of an altar table to celebrate the completed construction of her son's new house in a suburb of Đà Nẵng. Figure 3 is a video motion-capture of an elderly clan head ritually bowing to the ancestors at a village *chạp mã* (collective ancestor worship) ceremony.

Not unlike the lineage head, the grandmother made considerable effort to perform this bow and sanctify the celebration, traveling a journey of about 30 kilometers on the back of her son's moped to his house from her rural home on the outskirts of Hội An. To mark the occasion as sacred and perform with proper decorum and respect for the spirits, Bà Hai, like the lineage head, changed from her regular clothes to the traditional *áo dài* (long tunic and pants) just moments before performing the ceremonious bow. Her audience consisted of both the addressed spirits or ancestors to whom she was praying and a secondary audience,[36] namely, other relatives and guests, including her seven-year-old grandson. The grandson was treated as a "contemporary" rather than "consociate" in Schutzian terms and did not treat the occasion with the same sanctity as did his grandmother.

Performed bows, as embodied acts of self-abnegation, act as sign vehicles that indicate the spatial, temporal, or causal co-presence of another form: devotion to ancestors and descendants. As such, performed bows signal moral action. Indeed, the co-occurrence of the bow, special dress, and table laid out with ancestor-worship implements is iconic of an ancestor-worship ritual demonstrating filial piety, whereas each alone indexes (points to and recalls) the complex of respect within a social hierarchy. The women who prepare the feasts, the families who bring cash and gifts to support the hosts, and all those who light incense and kowtow at the altar after greeting their (living) elders with a slight bow and an appropriate kinship appellation signal their devotion and obeisance to the ancestors and elders.

Further, they signal their acquiescing participation in this moral economy of filial piety rooted in sacrifice and asymmetrical reciprocity. Participants explained that Bà Hai's effort to travel the long distance to her son's home and the ease with which she prostrated her aged body on the floor to seek the spirits' blessings were a form of sacrifice. Hers was an unspoken but willingly undertaken effortful (and faithful) performance for the sake of social inferiors (her son and his family); they in turn incur a moral debt to perpetually maintain her altar and feed her ghost on her death, as depicted in the earlier part of this chapter within Nga's family.

Contributions to and participation in these ceremonies are considered morally obligatory (and desirable) for adults of all ages whom I encountered, because failure to do so risks both offending living family members and making the ancestors "sad" *(buồn)*. Implicit here is the understanding that making someone sad, especially the ancestors, should be avoided through effortful devotion (i.e., demonstrations of respectful worship). Family members did not speculate what would happen if the ancestors became "sad," but in daily life they used the Buddhist logic of karma to link sadness to misfortune.[37]

BOWING ACROSS THE GENERATIONS AS
SACRIFICE IN ACTION

An analogous but pared-down practice of bowing to show respect (not unlike Nga's slight bow described earlier) is taught to very young children. Beginning around the age of eight months, infants are apprenticed into quotidian sacrifice and filial piety. They are expected to comport themselves appropriately and to prioritize the wants of social superiors. Caregivers use a simplified, baby-talk register[38] to constantly prompt infants to perform respect. Toddlers varied in how soon they might correctly and consistently perform respect but usually were able to do so early in their development.

I regularly video-recorded a toddler, Em, who from the age of 13 months, displayed competence in bowing appropriately in response to her caregivers' prompting directives to "perform respect."[39] I first captured this on film on an ordinary Wednesday, when Em was home with her grandmother and mother. Minutes earlier, Em had been prompted by her older cousin to "perform respect to Auntie" as she walked toward me. Now again, when her grandmother (Bà) and mother (Lan) sensed the camera turned on Em as she followed them into the kitchen, they reinitiated the directive. Without so much as looking backward at either of us, Mom prompted Em in a singsong, gentle voice, "ạ cô kia, ạ cô kia" (Perform respect to Auntie there, perform respect to Auntie there). As she did on other occasions, Em immediately turned to me, folded her hands, and bowed slightly while vocalizing the simplified, baby-talk respect particle ạ, which research participants explained babies are prompted to say because it is "easier" to produce than the full lexeme dạ.

The particle ạ consists only of a core vowel and nặng tone (a falling, abrupt glottal stop, one of the six tones in Vietnamese). In comparison, dạ consists of a consonant plus the core vowel and nặng tone, and typically appears as a sentence-initial respect particle in adult speech. The ạ particle may also be akin either to the sentence-final particle ạ that (older) competent speakers typically use to mark a sentence as deferential to their addressee,[40] or to the Northern sentence-initial compound vâng ạ, which also indicates deference to one's interlocutors in adult speech when answering in the affirmative or otherwise expressing agreement. Native speaker consultants explain that all three forms are initially taught to tod-dlers in the polysemic simplified form *ạ* to make it "easy" for the baby to learn and repeat.[41]

Em repeated "*ạ*" twice, perhaps for emphasis. When she had satisfacto-rily executed the respectful greeting, the adults barely acknowledged her competence. Instead, they directed her, when she lifted her shirt and exposed her belly, to pull it back down, presumably to show proper deco-rum. They signaled that although respect is to be prompted and learned, its correct performance (unlike the English *please* for toddlers in North America) need not be praised.[42]

Over the course of the year, I observed numerous other occasions on which boys and girls from infancy to age fifteen were prompted to greet their elders. For children and teens, these directives would take place at boundary-marking junctures, such as on first encounter and at leave taking, with the following prompt or question: "[child's kinship term, pronoun, or name] *chào* [elder's appropriate kinship term or compound appellation] *chưa?*" ("[Have you] respectfully greeted [addressee] yet?"). Children would promptly respond by folding their hands and slightly bowing to the intended addressee with the utterance, "*Dạ, chào* [addressee's appropriate kinship term or compound appellation]." This demonstrated their compli-ance and competence in honoring both the addressee and the initiator of the prompt, because to do otherwise than obey might lose face for the latter two.[43] Often, this meant reperforming a greeting the child had just per-formed because their parent or other relative may not have noticed that the child had already duitfully shown respect to the elder in the room. Adults in turn greeted their elders (e.g., great-aunts and great-uncles) in the same manner, and teenagers and young adults deployed the respect particle when addressing me and others verbally and in text messages, even while short-ening or cutting out other words altogether in digital media.[44]

In the case of toddlers, correct performance of only the contracted *ạ* particle was required to satisfy the prompting adult, who would issue the directive primarily, but not exclusively, at opening and leave-taking sequences. These prompts, like the politeness routines described for Japan,[45] Thailand,[46] and China and Taiwan,[47] help cultivate in children an attentiveness to their social surroundings beyond their individual desires or concerns. Such attentiveness helps subjects appropriately honor those who are superior and, eventually, respond beneficently to those inferior to them. It is consistent with the mutual but unequal expectations of asymmetrical reciprocity that caregivers strive to cultivate in themselves and in their charges. Toddlers sometimes simultaneously complied with and contested the requirement to perform respect when faced with the prompt *ạ đi* (perform respect), as a final, protracted social encounter with Em will demonstrate. Hinting at the hardship that such directives may pose for children, the encounter illustrates the ways in which performing *ạ* resembles elders' acts of filial piety, and it gestures more broadly to the dynamics of sacrifice rooted in asymmetrical reciprocity, as we saw earlier with Nga, Bà Hai, and the lineage head.

PERFORMING RESPECT PARTICLES: THE AUDIENCE AS COAUTHOR

During a routine family visit to the neighbors one Sunday, I recorded an interaction in which the now fifteen-month-old Em was asked to perform what conversation analysts would call a closing sequence.[48] At the level of vocalization, the requirements remained the same as in the previous social encounter. Ostensibly, Em was only prompted to use the particle *ạ*. This time, however, it was in the course of leave-taking. As a boundary-marking activity, leave-taking is a more consequential juncture at which to display (ritualized) deference by marking an interlocutor as worthy of recognition.[49] The prompt itself initiated an "on-stage" performance[50] that placed the face of Em's mother, who initiated the directive, on the line.

Step-by-step analysis of what transpires during this leave-taking sequence indicates how Em becomes enmeshed in her hierarchically structured moral world. The entailments of asymmetrical reciprocity combine both situation-oriented dynamics (requiring Em to adapt to the situation) and child-oriented attunements (requiring the adults to accommodate Em) rather than emphasizing, as in classic language socialization theory, one orientation over the other.[51] Filial piety and sacrifice, in other words, do not simply demand upward-directed respect, whereby children must adapt themselves to the demands of adults. As I repeatedly observed, adults also continually accommodated themselves to children's limited

Table 1. "Perform Respect to the Neighbors" Transcript

Line #	Speaker	English gloss	(Meta)pragmatic features	Vietnamese
1	Mom	Enough, [let's] go back	*Looking at Em*	Thôi về
2		Ready to go back?	*Matter-of-fact tone*	Về được chưa?
3		[Perform] *ạ* to Minh [before we] go back	*Minh walks over to stand next to Mom*	ạ Minh về
4		*ạ* to Minh [before we] go back	*Minh turns around to look at Em*	ạ Minh về
5	Neighbor Minh	Go "*ạ:*," "*ạ-ạ:::*"	*Nods his head, as does Mom*	Ạ: đi, ạ-ạ:::
6	Em	*ạ::: ạ:*	*Bowing head down, Mom and Minh looking at her*	ạ:::ạ:
7	Mom	Also *ạ* to Vi	*Pointing to Vi*	Ạ Vi nữa lại
8		*ạ* to Vi too [before] going back	*Em turns around to face direction Mom is pointing in*	ạ Vi nữa về
9		*ạ* to Vi over there	*Pointing to Vi*	ạ Vi kìa
10	Em	*Ạ:: =*	*Bending low to bow*	Ạ:: =
11		*ạ::::: ạ:*	*Almost falls, catches balance with her hands, Mom bends over laughing*	ạ::::: ạ:
12	Mom	Enough	*Em gets up*	Thôi
13		Go "*ạ*"	*Mom steps toward Em and flicks her gently*	Ạ đi
14		Fold your hands to perform *ạ* again	*Steps back as Em begins to bow again*	Dòng [vòng] tay lại ạ
15	Em	*Ạ:::*	*Bowing so low that has to balance on hands, hat falls, Mom steps forward*	Ạ:::
16	Mom	Bow to [perform] *ạ* just halfway of course	*Bends by Em, flicks her back lightly but firmly, picks up and puts Em's hat back on*	Ạ dừa dừa [vừa vừa] thôi chớ

Table 1. (continued)

Line #	Speaker	English gloss	(Meta)pragmatic features	Vietnamese
17		Fold your hands properly again to perform *ạ*	*Molds Em's hands into correct folded position*	Dòng [Vòng] tay đoàng quảng [đàng hoàng] lại ạ
18		Stand up!	*Tries to pull Em up to stand*	Đứng lên!
19	Em	*Ạ*::*.. Ạ*:::::	*Tries to bow as Mom pulls her up*	Ạ::*.. Ạ*:::::
20	Mom	Enough	*Holding Em, smiling and guiding her*	Thôi
21		*ạ*::*.*	*Em bows, Mom guarding her front with one hand and back with her other hand*	ạ::*.*
22		Ok, stand up	*Looks back toward Auntie An and Von approaching*	Thôi đứng lên
23		[Wave] bye-bye [to] older brother Kin [and let's] go back [home]	*Hands steadying Em to face neighbor boy*	Bay bay anh Kin về

capacities through downward-directed yielding actions. Both elements in concert are key to the ethic of sacrifice (see table 1).

I begin with a transcription of a multiparty social encounter involving Em, her mother, her neighbor Minh, Minh's wife, Vi, and five-year-old son, Kin.[52] The transcript features Mom directing Em to respectfully take leave of her elders. Although Em complies, she does so in an exaggerated fashion, leading Mom to ever more forcefully correct her daughter's infractions. As we see at the end, Mom at last yields to Em's presumed incompetence and, consistent with the entailments of asymmetrical reciprocity, reformulates and clarifies the instruction.[53]

The transcript immediately reveals several points of interest regarding sacrifice and hierarchy. First, the interaction has a noticeable top-down structure, as adults make up the vast majority of talk (18 of 23 lines, or roughly 80 percent). A plurality of these utterances are directives, mostly in the form of bald imperatives[54] that attempt to get the toddler to display respect to her elders. In rapid succession, Mom fires a predicative statement (line 1, "Enough [let's] go back"), a question (line 2, "Ready to go back?"), and two imperatives (lines 3 and 4, "Perform respect to Minh [before we] go back [home]"). Leaving no pragmatic space for the child to negotiate her own wishes, Mom expects and obtains compliance when she issues the subjectless, bald imperative *"ạ về, ạ Minh về"* (lines 3–4: "Perform a respectful good-bye, perform a respectful good-bye to Minh"). Neighbor Minh immediately reinforces this command, as he prompts and then models for Em the correct, expected form in line 5: "Perform respect, respe::ct::." Even before Minh has completed his utterance, Em displays her alignment with the adults by bowing and uttering the *ạ* particle (line 6). She thereby displays her knowledge of the social order and her place in it as a compliant, younger, and respectful person.

The first part of the leave-taking sequence may be read as analogous to North American parents' concern that their children learn to say "good-bye" or "please" and "thank you" to interlocutors. But this would be incomplete. As an honorific,[55] the *ạ* particle does more than just convey politeness. Along with the accompanying required (and corrected) bodily posture (slight bow), the honorific initiates children into a social and emotional order based on hierarchy and expectations of asymmetrical reciprocity that later implicates the ancestors as well as the living. This disposition requires a social consciousness beyond the utterance of politeness formulas. It exacts the production of specific greetings for socially differentiated audiences, through which submission is embodied and emotionally inculcated.

Discussing politeness routines in hierarchical settings, Yoshiko Matsumoto (1989) questions the universality of Penelope Brown and Stephen Levinson's (1987) politeness theory, which relies on an assumption of mutual (and symmetric) face wants.[56] Jack Sidnell and Merav Shohet (2013) alternatively highlight the "problem of peers," or the difficulties of linguistically encoding parity in Vietnamese interaction. And

Patricia Clancy (1986), Susan Blum (1997), Heidi Fung (1999), Kathryn Howard (2007), and Matthew Burdelski (2010) demonstrate how children learn to use honorifics in East Asian contexts to reify local relations of hierarchy and respect. Yet, across these discussions of filial piety and respect practices, scholars focus on the top-down nature of the interactions and neglect to note their reciprocal but asymmetrical nature, wherein social superiors are also expected to yield to their subordinates.[57]

The communicative model advanced in the Vietnamese social encounters that I observed, however, is not just top-down, where adults command and children comply. Rather, adults also accommodate to children, calibrating their expectations to what they believe toddlers are capable of doing and scaffolding the performance of their utterances and bodily comportment. Believing that Em is not fully capable of articulating the grammatically correct honorific, Mom and Minh prompt her to perform only the particle *q* to indicate respect to Minh. Mom then prompts Em to turn around and similarly greet Minh's wife, Vi (lines 7–9), gazing and pointing to clarify the deictic *kìa* (over there) after witnessing Em's success in performing respect toward Minh.

On the surface, Em seems to comply with Mom's imperative to greet Minh's wife, turning around (line 8), bowing, and uttering the respect particle *q* in the direction of neighbor Vi (line 10). Em, however, has bowed too low, essentially falling to the ground. Worse, it looks like she makes a farce of the respect gesture through her exaggerated display, uttering "respect" *(q)* twice and elongating the vowel as she bows low to the ground, almost falls, and catches her balance with her hands on the ground (line 11). In response to this humorous performance, Mom cries out "Enough" (line 12) and directs her daughter to (re)do the greeting (line 13) and fold her hands to reperform the *q* (line 14). Here, Mom intercedes not only verbally but also corporeally, rushing forward and reprimanding Em by flicking her lightly on her back. She then steps back to observe Em correct her transgression (figure 4).

Though seemingly banal, this correction sequence illuminates Vietnamese ideologies regarding cultivating toddlers' embodied moral subjectivity. Mom's insistence on proper comportment evidences a societal investment in respectful body posture in addition to vocalizations. Her insistence resonates with the Vietnamese expression, "Learn to eat,

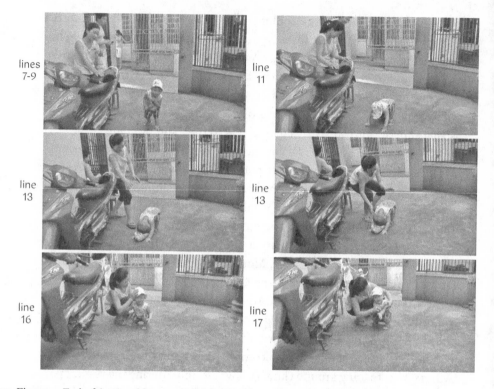

Figure 4. Em's objectionable compliance with Mom's directives to perform respect (Frame-grabs from video recorded by the author, April 11, 2007)

learn to speak, learn to wrap, learn to open" *(học ăn, học nói, học gói, học mở).* This is a pithy way of stating that everything must be learned, from these smallest tasks to bigger things such as gift exchange and, implicitly, proper ritual performance and obligations to the ancestors and the community. The inclusion of wrapping and opening in this saying, in addition to eating and speaking, points to the importance of gift giving and receiving as social acts that are deemed essential to one's personhood and that therefore need to be learned to be done properly. Correct posture, as the embodiment of virtue, is not just a symbol: it is an emotional mode incorporated in a display of obeisance that will be embraced and implanted ever more deeply as the child practices it over and over. Like other children, Em is expected to learn to correctly execute leave-taking practices and associate them with respect. Attaining competence entails learning particles, gestures, and their experiential valences by attending and responding to adults' prompts and commands, ultimately to develop one's ethical subjectivity.

The social exigencies surrounding Em's bow differ from those of Bà Hai's bow in figure 2 above. There, the act explicitly invokes the ancestors and implicitly addresses her living audience. Yet Em's display is mandated by her audience no less than was Bà Hai's, albeit with *prompting* to discern and appropriately address her different audiences. In Mikhail Bakhtin's (1981) sense, Em's exaggerated performance echoes and is populated with Bà Hai's deep prostration before her ancestors, suggesting that the toddler is developing an embodied understanding of emotionally laden symbols of her world even before she has full conscious command of what her action signifies. We may follow Clifford Geertz in calling Bà Hai's bow a "sacred symbol," which "function[s] to synthesize a people's ethos—the tone, character, and quality of their life, its moral and aesthetic style and mood—and their world view—their picture they have of the way things in sheer actuality are, their most comprehensive ideas of order."[58]

When Em exaggerates the gesture, she may be violating the Geertzian sacred symbol, bowing too much like Bà Hai and the lineage head in figures 2 and 3 above, a kowtow reserved for the ancestors and spirits, not for mere neighbors. In response, Mom lightly but firmly whacks Em on the back (line 16) and verbally and physically instructs her (lines 16–18) on the proper way of performing respect. That is to say, to bow with dignity, one bows just so: not too much and not too little. Mom's use of the particle *chô* (of course, line 16) morally frames the action as one that Em should know. It signals to the audience that Mom is performing her mothering role appropriately by insisting that Em (learn to) "behave."[59]

MODALITIES OF CARING: YIELDING IS AN ASPECT OF SACRIFICE

Alongside her situation-oriented, stern authoritarianism, Mom's facial expression and voice quality convey an alternative, child-oriented affective stance. Mom appears benevolent and even gently amused. The social relationship created is one of mutual, yet asymmetric, care, enhanced by Mom's squatting alongside her daughter to help and be on a level with her. Even as she utters, "Enough" (line 20), the rhythm of the act indexes an intent not to punish. Mom models the appropriate demeanor for her daughter by simultaneously directing Em's body and vocalizing the particle *q* for her (line 21):

20. Mom: Enough ((holding on to Em, **smiling and guiding** her))
21. Mom: Respe::ct. ((Em bows, Mom **guarding** Em's front with one hand and **guarding** her back with the other hand))

In this way, Mom mitigates the possible hardship demanded of young Em by the disciplining command to perform proper respect to her elders. Em witnesses that commands, while fierce, will be gently enforced. These moves in turn realize the relationship as reciprocally asymmetrical, involving both upward-directed disciplinary respect and downward-directed benevolent yielding.

Following the trajectory of benevolent yielding, Mom directs Em to "[wave] 'bye-bye' [to] older brother Kin." Perhaps sensing that her daughter will not or cannot properly perform, Mom here yields to Em by prompting her to enact what she considers an "easier" salutation of leave-taking: the English-like *bye-bye* (line 23). That this speech act is easier to perform than the Vietnamese *(d)q* reflects a local language ideology about what the Vietnamese form indexes rather than a judgment regarding its phonetic production. Vietnamese leave-taking is viewed as more difficult because it encodes more than mere politeness: ethics is not an empty practice but the combination of vocalization, corporeal comportment, and moral orientation.

Still, at this early stage in life, sacrifice remains more a matter of bodily comportment and limited vocalizations enacted in compliance with caregivers' explicit commands than an "intuitive" assumption of suffering in deference to others. Older children perform respect to their elders and ancestors without prompting, and they voluntarily (and relatively silently) anticipate and yield to others' needs above their own. Even in "new media" forms such as text messages and chats, junior interlocutors use honorifics and respect particles to address their social superiors. And at meals, children learn *not* to dig in before inviting elders to do so first. By around age seven, children routinely use the respectful utterance, *mời ông/bà* (invite grandpa / grandma) at the start of a meal, just as they proficiently use reference and address honorifics with kin and others, and they know exactly where to sit at ancestor worship and other such rituals, namely, at the outer tables, farthest from the altar.

Over time, children also learn to yield to their youngest kin, to minimize explicit conflict or confrontation with others, and to avoid making requests on their own behalf. Instead, they often request things like a glass of water or snack for a younger, seemingly more vulnerable family member and walk away or shift a conversation topic shortly after conflict begins.[60] As we shall see in subsequent chapters, young and older adults similarly engage in interactional routines in which the ethical imperative to yield to those below mandates that they provide substantial material support to poorer kin, using the justification of *tình cảm* (intimate feelings of care, concern, empathy, and love).

Caregivers do not lavish young children with praise for their appropriate displays of politeness, since they expect proper communicative behavior, and a reward is not accorded for what should, over time, become a naturalized, moral social action.[61] Instead, Mom's insistence on Em's correct performance may evidence a deeper concern to frame inequality as natural to the social order. This concern becomes salient when other adults, as secondary audiences, are watching (and judging), just as spectators are always watching adults' bows of respect and supplication to the ancestors, as we saw in the earlier set of examples of Nga, Bà Hai, and the lineage head. In all these occasions, any drama or suspense that I may have introduced by analyzing them in depth is muted. Ethical acts of yielding and respect are performed repeatedly as ordinary types of sacrifice that are essentially unremarkable. They become noticed only when absent or incorrectly executed.

SOCIALIZATION AS SUBJECTIVATION TO SACRIFICE

Readers might question the ethical thread that links the bows of Nga, the elders, and the toddler, Em. The elderly folks kowtowing and the little baby bowing were performing different acts in different settings. They belong to different generations, with distinct life histories and trajectories. The elders were raised in poverty and war, when the state called on women to sacrifice their husbands, fathers, sons, and brothers to fight for the nation's liberation and to display respect and yielding within the family. Em, in contrast, was born in a period of peace and rising prosperity, when old mud-and-wood shacks were being replaced by concrete-and-steel houses. Sacrifice now primarily meant devotion to the family, and the chief concern was no longer survival in near-perpetual peril but rather mastering English and the ways of the market.

Yet the elders' and the young girl's bodily comportment and communicative practices convey common moral subjectivities that regenerate sociomoral order. Even as contemporary ethnographic studies highlight new types of subjectivities that may be crystallizing in light of Vietnam's rapid development, elements of continuity remain through these sometimes effortfully achieved repetitions of customary practices.[62] Sacrifice in the form of ethical devotion to the family and community thus continues to entail forgoing food, medical care, or education and enduring poor health, loss, displacement, sexual harassment, or domestic violence to meet the perceived expectations of one's relatives or community.[63] At times, these expectations render sacrifice an insidious and iniquitous practiced value.

I have focused on routine displays of respect that range from the utterance of an honorific in the course of taking leave of one's neighbors, to slightly bowing to elders at familial events, to genuflecting in front of an altar. The involvement of young children in such ritual (and routine) practices apprentices them into filial piety (as upwards-directed respect) and the more encompassing interactional logic and social organization of quotidian sacrifice. Again, sacrifice need not necessarily involve high drama and violence, although it certainly can in circumstances of war, as recounted by Tan (see chapter 1). Em's socialization into sacrifice involves the cultivation of a set of psycho-moral dispositions habitually enacted by family members in their daily lives. These dispositions are rooted in the understanding that individual desires and needs cannot be separated from those of others with whom persons are normatively related in asymmetrically reciprocal relationships. The conventional anthropological form of sacrifice that calls for symbolic or real violence enacted to mediate a collectivity's relationship with the other-than-human world is supplanted here by muted forms of suffering that at times may go unrecognized even by the sacrificing agent.

In feasts such as those in which Bà Hai, the lineage head, and Nga kowtow or slightly bow, the labor and suffering of participants is more visible than in the setting in which Em is called on to demonstrate respect. All these enactments nonetheless emphasize willing, naturalized evocation of the social order.[64] The leave-taking scene involving Em, her mother, and other family members and acquaintances illuminates how a disposition to sacrifice is apprenticed early in life. Precise directives instruct young children in how to perform the language and comportment of respect to elders. At the same time, elders model an empathic willingness to accommodate the desires of children. These two prongs of socialization into sacrifice—adults' insistence that children accommodate to the moral constraints of social order and adults' accommodation to children—thus complicate the literature on hierarchy in society.

As attested in other parts of the world, children learn to attend to a multiplicity of semiotic channels to acquire communicative and cultural know-how.[65] Jean Briggs's (1998) account of the Inuit child Chubby Maata emphasizes the necessity of learning to make sense of contradictory messages, of harsh words and gestures accompanied by a gentle, smiling voice and a variety of scaffolding actions.[66] The model of socialization propounded in this chapter is neither primarily child oriented nor primarily situation oriented, as is depicted in the classic typology of language socialization studies.[67] Instead, it is a combination of both strands in equal measure. This combination of situation-centered and child-centered practices draws children into the version of hierarchy that I call asymmetrical reciprocity, which is foundational to the ethic of (quotidian) sacrifice.

More is at stake here than mere politeness to the neighbors or even filial piety to ancestors. As noted, babies are continually prompted to utter the simplified q particle and are taught the set of kinship appellations with which they are supposed to address their elders.[68] These prompts and instructions are so frequent that they become part of a child's "natural attitude"[69] regarding the world, a grammar and lexicon of respect and, by extension, sacrifice, which over time, and after considerable prompting, becomes nearly as invisible but just as compelling as are the rules of grammar themselves that underpin the local habitus or life-world.[70] For young and old, showing cursory respect becomes not so much a conscious, effortful undertaking as a "naturally" obligatory demeanor, with attendant emotional attitudes of self-abnegation and sacrifice. Over the life span, it accrues more onerous devotional obligations toward ancestors, involving dress, the preparation of food, and a number of other objects and actions, including patriotic acts for the nation when facing invaders and larger or smaller acts of suffering for others in the community.

The type of subjectivity created in these and like interactions is not monadic and self-contained. Rather, subjects are socialized to attune to the social surround: to a watchful audience that will prompt and correct the acting self should one infract the expected hierarchical social order and that will not tolerate explicit verbal negotiation or resistance. Em's interactions with her relatives and neighbors are but glimpses into this general pattern of embodied hierarchy and asymmetrical reciprocity through which habits of non-negotiation and yielding are apprenticed. This is a pattern that can be elucidated by attending to language, including not only its syntax and morphology but also its complex pragmatics in daily use, to clarify pictures and actions such as those of the elders and their rituals pictured in figures 2 and 3. The practices of language socialization brought to bear on Em's leave-taking comportment thus shed light on how suffering associated with the social asymmetries and obligations entailed by sacrifice may be normatively softened for infants and young children and how ordinary virtue ethics are cultivated in practice.

In the next chapter, I turn to the dynamics of *tình cảm* in relation to "modern love." Subsequently, in chapters 4 and 5, I describe situations in which family members carried out acts of sacrifice by muting, if not entirely silencing, their own suffering and forbearance. In each of the following three chapters, I show different dimensions of how adults' ways of embodying virtue are at once ordinary and yet troubled and effortful attempts at providing care.

3 Troubling Love

MODELS FOR GENDER (IN)EQUALITY?

I think . . . there are as many minds as heads and as many
kinds of love [as] hearts.

– Tolstoy, *Anna Karenina* (2014, 128)

On a warm night in March 2007, Hảo and I sat on her bed, chatting. Practicing her (better-than-most-people's but still somewhat stilted) English, she confided, "Usually I'm happy. But one thing I am sad. I have problem. I can't fall in love."[1]

"Mmm, that sounds hard," I said.

She switched back to Vietnamese. "I have lots of close friends. There's my friend Đức in Japan, and there's Hưng that I used to go to school with. Hưng always brings me books. He can give you some history books if you like? And there's my friend Đan in Australia, and there's Hoa in Singapore, and I have lots of colleagues."

"Yes?" I said.

"Cô Dung[2] thinks I should go out more," she sighed, referring to her boss, a woman in her thirties who, as I had learned earlier, had spent two years away from her own young children and husband to complete a master's degree in English abroad as part of my local Fulbright sponsor institution's efforts to broaden Đà Nẵng's international repertoire. Dung worked closely with Hảo daily, liaising between the local university's staff and its president, who I later learned was Hảo's mother's good friend. Work and home interests, I saw repeatedly, intertwined.

Hảo was not just boasting about the international and cosmopolitan makeup of her friendships. She was articulating a real concern she now suffered, having turned twenty-five with the passing of *Tết* a month earlier. Since December, when she returned home from her own studies abroad, she began feeling this little sadness sometimes, she elaborated.

"I'm getting old," Hảo continued, again switching to English. "I want to fall in love. Soon I'll be *ế* [an old maid]," she tittered, blushing. "Bà ngoại [maternal grandmother] is so good with children, she raised us," she continued in Vietnamese. "And mẹ [Mom] is retiring after next year."

Since both of Hảo's parents' families had joined the Communist Revolution and moved to Hanoi in 1954 during the partition period—when the country was supposed to have been only temporarily split—and returned to their natal Đà Nẵng only after the North's victory, Hảo was well on her way to following in her mother's footsteps. Born to Đà Nẵng's political elite, Hảo was ready to become a Party member and future cadre, and, despite her war hero father's earlier objections to learning the language of the enemy, she now also had an advanced degree in English from a foreign university, which gave her an edge in Vietnam's new economy. At work, she was favored by her superiors for her good family, work ethic, and tact. And she was pretty. As I would quickly learn, everyone agreed that Hảo commanded the Confucian "four virtues" of *công, dung, ngôn, hạnh* (good work, appearance, speech, and behavior) associated with "traditional" women and still valued in "modern" ones in market socialist Vietnam.[3] Her parents had even bought a plot of land on which to build her a neolocal house upon marriage. Nothing stood in the way of Hảo's success as a traditional-modern developed woman. Except for the fact that she couldn't seem to fall in love.

I focus in this chapter on gendered relations of love, sacrifice, and moral personhood to make sense of Hảo's predicament and to answer one of psychological anthropology's recurring questions about the cross-cultural study of emotion: simply, *What's love got to do with it?* Here, I trouble what we mean by "modern love" and the ways it is typically linked to capitalist individualism or transcendent desire by illustrating love's entanglement with ethics. In particular, I show how the idiom of ordinary sacrifice can enmesh romantic and family love.

In this way, I extend Jarrett Zigon's model, where he proposes that love is best understood as a quintessential moral experience around which moral subjectivity takes shape. It is an event, he writes, "that, once it occurs, shapes how people think of and live their lives."[4] Yet, in examining Hảo's story as a case study of family devotion, I shall propose that love in her case is not simply an event—an experience that either happens or does not. Love here is better understood as an ongoing *process*, one that can conjoin both so-called traditional (vertical) relations between kin, and modern (horizontal) relationships between partners. Subjects who love are not simply pursuing individualist goals of self-fulfillment that typically index "modernity." Their love involves at once morally acting, sensing, feeling, and reasoning in the world—a world of affective ties with others.[5] Emotion and judgment, intimacy and material provisioning are entangled here, revealing how experience, and likewise affect, action, and cognition, are simultaneously bound up, with uneven consequences for differently positioned subjects in Vietnam's development projects.

In highlighting how love entwines political economy, moral sentiments, and moral reasoning, I direct attention to *narrative practice*, as this focus reveals the interlacing of multiple layers of ambivalence and nuance that are at play. Here, ethics and morals do not stand above or apart from the messiness of life but are woven into the very fabric of living and loving.[6] This becomes particularly apparent when we juxtapose public proclamations of morality that strive toward a telos of predetermined norms, with personal sideshadowing narratives that embrace contradictory positions and articulate the contingencies of life.

As noted in the introduction, "sideshadowing" is a term I resurrect from Elinor Ochs and Lisa Capps (2001), who adopted it from two literary critics, Michael André Bernstein (1994) and Gary Saul Morson (1994), who sought to confront the problems implicit in teleological tales. These problems haunt memory work narratives that foreground hindsight, as in backshadowing narratives of the Holocaust (e.g., "Jews should have seen the writing on the wall"), or in the case of Vietnam, the idea that the United States should have known of the Vietnamese spirit of resistance and never entered the war. Such teleological framings similarly pervade narratives that are strongly ideological and imagine inevitable futures, as in foreshadowing narratives of progress and modernity (e.g., the Vietnamese Kinh majority's southward expansion, as manifest destiny). *Sideshadowing*, by contrast, emphasizes ambivalence,

ambiguity, and contradiction and thereby privileges the subjunctive qualities that lend narratives their open-ended, world-making qualities, as discussed in chapter 1.[7]

As ethnographers, we are well positioned to capture the flux and indeterminacy of ethical engagements, by focusing on the ways people struggle
to be virtuous, especially when "doing the right thing" is not so obvious and
outcomes remain uncertain. As I found from Hảo and others, "love" in
Vietnam entwines relations of *tình cảm, tình yêu,* and *tình thương* (care-,
romance-, and affectionate / pity-love[8]). Consequently, it seems wrong
simply to pit spousal or romantic (horizontal) "modern" love relations in
opposition to parent-child (vertical) "traditional" relations, since in daily
(Vietnamese) life these can intersect and converge, or occur sequentially,
rather than simply conflict. Both types of love relationships not only may
influence each other but also may be prioritized at the same time.

To understand "love" as a full experience, it is useful to bring the two
lenses together. I illustrate this by focusing in this and subsequent chapters on stories of "love" where people temporarily withhold judgment and
embrace contradictory positions. These stories expose compelling
moments of generosity toward the circumstances of others, who must
navigate volatile political and economic conditions as socialist Vietnam
increasingly embraces capitalist, arguably neoliberal reforms.[9] Hảo's
slowly unfolding story of finding love, recounted in detail in this chapter,
introduces some of the contradictions embedded in the nation's project of
nationalist modernization and gender equality.

To set the scene, I first highlight the intertwining of so-called modern
patriotic and companionate forms of love and the ways that Vietnam's
policy of gender equality in fact reinscribes gender and class difference. By
then focusing on the trajectory of an upwardly mobile middle-class
woman through the lens of sideshadowing narratives, I expand understandings of lived moral experience. Hảo's story in turn also illuminates
love as a moral process that unfolds over time in open-ended ways that
allow people to stake tentative claims over what or who is important to
them and how they matter to one another. These claims emerge from the
broader ethos of sacrifice in Vietnam, which is idealized as an everyday
moral practice. I begin by first relating Hảo's story to scholarship that continues to deconstruct developmentalist tropes (e.g., hoary "West and the

Rest" or "civilized-primitive" polarities) long questioned in anthropology,[10] and conclude with the story's unfolding.

MODERN TRADITIONAL DEVELOPMENT AND THE "HAPPY FAMILY"

Scholars in recent decades have continued to question the dichotomy often drawn between "modern" and "traditional," "developed" and "underdeveloped," "secular" and "pious." Saba Mahmood (2005), Lara Deeb (2006), and Ayala Fader (2009), for example, show how nonliberal Muslim and Orthodox Jewish women engage in practices of piety and "modesty" that are to be understood not as signifiers of women's oppression and cultural "backwardness" but as modes of mobilizing cultural constructions of "tradition" to confront changing social conditions and cultivate "modern," virtuous selves within their communities.[11] Ann Marie Leshkowich (2014a) shows how women in Ho Chi Minh City similarly subscribe to, and mobilize to their advantage, essentialist discourses of gender and piety formerly denigrated by the Communist state as "backward superstitions." To provide for their families and thereby embody market socialist modes of "modern," virtuous sociality, women draw on "traditional" tropes (e.g., women as both shrewd petty traders and devoted mothers).

As Harriett Phinney (2008) and contributors to the volume edited by Nguyen-Marshall, Drummond, and Bélanger (2012) demonstrate, decades of colonial rule, anticolonial and anti-imperial struggle, socialist revolution, and now efforts at market liberalization in Vietnam have brought with them various projects of "modernization" and "development" that can appear both continuous with and dissimilar to one another in their attempts to claim legitimacy at home and on the world stage. This makes it hard to date "modernity" or to determine what the term signifies, though Holly Wardlow and Jennifer Hirsch (2006, 4) helpfully suggest that key indices of "modernity" and modern love include the emergence of companionate marriage, "individualism, commoditized social relations, and narratives of progress."

Vietnam enjoys several markers of these forms of "development," including high literacy and recently achieved replacement-level fertility rates, as well as progressive legislation promoting gender equality. Vietnam's reading and writing rates of over 90 percent among both women and men, which place it close to par with other "developed" nations, are indisputable.[12] Similarly, national family planning efforts, instituted in late 1986 to limit couples to birthing no more than two children, have successfully led to replacement-level fertility in recent years.[13] Yet most significant, if controversial, are constitutional reforms that have asserted women's "equal rights with men in all spheres" at least since Vietnam's 1946 Law on Marriage and the Family.[14] Socialist laws designed to "liberate" women from their "traditional" Confucian Three Submissions (Tam Tòng), to their father, husband, and eldest son, have sought to integrate women into the workforce and eliminate "subordination." This has been attempted, for example, by outlawing polygamy and wife beating, forbidding men from divorcing their pregnant wives, and granting women special rights and privileges, including paid maternity leave, sick leave for childcare, and earlier retirement than men.[15]

The extent to which Vietnam's laws have succeeded in changing women's material conditions, however, remains debatable, as attested by continuing documentation of women's disproportionate suffering of intimate partner violence, trafficking, and butting up against glass ceilings, among other inequities.[16] Even at the level of theory, "gender equity" laws can appear problematic, since these reforms in effect also naturalize and reentrench difference, despite their having been crafted with the intent to legislate "equality."[17] Premised on the traditional Confucian morality the government sought to overthrow in the 1950s but revalorized since the 1990s, legislative measures place greater burdens on women than men to regulate their fertility and ensure compliance with biopolitical state goals aimed at uplifting the "quality" of the population, as Tine Gammeltoft shows in her studies of contraception (1999) and of responses to fetal anomalies (2014) in rural and urban northern Vietnam, respectively. In foregrounding women's "natural" tenderness and self-sacrificing virtue while declaring the family as the enduring basic "cell of society," both the laws and public discourse use essentializing language to associate women with the responsibility for the family's well-being and happiness, leading to uneven consequences for women themselves.[18]

The same standard discourse equates family happiness with the nation's success and development, first in the socialist bloc as against the "evils" of

capitalism and now in the capitalist world itself.[19] As the chairwoman of
the Vietnam Commission for Population, Family, and Children declares in
an article tellingly titled "The Vietnamese Family in the Cause of National
Industrialization and Modernization":

> [T]the family is always a sweet home, a primary environment in which vir-
> tues are born and nurtured and the Vietnamese personality created. . . .
> Precious traditional values . . . such as love for the country, solidarity, indus-
> triousness[,] . . . resilience, [and] undauntedness . . . have been kept up and
> developed by the Vietnamese family throughout the history of national con-
> struction and defense.[20]

Here as elsewhere in official discourse, the family is framed as the origi-
nary locus of happiness, patriotism, and national solidarity, a timeless virtuous institution that upholds Vietnam's progressive march forward while
avoiding corrupting individualism.[21]

Of course, not *all* Vietnamese affiliate closely with state proclamations
or take them seriously. But Hảo's privilege stemmed specifically from her
family's connection with state agencies, where they served as ministers
and salaried employees. Both her grandmothers had entered love marriages decades earlier and migrated North with their husbands to raise
revolutionary children; upon their return to Đà Nẵng with the Communist
North's victory, they were happy—and at times exerted efforts—to see
their grown children find lovers with whom to raise patriotic families not
blemished by unsavory affiliation with the South. Romantic attraction
leading to companionate love marriage and patriotic love of one's nation,
for Hảo, thus were linked through the practices and ideologies of her
exemplars. Finding (or falling in) love was part of continuing to be modern, patriotic, and worthy of privilege. This is not because romantically
based companionate marriage was unique to the Communist Democratic
Republic of Vietnam (DRV, commonly known as the North) or capitalist
South (officially known as the Republic of Vietnam), as both warring sides
(and likewise Vietnam's subsequent regimes) saw themselves as "modern"
and industrializing via different paths. Rather, we see here that marriage
based on "love" need not be linked to the pursuit of capitalist individualism and that affective bonds can at once encompass nation, family, and
individual love. In revolutionary (North) Vietnam, companionate love

marriages signified the throwing off of feudal bonds (and arranged marriage) in favor of entering into relationships where both partners were committed to each other as well as to the building of a more socially just independent nation.[22] Love, then, is a complicated affair that is at once locally variable and globally patterned, as recent gender, intimacy, sexuality, and globalization scholars also assert. Love can involve pleasure and closeness and commoditized and instrumental relations, both among the lovers and in relation to their broader context.[23]

SEARCHING FOR LOVE

Seen in this light, Hảo's complaint regarding her trouble accepting (and reciprocating) anyone's intense feelings of love—which she saw as a necessary first step to birthing and raising the next generation—indexed a deep existential dilemma. She expressed despondence because she was failing her elders, she later told me. Her family could not be happy without her finding love. Feeling pressed to live up to public moral conventions she had been raised to embrace, Hảo began to discipline her actions to try to reorient her sentiments. By finding love, she would be able to fulfill her cosmological, nationalist, and filial obligations. This was not a lone pursuit: her mother, friends, and supervisors quickly mobilized over the course of the year to help Hảo find love (to search for and to find a lover are one and the same in Vietnamese: *tìm người yêu*).[24]

For example, despite her own busy schedule, Hảo's cadre mother traveled with her to far-flung Buddhist temples and other shrines to meet fortune teller after fortune teller to discover when a suitable match would materialize, and how. Upon one soothsayer's advice, the house furniture and decorations were all rearranged to change the *phong thuỷ* (feng shui) of the place. And in addition to juggling two jobs, Hảo herself—with her supervisors' blessings—regularly made time to go out with her single friends to palm and tarot card readers who might divine the identity of her future companion and father of her children. These seemingly superstitious acts denigrated under high socialism as feudalistic and futile tradition, ironically now were excusable. They were now even embraced by Hảo's family of Communist cadres, who wanted to ensure their own continuity and her happiness *(hạnh phúc)* as a virtuous middle-class woman. And Hảo evidently acquiesced. She sought romantic marriage and its presumed attendant happiness through "traditional" channels rather than individualistically on her own, for example at beer gardens that could risk tarnishing her reputation.

The type of happiness Hảo sought, I learned, was more a protean family affair premised on essentialist gender assumptions coupled with ideologies of equality (and women's double shift) than a companionate project of "pure" intimacy (of instrumentalist egalitarianism) between women and men.[25] "Everlasting Happiness" *(trăm năm hạnh phúc)* was really a formulaic blessing given to all marrying couples. It meant "caring and being cared for" by loved ones (to appropriate a fortuitous phrase and concept from Borneman 1997). And it involved, in Hảo's Vietnamese case, interlocking webs of cross-generational responsibilities that were at once asymmetrical and reciprocal.

As I explain in the introduction and elaborate in chapter 2, asymmetrical reciprocity entails differing obligations and debts that reinforce bidirectional but differentially manifested care. It assumes not a liberal, autonomous subject of individual desire but disciplined hierarchical interdependence. Hierarchy in this context is regarded as natural and moral rather than antithetical to justice. Toddlers learn this even before they learn to speak, through language socialization routines such as bowing to elders and using honorifics. These are premised on a Confucian understanding of the boundless, unrepayable debt *(ơn)* children owe their parents (especially mothers) for giving birth to them and steadfastly enduring hardship to provide material care and support for them throughout life. The expectation is that children will in turn show respect to parents and materially care for and support them as they age. The type of personhood assumed here is akin to Michael Lambek's (2010c) ethical subject and Jarrett Zigon's (2014, 22) Heidegger-inspired Da-sein: it involves being enmeshed in relationships constitutive of your and others' worlds.[26] Throughout my research, asymmetrically reciprocal care was glossed as part of sacrifice *(hy sinh)* and as the essential building block of the virtuous "happy family" *(gia đình hạnh phúc)* steeped in *tình cảm*.[27]

This construct of the "happy family, prosperous and secure nation" (figure 5) itself was an official state campaign that rhetorically equated family

Figure 5. Vietnamese roadside propaganda billboard proclaiming, "Secure people, prosperous nation, happy families" (Photo taken by the author, July 3, 2004)

happiness (a "private" sentiment) with the public good—the nation's security and prosperity.[28] It went hand in hand with the demonization of women's extramarital sexuality, especially the sex work of lower-class women.[29] Standing in opposition to vilified materialistic promiscuity and the criminalization of prostitution, drug use, and HIV/AIDS as part of the "campaign against social evils" *(tệ nạn xã hội)*, idealized constructs of wifehood-motherhood are held up in Vietnamese institutional and public discourses of morality as exemplars of family happiness, development, and virtue.

Yet the opposition between virtuous wifehood-motherhood and vilified materialistic promiscuity does not quite hold up in the personal narratives of Vietnamese women. This is, after all, what anthropologists would expect: ideologies—like lives—are contingent in practice, and hegemony is never complete. As Michel Foucault elucidates, power relations are *historical* developments, not easily effaced through individual acts of "resistance."[30] What ordinary narratives can do, then, is point to the incompleteness and multiple ironies involved in relations of power and domination and how these implicate class positions.

Inconsistency becomes especially apparent in sideshadowing narratives. Again, these are often co-narrated, multiperspectival, open-ended accounts of events and conditions. Such narratives privilege, rather than obviate, the ambivalence and uncertainty of experience as lived in the moment, incidentally illuminating Jarrett Zigon's "assemblage" theory of the moral constitution of subjects.[31] In this account, personal moralities can be at odds with, if inflected by, official discourses of morality, since we cannot assume that all individuals at all times will adopt and abide by public proclamations of the good, the right, or what is at stake. To illustrate how the practice of sideshadowing refracts love in relation to class and state, I continue Hảo's telos-seeking story of searching for love in this chapter and recount another, contradictory narrative of neighborly and motherly love in chapter 5.

MODELS OF LOVE AND SACRIFICE

Hảo remained boyfriend-less as the year progressed and was increasingly absent from home. Often, this was attributed to her demanding job as an English teacher, in addition to her appointments with tarot card and palm readers, whom she visited with her friends. I wondered, too, whether her younger sister's courtship with a colleague didn't rankle Hảo a bit, as he increasingly spent time in their home. But Hảo didn't explicitly express jealousy. As she had told me, she didn't see having men take an interest in her as a problem; what she struggled with was how to feel more than platonic *friendship* toward one of them. *"Yêu không được"* (I can't love), she complained to me on more than one occasion when describing her various male friends. She could not or would not articulate why.

By April, Hảo had become fast friends with a thirty-one-year old single woman, Bình, whom locals defined as an old maid (*ế*). Hảo told me she wanted to avoid Bình's fate, and so together, they were in search of a partner. They had met through Hảo's former English tutor, whom they respectfully addressed with the honorific *cô* (teacher) Mai but interacted with as a peer.[32] Underscoring the slippage in "traditional" and "modern" modes of relating to people through their forms of address and pursuit of middle-class "leisure" (aimed, after all, at securing a mate), the three frequently joked with each other as they cruised on their new mopeds or sat at upscale cafés sipping strawberry shakes and munching on roasted watermelon seeds. A mate, for them, was *not* a necessary component of financial security, but he could promise or endanger participation in the broader moral community of intimacy, marriage, and reproduction, in addition to providing the thrill and satisfaction of passion and romance.

Mai was a beautiful, always well-dressed, cosmopolitan-looking unmarried woman in her forties who maintained a long-term relationship with a married man. She doted on his grown sons and frequently accompanied him to events while his shy and more matronly-looking wife almost invariably stayed home. To my apparently prudish mind, Mai seemed a strange choice for a chaperone in the event of possible dating, but she was close with Hảo and a good friend of Hảo's mother. And Hảo's mother was also a long-time friend of Mai's lover, who was also one of Hảo's bosses. Intergenerational friendship, love, marriage, and sex clearly were entangled here.

In due time, both Hảo and her mother privately (and separately) explained to me that Mai's relationship embodied sacrifice *(hy sinh)* on the part of all three involved in the love triangle: the two lovers for not being able to marry and officially ratify their love, and the wife for tolerating and accepting the situation. Mai, in her caring love for a married, high-ranking, privileged man, was in this moral economy *not* a prostitute. Mai instead was regarded, alongside her companion and his wife, as a virtuous sacrificing person.

Hảo's circle of friends evidently tolerated some ambiguity and fluidity in relational configurations, even while abiding by the constraints of conventional moral institutions that do not readily welcome divorce or extramarital liaisons.[33] Love, they implicitly accepted, is not delimited by marriage but ideally should lead to and flourish inside it.[34] For Mai, the union of love and marriage was not possible, condemning her to a life of sacrifice and childlessness; but like Hảo's kith and kin, she was working to help Hảo find a way to connect the two by meeting a suitable mate. And because she tutored many influential professionals in the now-desirable English language, Mai was able to gather useful information for Hảo about suitors' backgrounds.

As the months passed and Hảo remained single, her grandmother and aunts subtly voiced their concerns about her. Then in October, things came to a head, when Hảo's grandmother, who chronically suffered hypertension, landed in the hospital for several weeks. Following one hospital visit, my friend seemed unusually despondent and pale. Her concern, she confided, extended beyond her worry about an ailing, beloved grandmother: it was because this normally patient and nurturing Grandma had now warned Hảo that her ghost could not rest easy were she to die before a husband and grandchildren were on the horizon.[35] Faced with this sinister prospect, Hảo redoubled her efforts to at last fall in love. Moral sentiments and reasoning, it seemed, would have to unite to guide her actions and discipline her heart. Quietly, without the knowledge of most of her family, she began to have alternating coffee outings with two of her pursuers and sometimes with both together in a group, always in the company of Bình, Mai, or other friends.

The two suitors, Hảo noted a couple months later, were similar. Lâm was a handsome architect with a promising future income and a family living close by. Kiên, on the other hand, was a former student and fellow instructor at her university, also handsome and with a promising career. Earlier in the year, Hảo had shunned him, but he had persisted. Through Mai's reconnaissance, Hảo learned that not only was his family pedigree unobjectionable (they had supported the Việt Công and the North during the war), but there was an added bonus: his widowed father lived with Kiên's married older brother in neighboring Quảng Nam. This would mean that if married, Hảo and Kiên would not bear primary responsibility for Kiên's parents, as typically required in Vietnam's preferentially patrilocal kinship system.[36] Nor would Hảo face the prospect of caring for an ailing mother-in-law, as her own mother had had to do until Hảo's paternal grandmother finally passed away. Loving Kiên could afford Hảo a degree of freedom in both the immediate present and the projected future.

LOVE'S SIDESHADOWS

I present these details as though they were part of Hảo's rational, linear calculation. But this was *not* how she talked about the two suitors when we chatted in early January, as she was finally getting ready to make a choice. After having gotten to know both for some time, Hảo was still undecided and regarded the two men as two possible (and similar) roads toward the future. Love, she appeared to conclude, was not simply the force of individualistic if intertwined passion (tình yêu). True love would be less like the sexually charged desire associated with eros and more like agape, a love of that which is good, virtuous, and beautiful. More important, it had to involve deeply felt tình cảm that extended beyond the feelings between lovers to the sentiments shared between them and their families and friends.[37]

Tình cảm, as we now see, is the Vietnamese moral sentiment of care and concern for the other out of mutual affection and attachment. Rather than delineate a sphere separate from economic or material relations, tình cảm is rooted in a local model of the self as interdependent rather than independent of others.[38] Hảo, then, was searching for a partner with whom to share tình cảm, to preserve and build on, not disrupt, the tình cảm that she already had with her family. She desired a type of love that eluded Mai, her lover, and his wife. She sought a love marriage based on tình cảm between partners that would allow tình cảm relations with their broader network of loved ones to continue to flourish.

Hảo's case of finding love, I want to emphasize, was not unique. Other couples faced similar considerations. For example, I knew both Buddhist and Catholic young women who pined after a lost connection with a would-be spouse based on presumed religious or class incompatibility, and others who converted to their partner's religion to ensure acceptance by their partner's family. Still others were shunned by affinal kin after they married despite religious objections. Those who enjoyed happy marriages invariably attributed them to the sharing of tình cảm between partners and beyond.[39]

Increasingly since mid-December, Hảo seemed happier and more at peace. In earlier months, she often looked morose and tense and would sometimes even lash out at her father, railing against his cigarette smoking or excessive use of salt in his cooking; but these days she was better able to contain her temper. Through joking and bantering, preferences were expressed, and tình cảm was developing. Hảo smiled and giggled more and was even more frequently absent from home. By mid-January, when one day Hảo lay at home, ill with a cold, her and Kiên's mutual love could no longer be kept a secret. He had shown up at her door to see how she was doing. Blushing, she at once began to invite him to her family's home, so that her parents could meet and decide to approve or torpedo the choice.

A new phase had now started, in which she and Kiên regularly went on coffee dates with Hảo's mother to ensure compatibility and to make the union official. By early February, Kiên had also "dated" and been approved by Hảo's maternal aunts, who agreed that he was a good choice (*có tình cảm*, "he has *tình cảm*," they reasoned). As I was getting ready to leave Đà Nẵng in late February 2008, Hảo did not appear (to my American sensibilities) madly in love. Yet she seemed happy, and I sensed marriage was on the horizon. In less than two years, Hảo's mother would reach the age of fifty-five, Vietnam's mandatory retirement age for women. She had often said she would then be ready to care for new grandchildren while Hảo could continue to develop her career.

Laws promoting and protecting women's rights, especially reproduction, mothering and grandmothering, were on Hảo's side. These are in place to facilitate the formation of stable, working, multigenerational, traditional-modern families—families who did not need to rely on Vietnam's shadow economy, as we shall see in the next chapters. Commanding comfortable means in the new economy can evidently help women be simultaneously good subjects, mothers, citizens—and lovers.

To some, Hảo's loving a man who was not saddled by a nearby demanding family and whom her family approved may appear like quite a rational and calculating sentiment. While some might interpret her lack of florid and demonstrative passion as indicative of cold instrumentality, I am less sure. Is such a display necessary to signify passion and participation in "modern" forms of love? Or do our understandings of "modern love" (or even "love" generally) need to be reframed?

More intriguing to me is the extent to which Hảo seemed to attain freedom from disapproving natal and affinal kin, perhaps ironically through the "traditional" means of complying with societal and familial demands that she find a decent man to marry and love. Labels like "traditional" and "modern," "passionate" and "calculating" do not fully capture the complex intertwining of sentiment and material exchange involved here. At most, they might hint at the ways in which Hảo was fortunate that her desires were not substantially at odds with those of her community, as she did not, for example, insist on far less publicly sanctioned desires, such as single-hood or the pursuit of lesbian love.[40]

NARRATIVE INTERPRETATION AND LIVING IN LOVE

The couple married in autumn 2008 and moved into Hảo's old house where she had grown up. Her younger sister continued to be courted by the same boyfriend for almost two more years before finally marrying him, while Hảo went on to give birth to a baby son in early 2010. She had evidently dutifully and happily found a mate to love and with whom to build their mutual careers and family, clearing the way for her parents to retire in peace, her sister to marry, and her grandmother to dote on yet another generation. Their family, unlike others in my study discussed in subsequent chapters, was not beset by financial difficulties and conflicting child-rearing ideologies following untimely death and questionable connections. Their class and political affiliations had helped ensure family harmony in line with Vietnamese state goals.

Hảo's search for love can seem quite "traditional" in that she appeared motivated by a powerful desire to please her family and live out a normative destiny for contemporary as well as older generations of women. She had even resorted to "superstitious" means by which to find love, or alternatively secure an instrumental union with a man she could conveniently care for and be cared by. As I continue to follow her story from afar, Hảo and Kiên seem happily married, together accruing social and economic capital to support their only son.

Because she was not very demonstrative in her relationship with Kiên, one could wonder if Hảo's love was simply "bought," with social acceptability substituting for "authentic" or "passionate" intimacy once she reached the age and stage at which to marry. I cannot answer this, but I also believe that such questions are more ideologically relevant for those who privilege an autonomous, self-governing subject instead of the relational moral subject anthropologists have been positing for quite some time: subjects (or persons) motivated by multiple, entangled concerns. I prefer to refuse this reductive interpretive move and insist instead that we ethnographically attend to the multiple moralities informing subjects' being-in-the-world over time, as is the practice of person-centered psychological anthropologists.[41]

In tracing Hảo's story of success in romantic love, we see life and love unfold over time in ways that at once are constrained—but also facilitated—by structural, material conditions, including marriage and work laws that reinforce entrenched class relations. For those experiencing these, life and love remain open-ended and uncertain. Rather than present Hảo's trajectory as a foregone conclusion, a success story that could not have gone any other way, I have followed my study participants' lead in elucidating how living morally or pursuing "the Good"[42] can at first blush appear like a coherent project: that of forming an intergenerational, harmonious family that shares "love" horizontally between spouses, as well as vertically between parents and children. But as Hảo's and others' sideshadowing stories also attest, this is far from a linear process of merely following social conventions out of a feeling of obligation, or what Joel Robbins (2007a) terms a "morality of reproduction." Instead, moral lives are contingent and precarious, adhering to multiple forms of "what's at stake" and multiple, less than fully determined potentialities for how to behave, which can result in tragedy or trouble, in addition to family happiness. Hảo did not pursue a form of love that resembles Anthony Giddens's (1992) "pure" intimacy, which is based on egalitarian instrumentality, nor did she simply allow her relatives (or friends, or another entity) to choose a mate for her, nor did she give up the goal of finding "modern love" in concert with others, which would allow her to live in harmony with both her mate and her multiple loved ones.

Hảo's case, in addition to illustrating the advantages of privilege and the moral complexity that inheres even in such a "happy ending" situation, further raises a paradox akin to David Schneider's (1984) critique of kinship: Are we talking about the same forms of love cross-culturally? Anthropologists have indeed debated the universality or particularity of (romantic) love over recent decades. While some claim that romantic love is a cross-cultural, biologically driven universal,[43] others contend that this type of love cannot be explained simply in terms of the human species' reproductive needs or hormonal impulses. Instead, such theorists propose a cognitive-affective universal whereby humans seek partnership on transcendental spiritual grounds, whether in or outside of marriage and with or without sexuality; they qualify this claim by rejecting the possibility that such a universal could manifest in just *any* conditions.[44] Still others argue even more forcefully for the historical particularity of romantic love. But whereas some explain it in terms of social organizational or materialist principles and resort to theories of modernization or globalization,[45] others question the possibility of translating cultural terms or critique the loaded semantic content and historical baggage that ideas of romantic love carry across different contexts.[46] These latter anthropologists do not question all humans' capacity to love but object to typologies that distinguish "true" passion from "mere" lust or instrumental desire. They also object to attendant assumptions of exclusivity and instead highlight the ways in which recent descriptions of romantic love are embedded in political economic relations, particularly the spread of colonial and postcolonial Christianity and global capitalism.

My sympathies tend to lie with this latter group. In light of my ethnographic material, however, I reject an exclusive or linear linkage of romantic love to Christian colonial, postcolonial, or capitalist ideologies, even as I agree that it is important to acknowledge the profound influence of these discourses. One of my contributions here and in other chapters is to show that romantic love should not be cordoned off from other forms of love, but rather examined, at least sometimes, within the same frame. Yunxiang Yan (2016) has made a similar claim in a recent piece, where he revises his earlier (2003, 2009) dire accounts of the individualization of contemporary Chinese society to trace a new form of social cohesion that he attributes to "descending familism," or a refocusing of relations, from upward-directed obedience and deference to the elders and ancestors to "downwards" yielding to, and love and care for, the children's and grandchildren's generations. I take up the merits and some of my issues with Yan's (2016) argument in chapter 5, where I continue to insist on the importance of asymmetrical reciprocity, rather than unidirectionality, for understanding Vietnamese families and society more broadly. There and in chapter 4, I continue to comprehend love as an entangled web of relationships that involve spousal and other intra- and intergenerational ones. These complicate the polarities and linearities often assumed when describing "love"

and its often-invoked companion, sacrifice, as events rather than as ongoing moral yet quotidian practices and narrative-based processes. Together,
the following chapters more explicitly trace the contours of gendered
moral personhood in Vietnam and the conflicts and dilemmas it especially
brings up for women.

PART II   Care Narratives and the
Limits of Love

The chapters in the first part focused on elderly, adult, and young characters who aligned with Vietnamese state goals that link "happiness" to "development." Tan, Nga, Em, and Hảo each benefited from the transition to market socialism under *đổi mới* after Vietnam's "experiment" with socialist revolution, which they or their close relatives had embraced. Through their cases, I sketched the contours of sacrifice, asymmetrical reciprocity, and *tình cảm* as three organizing principles that fabricate a semblance of continuity across generations and across Vietnam's political-economic upheavals. The protagonists' verbal articulations or embodied actions demonstrated the relevance of these principles in organizing ethical life and engendering moral personhood.

The next two chapters focus on characters whose relations with the state were more tenuous. Their close relatives' connections with the Republic of Vietnam (the South) or outright alignment with the Americans figured in their backgrounds, whether directly or only subtly but still insidiously. Unsavory ghosts of the past left them morally suspect in the public eye and meant that they had not enjoyed the same benefits as did the characters we previously encountered. Yet the commitment to the three interrelated principles of sacrifice, asymmetrical reciprocity, and *tình cảm* figures no less strongly in their lives and affords them, too, a sense of continuity and a means of smoothing over past, present, and possible future conflicts. In what follows, I allude to family members' troubled pasts while focusing more explicitly on how gender ideologies and practices also construct continuities that complicate notions of ethical personhood in Vietnam. Building on Sarah Lamb's (1997) insight, I insist that moral personhood is not an acontextual construct, since we must understand it in relation to gender and the life course and, I would add, to politics.

4 Waiting as Care?

SACRIFICE AND *TÌNH CẢM* IN TROUBLED TIMES

The phone call came in late July. Nhu said simply, *"Bà Bảy bị đau"* (Grandma Seven is hurt / sick / in pain).

I didn't know at first what to make of it. I felt a bit guilty, having neglected somewhat the other families in my study while grappling with another family member's death and its ritualization.[1] I had planned to spend that morning at home, writing field notes and digitizing tapes.

"Bị đau?" (Hurt / Sick?), I repeated, trying to elicit more detail. The term could mean anything, from suffering a mild cold to more grievous conditions.

"Do you want to come with me to visit her at the hospital? I'm going soon," Nhu continued (all in Vietnamese).

"Yes, definitely," I said.

Bà Bảy was married to Nhu's father's oldest brother. The two lived, along with his other brother's widow (Bà Bốn), her son, daughter-in-law, and granddaughters, as well as one of their sons and his wife and their two daughters, in a rural part on the outskirts of Đà Nẵng. It had been three weeks since I last saw them.

I immediately remembered that Bà Bảy had been complaining of severe headaches since late April, when the summer heat had settled in, not to be dispersed until mid-September. Her blood pressure was high, Bà had explained to me, as she went on doing the household chores. She rarely rested.

"High blood pressure?," I hazarded.

"Yeah, she's hurt. See you soon," Nhu ended the conversation.

I revved up my old moped and drove to Nhu's shop, the whole time thinking of Bà Bảy. Unlike the houses of many of her relatives, Bà Bảy's house still did not have running water indoors. The pit toilet outhouse was in the back, a short distance from the small pigpen and chicken coop, shaded by jackfruit, starfruit, banana, and several other trees. It never smelled like a latrine, always taking me aback a bit, precisely because it did not smell. Neither did the pigs.

Just a few steps from the pigpen, there was a single, knee-high faucet in the space between the fire pit where all the frying and grilling were done and the kitchen, which itself was a large bare room with a counter on which the household stored all their pots, pans, and cutlery. Other than to lay out the countless dishes they assembled when preparing a death anniversary (đám giỗ) feast, family members rarely used this space.

Bà Bảy could always be found near the faucet, squatting over the fire pit to grill and fry. Or squatting alongside tubs filled with water to wash dishes. Or squatting on the sunny patch nearby, chopping vegetables and meat and rolling them in rice paper, teaching her fifteen-year-old granddaughter how to cook. She was a stocky and sturdy seventy-five-year-old, muscular from years of working in the fields, her back straight as a board.

But she felt too tired and weak lately to go to the market, she had told me in the spring. The heat was exacerbating her condition. She had also stopped farming their rice fields some distance from the maze of village houses. With income secured by her sons, Bà Bảy and her husband hired laborers instead. Her husband, the eldest of his siblings, was a wiry eighty-one-year-old whose skin looked like long-cured leather stretched over long lean bones. He had only stopped working the previous year. Until then, he had for years led teams of men in construction work. With his own two hands, he had built his house, his brother's old house, his children's houses, and many of the other houses in the hamlet.

These days, he spent much of his time lounging in a chair in front of their television in the bare living room or working around the house, sharpening knives, playing with his granddaughters, or donning robes and praying to the ancestors, whom the couple regularly fed at their altar room at the front center of the house. I wondered if he would be there at the hospital, sitting with Bà Bảy. Like all his siblings and his wife, he suffered from high blood pressure. Would the travel be too dangerous for him to make this short, 10-kilometer trek for his wife?

We left my Honda at Nhu's shop, and I mounted her newer Yamaha. Bà Bảy lay on a clean bed on one of the upper floors of a small private hospital. She shared the room with only one man, an emaciated cancer patient with a bloated stomach. He was walking along the hospital corridors, accompanied by his wife, whom we at first thought was his daughter. Bà Bảy's daughter, whom I rarely saw since she was usually too busy working as a hotel maid, stepped out for a brief break when we arrived, then returned. She and Nhu chatted nonchalantly during the rest of our visit. They barely looked at Bà Bảy but kept her cheerful company, waiting for her to feel better.

Bà Bảy looked pale and weak, her eyes rolling in their sockets. She did not engage in conversation and only repeated weakly in a whisper, "Đau. Đau" (Pain. Hurt). I was used to this refrain. With others, she would banter and joke, but to me she rarely said anything other than this quiet complaint. We placed on the bureau next to Bà Bảy's bed the carton of dry crackers and a row of juice-box-sized Vinamilk boxes, which were what Nhu insisted you bring to the sick. A large canister of Ensure, dry powdered milk, and a box of cookies—foods that adults never eat at home— were resting on the bureau, barely touched.[2]

Bà Bảy had already spent over a week at the hospital, having suffered a minor stroke. But it was only today that Nhu could finally free herself to visit and invited me along. On our way back, Nhu explained that her other cousins and siblings had been taking shifts visiting and staying with her aunt.

"Don't worry too much," she tried to reassure me. "It's just high blood pressure." After pausing a minute, Nhu elaborated, "Many people suffer. Especially the elderly."

It was true. Hypertension, diabetes, stroke, and cancer are increasingly prevalent in postreform Vietnam, just at a time when the public health care sector is shrinking and families increasingly have to provide care on their own. But Nhu was also referring to an ethical norm: suffering is, and ought to be, borne quietly and steadfastly—in Vietnamese, chịu. This was a form of nonverbalized, ordinary sacrifice made visible through acts of waiting, which themselves indexed care.[3]

Nhu and her cousin waited in the hospital, cheerfully chatting, feigning that nothing much was wrong. The family as a whole waited for Bà Bảy's condition to improve, letting doctors decide when to release her while they paid the fees, fed Bà at the hospital, and undertook all her work at home. They waited now, as she had waited for months, letting her condition get increasingly aggravated in the summer sun. As Nhu had said, "Many people suffer." Such suffering, especially when done silently, for the sake of others, was an ethical imperative: a good person was one who "bore" or "endured" *(chịu)*.

This chapter is about waiting, suffering, and bearing suffering quietly. Waiting, I came to realize, is not simply the passive passing of time, waiting for something to materialize. Waiting itself also materializes as a constitutive, sometimes painful, component of social relationships. Phenomenological states of directedness or intentionality, as in waiting *for* and waiting *to* care, I show in this chapter, can be troubled and troubling practices, and neither is necessarily based on willful or enforced or unwelcome stasis. Waiting fosters family members' efforts to enact affective continuity in their confrontation with rupture, such as that brought on by illness; but waiting also threatens to rupture certain continuities in these protagonists' taken-for-granted social and moral hierarchies. As such, waiting works as a form of moral navigation, wherein actors "shift back and forth between multiple perspectives in a constant process of adjustment to an uncertain social environment[,] . . . leaving potential trajectories as undetermined as possible."[4] The seeming suspension of time and judgments that result from waiting affords actors a space for ambivalence as they deliberate what constitutes "good care."

To further explore the role of waiting in understanding care, sacrifice, and love, I recount in this chapter stories of Bà Bảy and some of her kin. In speaking to and for others, people become evaluative and relational—thus ethical and caring—beings. These qualities are especially salient in the living narratives of everyday interaction, which can be fraught with moral peril and filled with silences.[5] Bà Bảy's case, discussed in the first half of the chapter, illuminates how illness and attendant feelings of loss are managed in subdued and yet effortful ways. These reveal the multiple layers of waiting and care, which some narrate as fulfillments of sacrifice. And yet, as I show in the chapter's second half, others' stories trouble typical linear connections assumed to link sacrifice to family love *(tình cảm)*. In narrating their relatives' shortcomings, some of Bà's kin instead point to the complex ethical entanglements of sacrifice with *tình cảm*.

WAITING AS CARING AND CAREGIVING

Writing of the ways in which the extension of credit to the poor entangles kin, neighbors, and friends in cycles of debt and violence—as well as hope—as they care for one another in the face of mental illness, addiction and the everyday struggles of making a living, Clara Han (2012) suggests that waiting is a form of care. In waiting, both for the unknown and for a not-yet-realized but hoped-for known, subjects embrace subjunctivity, or the inherent open-endedness of life, by imagining (narrative) possibilities. This is because subjunctivity can render the future hopeful by foregrounding possibilities over probabilities and actualities.[6] Facing harsh realities, subjects like Señora Flora in Han's (2012) ethnography express their desire to be infinitely responsive to the needs and desires of those about whom they care through acts of waiting, hoping that in time relations might smooth out, even as they experience this waiting as a form of assault and violence on their very being.

Waiting, Han learns, is a way of anticipating new possibilities not yet on the horizon. It is an orientation to the future as unpredictable and open-ended, leaving space for the hope that in time a family member who has disappointed in the past might yet show a different aspect of themselves. By waiting, kin refuse to foreclose the possibility that the present—and the future—could be otherwise. They "buy time" by literally extending their credit, getting another loan on life by taking on further financial debt, waiting for a better present-future to perhaps emerge.[7] Or they refuse treatment and deny that they may be ill, by taking a wait-and-see approach, as an Acehnese AIDS-afflicted woman does in Annemarie Samuels's (2018) ethnography, hoping that the future might yet render the unexpected, mysterious, even miraculous possible.

Yet waiting as a form of care works in other contexts as well, even when life is not framed as open-ended and glimmers of hope for a future that is other than what is predicted by the present are not foregrounded. Felicity Aulino (2016), for example, writes of the ways in which two middle-aged sisters care for their elderly comatose mother in Thailand. They ritually cleanse, medicate, and nourish her four times daily over weeks and years, not because they hope for any miraculous recovery, or because they see this as the expression of any deep sentiments of love and respect, but because the ritual of caregiving embodies for them a moral being-in-the-world. Sentiment and action, Aulino forcefully argues, need not be coupled when trying to fathom care.[8]

What matters is not caregivers' affective orientations or sincerity but rather the practices of caregiving performed daily over the long term. Through these habituated acts, the sisters pay off their karmic debts and gain merit in possible future lives, regardless of the ambivalence and even resentment that they may harbor for their all-but-dead mother.[9] Here, as in Vietnam's somewhat different Buddhist (and sometimes professed atheistic or agnostic yet nonetheless ritually devotional) context that I describe in the following pages, waiting for—and accepting with equanimity—the seemingly inevitable was also regarded as a form of care and sacrifice that family members enacted when facing illness and the prospect of death.

Like waiting, care can be fraught. It is both ethical and embodied, both a "moral intersubjective practice and a circulating and potentially scarce social resource."[10] It can be enacted or withheld in medical and state institutions,[11] in institutional interactions with families,[12] and also within homes and families themselves.[13] Further, care inherently involves a temporal dimension and is central to notions and practices of sacrifice. By focusing on waiting as care, I draw attention not just to the phenomenological nature of temporality, where the experience of time, or passing duration, depends on the point of view and actions of the experiencer and his or her relations to their phenomenal world.[14] I also direct attention to the multiple layers of care and sacrifice involved in acts of waiting: of being in time and in relationships.

Waiting, then, is not just temporal: a waiting for. We might also think of the ethical moments of suspended temporality: a waiting on, a dwelling with, in a liminal state where the usual order of things is in disarray, where temporality is backgrounded, and care may be achieved by reformulating norms. When considering waiting in its less temporal dimensions, what is the logic that links it to sacrifice, and how does this in turn relate to care?

People had often told me, when I asked them to reflect on what *hy sinh* means and how it is enacted, that it can be a patriotic act, but that it is also many other forms of embracing and undertaking difficulties for the sake and benefit of another. They added, however, that should they call their own actions "sacrifice" and demand recognition and compensation for them, then these acts could not really be sacrifice. Sacrifice has to be willingly and quietly embraced, without too much fanfare. As we saw in the introduction, Loan, a retired cadre now living in Ho Chi Minh city, articulated this as follows:

> Sacrifice refers to difficulties that [one] directs toward oneself, whereas when there's something advantageous [one] secures it for [one's] father, for [one's] mother, for [one's] husband and children . . . Sacrifice doesn't just mean fighting in wars; the term includes a lot of meanings, so when you talk of sacrifice it means accepting suffering for oneself . . . hoping that [the beneficiaries] don't know about your sacrifice, right? For example [if] you sacrifice but you have to say that you sacrifice that's really ugly . . . Sacrifice is mute and secretive.

Sacrifice, I learned from her and others, was most often a familial act of care. It was an act not named by its initiator (hence "mute") and only rarely described as *hy sinh* even by others (thus "secretive"). Sacrifice as a form of ritualized care was what Bà Bảy's family now mobilized to provide as the old matriarch rested in the hospital, waiting to regain her strength.

*   *   *

Bà Bảy stayed at the private hospital for another week. Upon leaving the hospital, she returned to her usual spot by the faucet in the back of her house. She squatted to cook and clean, as she always did. And she suffered another stroke within days. This time, she arrived at a larger Đà Nẵng hospital in a coma. This hospital was supposed to be better equipped to treat patients in her grave condition.

Nhu's brother Lộc invited me to visit Bà Bảy shortly after her admission. We entered a busy, crowded room, filled with cots on which patients in various degrees of consciousness lay, hooked up to oxygen tanks, IV drips, and other machines. Bà Bảy lay naked and unresponsive on her bed, covered only with a white cotton sheet. After a few minutes, during which we observed another patient's relative angrily explode in the otherwise quiet room, only to get restrained by hospital staff, Lộc insisted we step outside.

I wanted to understand the outburst, but Lộc was in no mood to talk about strangers' transgressions. Making a scene was not what one does, he implied. Smiling but spinning his finger near his head, he shuddered for a second, then said, "*Thôi!*" (Enough!), and grinned widely again. We spent the rest of the visiting hour chatting with Bà Bảy's son and next with her daughter and son-in-law, who also stopped by to visit. There was not much to do, Lộc told me. You just go in to keep the sick company, to show them *tình cảm,* he elaborated.

We waited with Bà Bảy's son, son-in-law, and daughter until the end of the visiting hour. Later that night, Lộc went drinking with the men. It was all part of showing *tình cảm*. Caring and family feelings of love, I saw, were in some senses mute, much like *hy sinh*. They involved acts of being-with others, an ordinary sociality.[15] Emotional and verbal restraint were what most situations called for. Maybe I should not have been surprised not to hear family members talk about Bà Bảy's diagnosis, prognosis, or ways of caring for her; what mattered more was that they were there, present with her and with, and for, one another.

SILENCE IN SACRIFICE

I visited Ông Văn, Bà Bảy's eighty-one-year-old husband, a few days later. He lay in his bed, sleeping. I waited for several hours, but he slept, and slept, and slept. And slept. His son Nguyên, who lived with his aging parents but normally spent the week working for a development nongovernmental organization in a neighboring province, was home, along with his wife, who also usually was away at work. Now they both undertook the housework and childcare labor that Bà Bảy had been doing for years. They did not complain, nor did they elaborate on their mother's palpable absence. Bà Bốn, who was Bà Bảy's sister-in-law by marriage and had lived in the adjoining household, sharing in the family's labors for decades, likewise seemed unfazed. She poked fun at my concerned face. No one engaged in talk about Bà Bảy. Not even her granddaughters, who during the day were normally under her care.

"*Cực*" (Tough), the adults shrugged and smiled again. Life is hard.

"Come back again in two weeks," Bà Bốn and Nguyên said as I left. "Ông is just tired."

When I returned in early September, Bà Bảy was still away at the hospital. Up the dirt path, Ông Văn joined the other elders, including his siblings as well as his cousins from his mother's side, in celebrating the rededication of the family altar, which they had just completed refurbishing. Dressed like the other men in dark trousers and a light-colored button-down shirt, he genuflected nimbly in front of the three newly painted altars, each dedicated to the collection of ancestors from his mother's clan.

A younger cousin who was more senior at the lineage level (son of an older brother to Ông Văn's mother) donned mandarin robes and led prayers in front of the three altars, uttering words of devotion to the ancestors and asking their blessing for health, prosperity, and good relations among their descendants. The others stepped up to each altar one by one, each in their own time mouthing silent prayers, genuflecting three times in front of each altar, and placing their joss sticks in the urn prepared at each richly laid-out table serving a feast, rice wine, and fresh hot tea to those long-departed ancestors.

Like the others, Ông Văn partook of the ritual feast after the ancestors had been fed. He sat sandwiched between his brother and nephew and spoke and ate sparingly. He smiled at the bevy of children thronging around my camera, perhaps remembering happier days of his own youth. Soon after the feast was over, he walked back to his compound, discarding his dress pants and dress shirt on his bed. He played for a few minutes with Bà Bốn's two-year-old granddaughter, cradling her affectionately in his lap. But he did not seem up to the task of greeting his grown nephews and nieces as they returned from the feast to rest a bit before going back to work. The afternoon sun beat hard. Ông Văn soon retired to his compound for his afternoon nap. Again, other than pleasantries exchanged at the feast, we did not talk.

Grief and loss are not unique to death. Bà Bảy was not yet dead, just gone, away now for over a month, in and out of private and public hospitals. Alive but not conscious. Absent from home, her loss now felt like a palpable presence. As Robert Desjarlais writes, "Form comes of loss. Something is made present when something else is no longer present."[16] Bà's was an unnamed presence, an unnamed loss, a loss not yet ritualizable, mournable, acknowledgeable. It called for a kind of care that is silent, unspeakable, secretive almost. It called for suffering in silence, waiting for her to recover or to pass away. It called for sacrifice *(hy sinh)*. Neither expectation, of recovery or of death, was spoken now. Life in her household went on. Sons and daughters, nephews and nieces stepped up, visiting the matriarch at the hospital while her husband went on, too, participating in the everyday and the ritual—which itself was part of the everyday—as he could, walking in a kind of daze, sleeping a lot, smiling little, saying less.

Writing of Hyolmo rituals of death, Desjarlais points to the similarities of the experience of loss across communities despite its cultural patterning. He quotes Proust: "People do not die for us immediately, but remain bathed in a sort of aura of life which bears no relation to true immortality but through which they continue to occupy our thoughts in the same way as when they were alive. It is as though they were traveling abroad."[17] Rituals of mourning help manage this transition, this present-absence. In Hyolmo, as in Vietnamese belief and practice, mourning rituals help the soul of the deceased travel to the land beyond. The deceased's survivors embrace ritual to assist the loved one achieve a good death and also to manage their own pain and forge a new existence with this loss.

Alive yet not quite alive, Bà Bảy did not die immediately. Her absence, I could not help but think, continued to occupy her husband's and other loved ones' thoughts and now altered their actions. Daily, they performed much of the work she now could not. And yet talk about her seemed proscribed. Life had to go on.

Vietnam's shrinking public health sector and limited insurance options made it impossible for the family to keep Bà in the hospital indefinitely, so she returned home in early December. As everyone knew, a good death is one completed at home, in the comfort and embrace of one's family, not in a cold hospital room (or, worse, a battlefront).[18] The family hired a nurse to help with the tasks of care, daily checking her vitals, changing her clothes, swabbing her clean, rubbing her legs and arms, shifting her in the bed in the living room where Ông Văn used to watch TV. Bà's daughters and daughters-in-law took turns performing these tasks, too. By January, when the time had come to celebrate Ông Văn's father's death anniversary—an annual event for which the whole brood gathered—the women were well versed in these tasks and performed them without the aid of the nurse.

All year I had heard talk and planning about this great feast and the one that would follow it a few weeks later, to honor Ông Văn's mother, who had died ten days after Tết decades earlier, in 1972, before the war had ended. Ông Văn's father had passed away much earlier, in 1947, a young father of seven. He was barely remembered even by his own children, except for Ông Văn, the oldest, who recalled his father as a gentle and noble-hearted man. The ancestor's grandchildren often talked with great excitement about the feast honoring his death. This was a time to gather the elder's five remaining children and their spouses or widows, many children, and now also grandchildren and great-grandchildren.

It was, I was repeatedly told over the course of the year, the clan's biggest death anniversary. Together with the large feast honoring his deceased widow and the Tết holiday sandwiched in between, it was a time of merriment and feasting, when beer would flow and delicacies would be consumed. Nhu and her sister Nhi, like their sisters-in-law and various cousins and other in-laws, had for months planned to close their respective shops so that they could provide the labor needed to produce this event. Repeatedly, they insisted that I was not under any circumstances to miss this gathering.

MUTED RITUALS AS ACTS OF CARE

I came on the second day of the twelfth month of the lunar calendar, ready to participate in and film the clan's preparations and activities honoring the death anniversary of Ông's father, who had passed away more than sixty years before. It was a crisp sunny day in early January, less than a month before *Tết* and just over a week after the wedding reception of one of Bà Bảy's granddaughters. At that reception in a restaurant in Đà Nẵng proper, Bà's sons, like her nieces, had again reminded me to come with my camera in tow to document and share in one of the family's largest collective gatherings. In the pages that follow, I provide a detailed snapshot of the ways in which Bà was cared for based on the footage I recorded that day, to illustrate the role of silence, muted speech, and embodied action as the family gingerly managed a prolonged period of waiting with Bà's illness.

Unlike the Thai patients with whom Scott Stonington (2011, 2012) worked, Bà Bảy's kin did not speak of her coming death. They faced the rupture that her illness had engendered with relative silence, acting in ways that displayed efforts to sustain order and maintain continuity. Their rituals and routines embodied care in ways that paradoxically both challenge and uphold normative ethical commitments to, and hierarchies of, loved ones, whether alive, dead, or somewhere in between. This evidently unfolds even in the brief moment of caregiving that now follows.

Bà Bảy lay on her bed in the living room, bathed in sunlight, motionless as usual. There was no hired nurse that day. Bà's knees were upright, locked in place. Her daughter-in-law, Lan, stood on the bed, pleading with the comatose elder to straighten out her legs. She had started from Bà's top, adjusting her head and back on the pillow and moved downward to the legs. As these dangled close together toward the left, Lan let out a little laugh tinged with sad frustration, looking at her mother-in-law's helpless yet seemingly stubborn body, and said, "Relax / Easy, missus" *(Nhàn cô)*, as though to cajole the legs downward, addressing her mother-in-law with the somewhat distancing pronoun, *cô* rather than *mẹ*.[19]

Lan then placed her hand gently but firmly on Bà's right knee, pulling it open from the left one, and adjusted each foot on the bed, aligning the legs with the torso to ready them to stretch out. Placing a pillow between the recalcitrant legs, she tried to coax them gently downward to straighten out. These acts of care through gentle coercion were ratified by Ông Văn. Approaching the bed, he addressed Lan, repeating several times the nondeferential second personal pronoun, *mi,* which typically only status-seniors use toward status-juniors,[20] until Lan looked up at him. In these

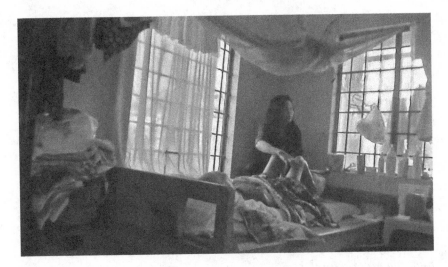

Figure 6. Lan attempting to straighten the legs of her comatose mother-in-law, Bà Bảy (Frame-grab from video recorded by the author at the family's request, January 9, 2008)

subtle ways, both he and she ensured that they had each other's attention while also reinforcing their taken-for-granted status hierarchies.

Having secured Lan's eye contact with the repetition of the pronoun, "Yo-yo-yo-you:: *(Mi-mi-mi-mi::),*" Ông Văn asked Lan if she could get his wife to stretch out her legs. With a smile, Lan answered in a plaintive voice, "She keeps grimacing." She then added, "This morning I was able to stretch her a bit. But she's really struggling."

Without a pause or lull in this stream of talk, Ông Văn replied, "That's ok," reassuring Lan that she was right to try to stretch out his wife's legs.

But as she continued trying to rub and coax the legs downward to stretch out, Lan also continued with her complaint, voicing her concern, "Actually, she's mad at me, I'm hurting her terribly."

His hands clasped behind his back, Ông had approached the bed, entering the frame of my camera. After muttering, "*Đau*" ([She's in] pain), he gazed at his wife for several seconds in silence, while Lan continued to try to work on Bà's legs.

Ông then bent over Bà and stated in an authoritative, paternalistic, matter-of-fact voice, his face directly over hers, to clearly address her, "It doesn't hu::rt." Bending even closer, he exhorted Bà to endure the pain and comply, stating in a scolding voice:

> Endure the pain.
> Stretch out the legs,
> why stay cramped up?

He then added in a gentler, quieter voice, raising and lowering his chin in a kind of entreaty to her, his eyes focusing on hers, "Stretch out. Stretch out."

Lan continued to try to gently straighten out her mother-in-law's legs throughout this short interaction, working to make Bà cooperate with Ông's directive. Overlapping with this command to stretch out *(duỗi đi)*, she protested quietly, "I *tried* doing that [straightening out her legs]" *(Ý là duỗi con làm rồi ấy chứ)*.

Meanwhile, Ông's sisters-in-law, who had come to watch from the side, approached the bed and similarly told Lan, "Stretch out her legs so that her legs lie on the bed."

Ông turned to his brother and sister-in-law at this instance and then quickly turned back to Lan and also repeated this directive, saying, "Try to straighten the legs out."

His brother's wife repeated, as though clarifying, "Meaning, do something so that her legs lie on the bed" *(Tức là làm thế nữa duỗi ra được tới cạnh giường ấy)*.

Lan answered, "[I] can't, her legs only go this far" *(Có đâu xuống tới được dưới đây)*, as she shrugged her shoulders and let out a little laugh, looking up away from Bà's legs and straight at Ông's sister-in-law.

Ông, his back now straight and looking at Lan, exchanged a smile with her and said in a quiet, reassuring voice, "Ok, keep doing it so that they will straighten" *(Thôi để làm tiếp cho nó xuống)*.

Lan then simply repeated, looking down again at Bà's stiff legs, "They only go down to here" *(Xuống tới được nhiêu đây)*, and continued to coax Bà's legs down onto the bed.

Erving Goffman (1981) and followers have written at length about the ways in which participants in interaction can take on multiple and partial roles. For example, a speaker can be the "author" of a strip of talk, or simply the "animator" of another's utterance, depicting the latter as the "principal," or person socially responsible for that utterance through the device of reported speech. Audiences, or "hearers," too, can be analytically broken into different categories, from ratified "addressees" to "bystanders" and "overhearers." In the present case, Lan at first directed her speech at Bà, treating her as the main addressee, though it is plausible that the utterance was also directed at the bystanders and overhearers—Ông Văn and his siblings—who also milled about the room and could observe her solicitation toward her mother-in-law as they approached Bà's bed.

In focusing on speakers and hearers in their various participant roles, Goffman's (1981) model allows us to see how the two generations in this scene organize their interaction in gendered and age-graded ways. It is the daughter-in-law (Lan) who physically takes care of the ill woman (Bà), while the seniors—including both Bà's husband and his brother's wife—direct Lan to keep doing what she has in fact been attempting to do. She in turn has little recourse than to smile, comply, and only weakly protest that she has been doing as told.

Significant here, however, is not just the semantic content and delivery features of the utterances produced. For as Charles Goodwin and Marjorie Goodwin (2004) note, Goffman and followers tend to overly privilege speakers, rightly representing them as "endowed with rich cognitive and linguistic capacities, and the ability to take a reflexive stance toward the talk in progress"; such representations, however, tend to leave others—as fully embodied presences—underanalyzed.[21] Yet as the Goodwins show with the case of "Chil," an aphasiac man who can only produce the three words, "yes/yeah," "no," and "and," he *is* able to participate in assessment activities. With his limited vocabulary and body, he expresses approval of a beautiful calendar and is thus understood as still displaying his rich cognitive life despite new verbal limitations.[22] When the analysis takes into account participants' gestures, movements, bodily use of space, facial expressions, gaze, and interaction with the material environment, in addition to the content, prosody, and tone of utterances, then "participation" is better understood as a form of embodied social action. The Goodwins' model of "participation" thus works as an analytic framework that allows us to discern who is interpellated as a ratified participant and how. This tells us about local understandings of personhood, resposibility, gender roles, morality, and power.

From this perspective, the exchange looks less like a harsh or unsympathetic gesture on the part of those tending Bà and more like potential acts of care and sacrifice. Despite Bà's grave condition, they treat her as a ratified participant: someone to whom they attribute a will, emotions, and agency. Ông scolds; Lan pleads and imagines (or experiences) being scolded. In contrast to those who are not there daily to attend Bà, the two at times address her directly, not just as a mostly-but-not-yet-dead body.

They know that Bà cannot respond, either verbally or with her body, yet they "read" her knotted brow and stiff limbs as expressions of pain and stubborn reproof. They treat her, in other words, as still endowed with a rich cognitive life, even though she is motionless, essentially unresponsive, and on the verge of death.[23] In this incipient narrative, I interpret Ông's exhortation to "stretch out" as modeling for Lan—who had complained that Bà would "scold" her—how to act in this difficult and morally fraught instance, where the daughter-in-law is afraid to hurt and earn the wrath of her mother-in-law. In addressing Bà, in place of Lan, who cannot issue directives to her mother-in-law due to her inferior social position, Ông attempts to help Lan and indirectly enjoin her to keep on tending to the old woman, not to allow Bà's limbs to stiffen and suffer even more. His sister-in-law's directive to Lan, while seemingly extraneous, buttresses Ông's action and is her way of showing that she cares about the ill woman and wants her (body, as well as moral status) not to suffer.

Novices at this type of intensive caregiving, both Lan and Ông struggled to make Bà comfortable and to manage their own discomfort. Most days, they did so in muted ways, Lan smiling and Ông sleeping in the face of Bà's calamity. Like the Thai family that Felicity Aulino (2016) describes—and less like Scott Stonington's (2012) Thai interlocutors, who did allow kin to be disconnected from life support at home—Bà's kin appeared more concerned with embodied forms of care that maintained her life until she expired than with reflexive discussion of her impending death, including whether or how to bring it about or their feelings about it. In the absence of prescribed rituals—which are in place for tending and honoring the dead—they worked instead at treating with respect and care this matriarch who for so long had herself managed the smooth running of the household.

In these ways, Ông, Lan, and other caregivers interpellated not just each other but also the comatose Bà as capable of moral action—as immanently competent, yet imminently incompetent beings who are engaged in an ethical project of care for and about one another. This is why their interactions seem so fraught, I think: we see the family deliberate, through fleeting action, over what the "best good"[24] is for the nearly dead. Stretching out Bà's legs causes the inert but recalcitrant body and the person inhabiting it pain; but because she is still a living person, the family instructs Bà to endure this pain and act ethically in *this* world.[25] As elsewhere in Vietnam, worry and care are essentially synonymous ways of displaying one's morally upright status, the affect of worry *(lo)* concretized through material acts of caregiving.[26]

Ông's siblings and children followed suit. In place of the usual festivities and large feast where alcohol would have been drunk in copious amounts to honor Ông's father, who had passed away over sixty years earlier, kin and friends now took part in a muted affair. The women still cooked the requisite number of dishes to feed the ancestor and honor him at the ritual altar and table, and the long-dead patriarch's children and grandchildren still lit incense and prayed. But in place of the usual five to seven round tables that would have seated upwards of fifty guests, only three were set that day: one around the altar for the men, one next to it for the older women, and one for some of the younger children.

All morning, as Lan took care of Bà, her other relatives had busied themselves preparing a feast that now felt like a burden. Off-camera, some of the women cooking at the fire pit outside in back of the house had grumbled about the cost and hassle of this occasion. When it was finally time to sit and feast, Bà's immediate family circled around the three set tables and ensured that everyone ate and enjoyed their meal. None of them sat down, save for Ông. They carried out the ritual clearly halfheartedly at best.

Their extended family, Bà's three generations of in-laws, consumed the feast while engaging in the usual banter characteristic of such occasions, but no one drank alcohol or the sugary sodas typical of these feasts, and the meal was over faster than usual as a result. Having worked all morning to prepare the feast, Ông's extended family ate relatively quickly, said their good-byes and left, returning to work. Bà's immediate family and just a few of her in-laws stayed to clean up and eat later. They spread out mats in the living room next to Bà's bed and sat cross-legged, eating and chatting quietly, like the others drinking neither beer nor Fanta or Sprite, the usual death anniversary libations. They spoke in hushed tones, as though not to disturb Bà while she rested on the bed next to them and only very quietly showed off the photo album that had already been assembled from Bà's granddaughter's wedding just over a week earlier.

The large gathering that I had been led to anticipate all year long was over in what felt like no time, overshadowed by the illness and impending death, which could come soon or in years. No one knew when, and no one ventured to guess. I did not quite know how to ask about it and feared it would be too indelicate to do so.

A month later, on the first and the eleventh days of the first lunar month, I joined the clan as they gathered again: on the first to celebrate the new year (*Tết*), on the eleventh to celebrate Ông's mother's death anniversary. And again, the family performed the formal ritual acts as prescribed by custom, preparing the requisite foods, lighting incense, greeting their guests. And yet again, despite the smiles, treats, and warm greetings, Bà's condition cast a shadow over these merriments. Though they went on with their lives, mostly as if nothing much was wrong, Bà's household members, along with some of her children and grandchildren nearby, seemed to be in a perpetual state of quiet suspense, waiting. In the relative absence of state support for her kind of constant need for tending, they had to alter their routines, pool their resources, and provide care.

WHAT GOES AROUND COMES AROUND?

I could end by concluding that these occasions, like Bà's earlier, quiet endurance of pain, where for months she did not seek care for her high blood pressure, engender and reflect local understandings of virtuous care and daily sacrifice. But the story does not end here. Not everyone regarded Ông and Bà as morally innocent. Their niece, An, for example, accounted for their present suffering differently, surprising me one December day after we returned from a visit to the elderly couple with a story of past wrongs and transgressions. As her account unfolds in contrast to that of Ông Văn, waiting also appears as a form of withholding or suspending care. Their narratives' differential trajectories underscore the morally fraught ways in which local enactments of care and love entail waiting, often at different temporal scales and with different gendered expectations. These not only sustain but also threaten to rupture shared understandings of who is (or was) virtuous and why.

As I began to suggest in previous chapters, moral personhood in Vietnam is gendered, but this is not the only dimension along which cleavages congeal. The first half of this chapter hints at the ways in which protagonists are not all equally burdened with the moral work of enduring suffering for the sake of another silently. Tracing the unfolding emplotments and intersections of Ông Văn's, An's, and An's mother Bi's stories, in this second half we continue to see, now through narration rather than interaction, how fragile and precarious the work of enduring and waiting in the name of love or care is, even when (and perhaps precisely because) protagonists share a telos of the "good."

An, whose mother was Ông Văn's only remaining sister, used the same logic as her uncle had time and again to account for misfortune. Whenever I asked Ông about his childhood—a period during which the countryside was divided in struggle against the French—he emphasized his parents' gentle forbearance and courage, concluding with a mantra that he attributed to Confucius's teaching, "If you are kind and do good, you'll receive kindness and be fortunate; if you are wicked and do evil then you'll meet with misfortune and wickedness" (*tích thiện phùng thiện, chứa lành gặp lành; tích ác phùng ác, chứa dữ thì gặp cái dữ*).[27] He would repeat this mantra several times more, as though to ensure that I learned it by heart.

Ông did not dwell on his own father's untimely death in 1947, which he did not explain in terms of bad karma but rather attributed to a lack of medicine and medical knowledge at the time. Repeating the mantra, he also told me with pride about how for years he had taken care of his younger siblings, as well as his own children and now grandchildren. When I tried to probe for more concrete examples, he instead listed all his siblings and children by name, recounting their achievements at school. He concluded by emphasizing that this was the moral story I should learn: *always do good and be kind; don't be wicked or exploitative.*

Ông talked most about his youngest brother, whom he described as the best student of their lot. The boy, Xin, had been quite young when they lost their father and had had to tend the family's water buffalo as they grew. Pitying Xin, Ông sold the beasts in order to relieve his most precocious brother of the duties to tend them and instead sent him to school and even university.

Later, as the war took over everyone's life, Ông continued to care for the family's well-being, together with his wife. Worried about his youngest brother, he had helped enroll Xin in the police force, to prevent him from going to the front to die in battle.[28] With one brother gone North to join the DRV Communists and the other three drafted or volunteering to serve the ARVN (Southern) side, Ông and Bà were the ones tending to Ông's mother, their own children, and their brothers' widows or young wives and children. They were committed, he emphasized, to make sure that all the children received a good education, for this, too, was one of Confucius's moral pillars.

It was not his fault, Ông had implied, that after the war Xin was sent off to reeducation camp by the winning regime.[29] Xin had, after all, been on the police force rolls of the enemy. Bà Bảy had chimed in throughout this narrative, saying it would have been better had Xin gone abroad in 1975. Instead, Xin had stayed, reluctant to abandon his young child and pregnant wife. Ông and Bà's joint story did not praise Xin. Their point was that they had done the best they could for the extended family during all those years of war and struggle. Their sacrifices for the family and Xin's sacrifices for his wife and children had simply not been enough to prevent or avert their loved ones' suffering and misfortune.[30]

On many occasions since we met in 2005, Ông and Bà had presented themselves as virtuous caretakers who had assured the younger generation's education and success. Ông's sister and her daughter, however, told a different story that implied negligence and even greed. It wasn't just that neither Ông Văn nor his wife had visited the younger brother when he was imprisoned by the Communists after the war, nor that they had *not* helped his wife and her two young sons. In recent years, An and her mother implied, Ông Văn and his wife had also mishandled the family's inheritance. In simply waiting and *not* caring when postwar relations upended certain lives, they may have contributed to the exacerbated misery of some of their kin.

The day after An and I returned from a visit to the now-comatose Bà (before the long-anticipated death anniversary described earlier), An launched into a story that linked her aunt's prolonged suffering in her present comatose state to disputed landholdings within the family. She came to this story slowly and circuitously, as if by accident. Her initial concern had been to explain, with what seemed to me like surprising optimism, how her mother's newly renovated house would have to be demolished to make room for the city's rapid development project.

An told me with apparent patriotic pride how Đà Nẵng had just gotten foreign investors to sign a contract to build a new bridge and six-lane highway connecting the central part of the city, where her mother lived, to the city district across the river. The family had bought their house in 1968, when times had really been hard; they had only completed renovating it by installing tile floors, electricity, and a flush toilet in 2006. But soon this new house would be razed to the ground. An's mother and three brothers, who presently lived in adjoining households, would have to relocate to the city outskirts to make room for the new bridge. Because the amount of compensation was uncertain and their means unequal, the brothers would likely build separate, nonadjoining new households.

We had heard news of this plan just a couple of months earlier, when An's sister came running in with the "happy" news. I had expected them to express shock, dismay, anger, or even regret. How could they not feel negatively about this development? But on the day that we heard the news and again today, An did not dwell on what to me seemed like the difficult prospect of moving and separating. Instead, on both occasions she narrated her excitement for the city's future.[31] In reviewing our recorded conversation, I came to wonder if this, too, was another form of sacrifice, framing the city's collective good as transcending her family's individual hardship.

An waited now for the Americans to make good on their promise to rebuild and invest in the city. This was a type of waiting filled with anticipation, where if there were traces of dread, they remained muted. Waiting, for her, was not just an empty time of sitting still, or of being in limbo and extended states of liminality: it can be impregnated with positive and negative affects such as hope and fear, anticipation and resentment.[32]

PAST WAITING AND SHIFTING ALIGNMENTS OF CARE

The story of the bridge now reminded An of the hardships that her family had undergone years ago, during the war. Her mother, Bi, newly married, had just moved in with her husband's family. Bi then went back to her own kin to give birth at her natal home, and they took care of her there because the siblings loved each other *(anh em thương nhau)*, An narrated. These siblings, including Ông Văn, had been good to An's mother. They helped her with everything, unlike the new in-laws, An elaborated. This is why to this day she feels closer and loves her mother's more than her father's relatives, An added, repeating that she cherishes her maternal kin *(quý bên ngoại)*.[33] Patrilocal residence norms, she implied, do not overcome matrilocal affective bonds. And resentment that may have crept in later does not negate memories of love and cherishing fostered earlier on. Her story, meandering and encompassing multiple, at times inconsistent and nonlinear positions, thus featured sideshadowing prominently, allowing for contradictory moral and affective stances to coexist and complicate the "truths" narrated.

During those war years, conditions were harsh. Children died. There was not enough food, or enough medicine. Everybody suffered, An emphasized. "We were not the only ones," she added, not unlike Nhu earlier in this chapter and many others whom I followed who minimized their own personal suffering by emphasizing instead the collective suffering of others. Familial relations were essential and nourishing ingredients to survival, tightening bonds between loving kin. With animation, An recounted how her mother's youngest brother (Xin) saved her when as a young child she had been really sick. He used his connections to take An to the hospital. This was because Xin loved her mother, An explains: he had declared his devotion to her, over and above that to his oldest brother, saying, "I will only go with sister Bi. I don't want to go with anyone else, not even oldest brother [Ông Văn]."

Had there already been a dispute back then over who would shelter him? Was his move from their natal home outside the city to the center of Đà Nẵng related to more than just Xin's professional post in the military?

After his marriage, Xin continued to live with An's family. He brought his wife and, not long after, their infant son, to occupy a room in An's mother's house. Though initially beneficial, Xin's devotion to his oldest sister (Bi) would cost An's family. When the war was over and the Communists had taken over, the new regime wanted to confiscate Bi's house, reasoning that it belonged to and had harbored *Ngụy* (Puppet Regime Enemy soldiers). Yet An does not narrate this turn of events in backshadowing form, with the hindsight of the future that might lead her to criticize having harbored her uncle and nearly costing her family their home. Instead, she emphasizes the loving bonds of kinship between brother and sister and their respective families, quoting her uncle's declaration, "I love / care for sister Bi" *(Em thương chị Bi)*. She also explained this love in terms of the place his sister had made for him in her small house. In classic Maussian fashion, brother and sister placed moral claims on one another.[34] Bi had to respond to Xin's declaration of devotion with reciprocal material care:

> Because he always followed her,
> the *tình cảm* between us was stronger than between him and the others.
> [She] was closer to him.
> That's why Aunt Bi loves/cared *(thương)* more about Xin than about the others.

Having explained how her uncle Xin had helped her parents pay off the loans they had taken to buy their house during the late 1960s and early 1970s, when he was an officer for the Army of the Republic of Vietnam, An recounts the sharp turn of luck upon "Liberation" *(giải phóng)*, when Xin was taken away to reeducation camp and the government almost seized their house, thinking it belonged to him. It was only through the intercession of her father, who somehow managed to convince the new authorities that the Puppet Enemy Soldier *(lính Ngụy)* had just been staying with them but did not own the house, that the family's hard-earned hut was spared. Xin's wife, meanwhile, returned to her own parents' home, suffering greatly due to her father's abusive and aggressive nature, An recounts. No one, one might surmise, wanted to harbor the pregnant wife and young son of a now-captured former Puppet Enemy Soldier. Ông Văn and his wife are not described here at all.

Yet contact between the families had not ended. During Xin's incarceration, An would sometimes visit his wife, Mợ,[35] at Mợ's parents' house. And on those three or four times when Mợ received permission to visit her husband up North, she always came first to Bi's house to cook for him there, not at her own mother's house or at Ông Văn's. It was always An's mother and one of An's siblings who traveled with Mợ the long distance to the reeducation camp where Xin was being held in "very rough, fearsome conditions" *(cực lắm, sợ lắm)*, An recounts. She implies that the act of cooking at her mother's house, rather than elsewhere, was yet another way by which her family helped her uncle in ways unparalleled by the others. Pausing to reflect later in her narrative, An muses that she had in fact loved Mợ even more than she loved Uncle Xin.

GENDERED LOVE, CARE, AND BETRAYAL

From the start, An explicitly describes her uncle's wife as moral and virtuous, for she had not left her husband but stayed with him, waiting for many years until he was finally released a decade after the war's conclusion. An repeats several times, using the third-person plural pronoun, *họ*, to indicate an amorphous person who does not at all resemble her beloved Mợ, who had virtuously waited.

You see?	*Thấy hông? ((không))*
Certainly if [you] met other wives	*Chứ gặp như những người vợ khác*
They would leave [their husband]	*là họ bỏ*
They'd leave.	*họ bỏ.*
It's too burdensome.	*Cực quá.*
For example, if they were already busy working to take care of their kids . . .	*Thí dụ họ làm lũ họ làm họ lo nuôi con . . .*
they wouldn't be able to visit.	*Là không có đi thăm được.*
There were many people	*Còn có nhiều người*
[who find] these conditions too tough	*cực quá*
and leave their husband for another one.	*là họ đi lấy chồng khác.*

An contrasts such wives with Mợ, who, unlike others, was "really good" *(mà mợ rất là tốt)*. She adds that this is why she goes to the pagoda to worship her, because she really loves Mợ, and then continues with this story, describing how she had cried when her uncle's wife died, having loved/pitied her so much *(thương dễ sợ)*. Recalling a range of negative stances that she adopted about her uncle, she repeats that she had not liked it at all *(không ưa)* and even turned angry *(cũng tức)* when she heard that her uncle Xin had gone on to remarry abroad after his wife's death. An felt it was an injustice to her beloved Mợ, who had waited so faithfully for her husband to return. Xin, An felt, had not loved his wife in the same way and had not stayed faithful. With these words, An protests what seemed to her a gendered double standard of love and care, where the wife stayed faithful, but her husband did not.

And yet immediately, An corrects herself, recounting how her mother, Bi, disputed this account of Xin. Bi said that An was all wrong in her interpretation, explaining that it was not for lack of love that her own beloved brother had remarried: it was in order to find a mother to take care of his children, someone to cook for them and for him in his widow's absence. An did not argue. She simply started going to the pagoda to worship her aunt there; she continued to love / pity Mợ, she said (*thương Mợ lắm*).

Mother and daughter disagree in this instance over what constitutes moral care and love, or how it ought to be expressed or preserved through acts of waiting. An's sideshadowing account, rather than foreclose or privilege her own interpretation, highlights the moral permeability involved in judging and enacting love. It effectively suggests that relations of care require moral navigation through at times turbulent waters.[36]

One might wonder what all this has to do with Ông Văn and his sick wife. And yet, as the narrative continues, An weaves a moral tale that enfolds all her uncles in the end. Here, women are positioned as the virtuous caretakers who stay faithful to their husbands and brothers while the men engage in seeming acts of betrayal. It is not just Mợ's husband who betrayed, I learn. Ông Văn, in essentially abandoning his brother since he left to live with his sister (Bi, An's mother), had not really done right by Xin. And Ông continued to do wrong. Moral retribution can wait a long time, An ultimately recounts.

At this juncture, An initiates a story that morally frames her oldest maternal uncle in a negative light. She first provides the background, recounting how her uncles' mother had not left the youngest uncle (Xin) a piece of land on which to live when she died, for he was not yet married. When Xin finally returned after reeducation camp, never once having been visited by any of his brothers, his sister alone stepped in to help. In anticipation of his return, Bi borrowed some money from Mợ and in return gave Mợ rights to a portion of her own land, on which Mợ and

Xin would build their own house, apart from Mợ's parents and brothers. Mợ's father, however, had been perfidious. He kept for his family the paperwork that established legal claims to the land deeded to his daughter and son-in-law.

When Xin and Mợ and their children received permission to emigrate from Vietnam under the auspices of the Joint US-Vietnamese Humanitarian Resettlement Program,[37] Ông Văn had wanted his sister to buy back the land so that it would stay in the family. But Bi would not. She had no money, she said. This should have been land, An notes, that Bi could have sold and herself become rich; instead, now she could not even afford to buy it back. Nor would she take it back by force when Xin's father-in-law refused its sale to Ông Văn's son. Instead, Mợ sold the house to her own brother, who paid only half the selling price. Ông Văn got angry. He blamed both his sister and his brother for being foolishly taken in by Mợ's family. He berated Bi, "Why won't you take the land back? Why did you let him sell it?" As An tells it, Bi stood up to her older brother, answering with the colloquial pronouns *tui* (I) and *hắn* (he) that indicate intimacy:

I already gave [it to him].	*Tui cho rồi.*
He can do whatever he wants.	*Hắn lo làm chi hắn làm.*
I can't . . .	*Tui không . . .*
can't take it back.	*không có thể lấy lại được.*

Ông Văn's household got angrier and angrier, getting into a "feud" *(đại khái cũng ồn ào)* with his younger brother and Xin's in-laws. Xin, An recounts, became afraid: Would the government now not let him leave Vietnam if they heard that he was at the center of conflict with kin? Could they detain him again? Whispering to his sister, he begged Bi to side with him and not to say a word. Having sold the house and land for just three taels of gold, Xin left these to his sister Bi to distribute among her children. He left the country with his oldest brother still angry at him and his brother-in-law the winner of the land dispute. Over twenty years after this saga, An still sounded upset.

Her mother, she intimates, was the only one who really cared about poor Uncle Xin and his wife, Mợ. Whereas An's mother had accompanied Mợ to the reeducation camps or sent her daughters with Mợ on these perilous journeys, Ông Văn and their brothers never went and did not even pay attention to their youngest brother wasting away after the war. It is because of this closer and more intimate bond between her mother and uncle, An explains, that upon his return from reeducation camp, and, later, upon emigration from Vietnam, Xin would always give more money to and prioritize his sister over his brothers. He knew, like no one else, how hard his sister worked and how she had suffered.

In nonlinear, sideshadowing fashion, An's narrative weaves back and forth through time, emphasizing moments of connection, love, and hurt. She returns to the immediate postwar years, when her mother, Bi, used to sell snacks at the corner of their alley. People were not at all nice back then, chasing Bi away. Mean-spirited neighbors went beyond egging her mother on to leave: they hung a bird cage from their house above her stall, whereupon birds would defecate on Bi's head. Only years later, An recounts, did her mother tell her of these hardships; at the time, Bi had hidden her sorrows and humilations, enduring and suffering in silence.

An's message was clear: Bi had stood by her brother Xin for decades. She steadfastly waited and acted virtuously, caring in quiet, helpful ways for her brother. Upon returning from his prolonged incarceration and beginning to work, Xin regularly paid Bi. And in the midst of the dispute over the sale of his house, Xin promised to make a fortune abroad and send it back to Bi to help her retire. After Xin managed to leave legally with his wife, two sons, and young daughter, Bi kept to herself knowledge of his promise. Perhaps in an effort to save her brother's face, or because she feared the cruelty of optimism,[38] Bi did not share it with the rest of her children until after Xin's death. An recounts how Bi waited in silence and without true anticipation for the day Xin might make good on his promise, elaborating:

> Bi never mentioned it. [...]
> This was not because she regretted that piece of land.
> She didn't.
> What she meant was ...
> siblings love/take care of each other *(chị em là thương nhau)*,
> no matter what happens.
> [They] don't concern [themselves] with money.

Yet this was a contradiction, since not concerning oneself with money was not an ideal that I observed practiced within families. Usually they framed refusal to give as betrayal and lack of *tình cảm*.

Soon after Xin left Vietnam, he lost his wife, remarried, and passed away several years later. Bi's kindness and investment in Xin and Mợ had never paid off. They each left the world too early, orphaning their children in a land distant from their kin. Here, too, misfortune stands unexplained: Xin, Mợ, and Xin's father all died young, leaving bereft children behind. An was a more devout Buddhist than Ông Văn, but like him she did not explain why someone who had not been "wicked" met with misfortune.

Nearly forty years had passed since Xin had left Ông Văn's care, first to be with his sister and decades later when he headed abroad. And yet An recounted their story of muted family rifts with a rawness that still stung. Ông Văn's present misfortune, which involved the liminal loss and possible suffering of his wife, Bà Bảy, and the rest of their household, had rekindled the pain of past losses and fissures. It now left an opening to air out long-gone relational difficulties and fracture the narrative framing of Ông Văn and Bà Bảy as moral exemplars who had taken care of all their younger kin and who yearly on Xin's death anniversary worshipped him on the altar next to Ông Văn's parents. From other family members I had only ever heard of how Ông Văn had taken care of his brother Xin after their father's death. For An, however, the present affliction (in tandem with my curiosity) provided an excuse to reframe her own mother's long suffering and waiting for a more "just" fortune to meet her unrecognized deeds of kindness and the love she had shared with her brother Xin. Maybe Bi's sacrifice no longer had to remain so secret and mute.

An might have continued the narrative, but at this point her mother returned home. Seeing us speaking with the audio-recorder on, Bi expressed concern that we were gossiping and interrogated me about my visit to Bà Bảy. She asked if Bà was opening her eyes, whether she recognized me, and who else was there. Reluctant to disseminate information about others and mindful that An could tell her much more than I could, I mumbled that the usual caretakers were there: Bà Bảy's sister, sister-in-law, hired nurse, and Ông Văn but not his sons (who could only come on weekends).

As Bi stepped out again and we continued to chat, An warned me never to speak ill of Bi's brothers. "She will scold you," An repeated. "[You're] not allowed to speak badly of her siblings. She's very protective. Very protective. If you say something bad about Ông Văn, it doesn't sit well with her. [You'd] get scolded. We'd get scolded."

"Do you get scolded?," I asked An.

"Yeah. Anyone. Not just me, but anyone. If anyone talks—[they'd] immediately get scolded by Aunt Bi." Bi, An explained, was very loyal to her brothers and was committed to upholding the moral and social order in which siblings are supposed to love and protect one another and not allow outsiders to air family rifts. But Bi herself, An added, could speak ill of her brothers. Coming from her, it would be acceptable. "But we can't say anything."

I probed, asking for an example of when An got scolded. She volunteered the latest encounter, when one of Ông Văn's daughters-in-law had mentioned that he had sold off some of the family's collective lands.[39] An had protested to her mother, saying that it wasn't fair. She had objected that her uncle should have first consulted with his brothers, including Uncle Tan, who had returned from the North after the war, and with Xin's orphaned children, since they had never gotten a share of the family lands. Her voice quiet but quivering with emotion, An explained, "Don't you agree? It's a matter of fairness! Even if the sons are abroad. Even if Uncle Tan is rich, he should have called them in."

To buttress her principled rather than contextual approach to justice, An next authored for Ông Văn the type of discourse he should have initiated, animating him as the fictive principal[40] of her imagined dialogue: "In the past, Grandma left this much land for you. Now I am giving it to you." Returning to her own voice, An continues:

If they didn't claim it, then Ông Văn would have the right to sell it.
[He could] sell it.
And build an ancestral worship shrine.
Right?
But chị Ngọc [Ông's daughter-in-law] said that he gave to this guy and
    that guy.
He gave it to his grandchildren, to his children and grandchildren.
He took our land and gave it away.
And he never thought of Uncle Tan and Uncle Xin.
That's why I disagreed.
And got scolded.

"You brat, you don't know anything," An imitates her mother scolding her, using the same nondeferential second personal pronoun, *mi*, that Ông Văn had also used to address his daughter-in-law, Lan. "You don't know anything, you shouldn't speak."

An does not stop to comment on how she felt in the face of her mother's rebuke. She simply continues her story, adding that it was only after he had sold the land that Ông Văn called Aunt Bi and Uncle Tan back to give them each a million *đồng* (about US$40), out of a sale of 200 million *đồng* (about US$8,000). Their younger brother Tin, who was sick, asked for more.

Bi had at this point returned, but this time she did not interrupt our "gossip." An continued:

> Aunt Bi and Uncle Tan would not take the money.
> They didn't take it.
> They said they wanted to leave it for their brother [Ông Văn],
> so when he builds the ancestral worship shrine,
> they will have already contributed like that.

Murmuring, "Ah," I let An continue, her discourse filled with parallel structures, repetitions, and direct reported speech that pull the listener into the scene and convey An's sense of injustice:

> After that, well, then, Uncle Tin was sick.
> He asked for ten million [about US$400].
> He asked for ten million.
> But Bà Bảy, Bà Bảy who is sick now, she said,
> "Ten million, where would [we] get ten million from?
> [We'll] give you five million.
> After you've used up five million,
> come back and ask for another five million."
> Well, Uncle Tin used up the five million,
> So he came back to get five million more.
> But Bà Bảy said they were out of money and didn't give him any.
> In the end they only gave him five million.
> You see.
> So that's about the land.
> See?
> And [Xin's] children abroad got nothing.

Addressing me directly by name, An asked pointedly, "You have to agree, they were taken advantage of, right?"

I feigned misunderstanding, repeating, "Got taken advantage of?"

Bi now joined the conversation, taking over from her daughter to summarize:

Ông Văn sold the land.
He was wrong.
You see?
He's older, but he was in the wrong.

No longer at odds, mother and daughter now collaboratively narrated a unified moral stance that placed blame squarely with Ông Văn and emphasized the seeming paradox that their senior male kin could so egregiously violate the expected order of things. Like her daughter, Bi formulated what she thought Ông Văn *should* have said: "'I -I want to sell that piece of land, what do you guys want to do?' Like that." Continuing with a firm stance that outlines why her older brother was in the wrong and ultimately came to suffer misfortune, she makes her case more resolutely than in An's circuitous narrative by asserting:

If he'd just said one more sentence like that,
it [the rift] would be over.
But he sold it [the land] first,
and then he called the uncles.
He called them back to give them the money.
You see.
He'd already given a lot away to his children and grandchildren.

There was no turning back, Bi implied. She elaborated that Ông Văn should have given each one of her parents' descendants a share. But instead, her brother had prioritized his own closest kin: he gave each of his grandchildren two million apiece, but barely left any proceeds for his own siblings and their children. And as for Xin's children, he left them nothing. As though to conclude, she states point blank, "So I felt sad. I felt sad because he left them nothing." Bi does not say that she felt sad that her own children were deprived of their rightful inheritance, but I read her moral outrage as involving them as well. Bi continued, enumerating why Ông Văn was in the wrong and articulating how she would act differently.

She explained that since the land was not really Ông Văn's but belonged to the siblings' grandparents he did not have permission to sell it without her and her brothers' (Tan's and Tin's) prior consent. Alluding to karmic retribution for violating the principle that family land should not be sold off, Bi continued, "But these are Ông Văn's deeds, so he will have to bear the consequences." She contrasted herself with him and implied that she was more filial, by adding that were he to have given her ten million *đồng* (which should have been her equal share from the land sale), she would have accepted it but only to return the sum to him to help defray the cost of refurbishing their grandparents' ancestral shrine.

Struggling to follow Bi's logic and the time frame of their dispute, I said, "Oh," and asked, perhaps foolishly, "When was it resolved?" I could not tell if she was more upset about the process or the outcome. Disregarding my question, Bi went on in a tone of righteous indignation:

> Ông Văn said so, it was an example.
> And Aunt Bi [I] didn't take it.
> I was poor,
> a poor laborer,
> but I didn't want to take our grandparents' money,
> nor their land.
> But he didn't tell me anything.
> He only called us back to give us each one million.
> I didn't take it.
> And Uncle Tan didn't take it.

Futilely, I tried to clarify, "But where is the ancestral shrine?" Bi barely stopped her tirade:

> It's there at his house.
> And if it's damaged, Ông Văn will have to fix it.
> We don't have to worry about it, understand?
> If it deteriorates, he has to fix it.
> Even if he doesn't fix it up,
> I am not going to take our grandparents' money.

Continuing with this confusing he-said / she-said[41] moralistic story in which she casts her brother and his wife in a dubious light, Bi elaborated:

> He told me, "You're old,
> if you criticize and you don't want to take it, it's fine.
> I won't say anything."
> That's what he said.
> Well, he's older,
> but he didn't do –he did not do the right thing.
> You see?
> I don't know if he said that he would give the others five million or something.

Bi next implicates not just Ông Văn but also his wife, Bà Bảy, whom she implies was behind the unfair distribution of the sale's proceeds:

> But Bà Bảy, she said, "Those relatives are rich,
> so it doesn't matter if you give them any money."
> Their relatives told this to me.
> I don't know about this affair.

"Who said it?," I asked. Impatiently, Bi retorted:

> It doesn't matter who.
> Someone in their household told me.
> I didn't see it.
> And I don't have that land,
> I don't have any money from our grandparents,
> but I still live fine.
> We can still raise children and take care of them.
> Such gifts are gifts of sentiment,
> they signify our bonds of love as siblings . . .

Bi trailed off, having made her point that unlike her (greedy) brother and his wife, she did not need the money from her grandparents' sold land. But then she immediately continued, elaborating in a quietly plaintive tone:

> He sold it for a hundred something, the land nearby.
> When I was fixing up my house,
> I came to ask for some tens of million to borrow,

he wouldn't give me.
He said he was out of money.
He'd put it all in the bank already.
So I said OK, then five million [about $200].
He still said it was in the bank and he couldn't get it.
Then.
Then I got irritated,
and I asked for five hundred thousand to borrow.
I only asked for five hundred thousand [about $20],
like you gave me the other day.
I only asked for that much, but he wouldn't give it to me.
This was recent.
Before Bà Bảy got sick.
Ông Văn said he didn't have it.
Fuck.
We give him whatever he wants.

Surprised that she had sworn, I foolishly interrupted, "You said *Ông*, meaning Ông Văn?"

"Yeah," she answered, as An began instead to explain to me about terms of address and about the need to worship the ancestors properly.[42] The time for expressing anger had passed. An and Bi did not return to their story of grievance with Ông Văn and his wife. Yet in that brief tirade, it became clear that I had not just imagined Bi's anger. It had bubbled over, and, just like her daughter, she connected the misfortune now afflicting Ông Văn's house to past acts of stinginess, perfidy, or exploitation. The silence had cracked, if only briefly. Their waiting was not entirely peaceful. Family fissures had creeped to the surface, threatening to erupt into a full-blown feud, perhaps not unlike the one that had almost prevented her brother Xin decades earlier from fleeing their homeland.

And yet, as I continued to attend the households' death anniversaries, engagement parties, and weddings, these dark rumblings subsided. In a few weeks' time, we all went up to Ông Văn's house to worship their father and later their mother, as described above, pretending, at least, that chasms had not opened up and would not swallow their shared *tình cảm*. An and Bi, much like Như, Lộc, and the other relatives, treated Ông Văn and his comatose wife with outward respect. Silently waiting for death, they remained persons who reciprocated care.

NARRATIVE AND MORAL PERIL WHEN WAITING IS CARE

The enacted stories of waiting as care embodied by Bà Bảy and her kin—Ông Văn, Lan, Nhu, Lộc, and the others—are entangled with the narratives told by An and her mother, Bi. If in chapter 2 it was corporeal practice that points to the ethics and labor of sustaining sacrifice that connected seemingly disparate cases, here, too, the chapter's characters are connected by more than merely the bonds of reckoned common ancestry and kinship. The stories all evince moral peril. Uncertainty pervades not simply the future: the suspense of what will come to pass (or when), as characters at different points wait for what will be, and struggle to make bearable their present difficult circumstances. Uncertainty and even incommensurability also pervade these accounts as existential conditions, as protagonists strive, in Cheryl Mattingly's (2014a, 2014b) neo-Aristotelian virtue ethical terms, to arrive at the "best good" for themselves *through and in caring for* others while mired in the liminality of waiting. In waiting, they learn that what seems "good" on the one hand can also make another relationship or cherished connection vulnerable to fraying and even breaking.

Should or could Bà Bảy have demanded treatment for her overwhelming headaches earlier? How might that have upended her claim to enacting virtue by suffering silently? Why was it so important for Bà's daughter and Nhu, Lộc, Ông Văn, and the others to minimize the elder's suffering or their own hardship and loss? Why the insistence that Bà straighten out her legs? At what cost to the comatose elder and to her struggling daughter-in-law Lan?

The protagonists of these fleeting actions did not pause to reflect and explain to me (or themselves) the rationale for their actions. Yet I interpret the relationships recounted here as premised on the logic of *tình cảm*, which requires acts of care to sometimes be achieved by feigning, or even feeling, its lack. We witness this, for example, when Nhu, together with Bà's daughter, pretends that the hospitalization is not a major cause for concern, or when Ông Văn urges Lan and admonishes his comatose wife to straighten out her legs. We also see this with An and Bi, who narrate how the presence of *tình cảm* with some (Xin and his wife) threatened the maintenance of such relations with others (Ông Văn and his wife); this also threatened their own well-being, as when Bi almost lost her house and lost family lands in the name of family love. What might they have risked or suffered had they severed relations with Xin and Mợ back then or cut off relations with Ông Văn and Bà Bảy now? If they ever asked themselves such questions, they did not share these with me or with those in their social circle whom I knew.

While the struggles of mixed allegiances and ambivalent feelings pervade the everyday, their thematization as narrated stories are, for the most part, kept under wraps and silenced. They are mute and secretive, affirming sacrifice by minimizing explicit attention to one's own loss and affirming that of others. Sacrifice, we see again, requires silence. In these narratives, it is not just (or even primarily) a teleologically driven temporality that guides action. As elsewhere,[43] the characters here wait for care, or for the world to become otherwise, and meanwhile resent the sense of suspense.

But also, and more important, this chapter's cases highlight the sideshadowing quality of ethics in the everyday, where the extraordinary is turned (back) into the everyday through the ethical work involved when characters must contend with multiple, competing, ambivalent bonds and claims on their sense of the good and the right. Ethical reflection and narration may well be called for in these moments of "moral breakdown."[44] And yet the cases here also suggest that ethical work becomes ordinary through the cultivation and invocation of sentiments *(tình cảm)* in prolonged periods of waiting during which characters manage the upending of the ordinary by altering routines to simulate continuity. Ethics across these cases is ordinary and achieved in interaction.[45] Ethics need not be solely or even primarily the result of reflection.

Further, sacrifice in Vietnam is not straightforwardly an act of affirmation through abnegation or violence, as anthropological canonical knowledge would have it. It is rooted in largely kin-based sentiment and social hierarchy, with multiple vectors that involve moral conflict and peril, contradiction as well as resolution. Much like the comatose Bà, the deceased Xin serves as the instigator and foil for moral deliberation, narration, and action. As politically tainted and at once vulnerable and threatening—first because of his premature orphaning, then for his retributive incarceration, and finally in his premature death—Xin is an analogue to Bà in her liminal state, alive but not quite alive. Both are present absences whose consequent inability to narrate a plot to counter their past deeds as "wicked" (or insufficiently kind) open a space for critique and articulation of preferred norms. Bà's family is threatened by her condition of vulnerability. Her relatives wait for her end in silence, giving care through words or embodied actions such as caressing or scolding or ignoring, upending their routines and scaling back rituals in order to maintain a semblance of continuity and order, pretending that nothing much has changed when almost everything has. Bi, meanwhile, laments Xin's unfulfilled promises only after his demise, having earlier waited and suffered in silence.

As in the stories that Cheryl Mattingly (2010, 2014a) tells of families struggling with their children's illness and with how to navigate the multiple, contradictory claims made on them (e.g., as an expert caregiver who can earn the respect of clinicians by being as knowledgeable as they are but at the expense of being a loving mother attuned to her daughter's needs), Lan and Bi (among others) in this chapter struggle with the duties of love. They risk hurting and being hurt when they care for the other and abide a Levinasian moral imperative to prioritize the other not because it is a duty to insist on the singularity of the self or the other, as in Emmanuel Levinas's (1998) philosophy, but simply because it is an existential condition of life to be entangled with the other.[46] Their struggles in the everyday and in moments of breakdown expose the tension—but also possible convergence—between the quotidian and the extraordinary, belying claims by theorists of morality and ethics in either camp about their mutual exclusivity.

Through ethnography, we see instead how efforts geared toward the ordinary and cultivated through habit[47] emerge; they are engaged in extraordinary circumstances of disalignment, dissonance, or even attempts to reaffirm transcendence,[48] to create continuity out of change. The dynamics that shape protagonists' ethical frameworks, I have continued to show, are gendered and deeply fraught with clashing expectations by differentially positioned kin, who in turn carry the weight, and sometimes scars (as we saw in the case of Xin), of Vietnam's entangled internal and geopolitical conflicts. Following other psychological anthropologists interested in care and the dissolution or reconstitution of "the ordinary,"[49]

I continue to explore these tensions in the following chapter, where I attend even more explicitly to the discourse of family love or *tình cảm* in action and, again, in interaction with the looming history of war and promising future as Vietnam as a state and society embarks on its particular courses of national development.

5 Children and Lovers

"WHAT DOES FAMILY GIVE FOR YOU?"

Lộc and Hiệp's son Ri was a typical sixteen-year-old high school student usually only interested in comic books, soccer, and physics. Yet as a scholarship student at one of Đà Nẵng's best high schools, he possessed better writing skills in English than most students, and he diligently completed his homework each night. When instructed at school to write an essay about "the most important thing," he emulated philosophical tracts that strive to arrive at truth by posing questions and immediately answering them. I quote at length from one of Ri's English-language compositions to show how ingrained are the ideas that family is central and rooted in feminine virtue and labor. Even in his understandably less than professional prose, it is clear that Ri used his cultural knowledge to craft the type of essay he knew his teacher would approve and reward with high marks.

Ri declares "family" is the key to a good life in this essay, articulating cultural tropes that link well-being to familial care, material provisioning, and devoted wives and mothers, as excerpted here:

> What do you want from the life? Life gives you many things but what's the most important thing? I think it's very hard to choose the most important

thing, such as: family, health, friend, money, job, . . . so on. If I must choose
the only answer, I'll say family. That's the most important thing to me. When
I happy or sorrow, family is the place make me better.

[. . .]

What does family give for you? Family likes a close friend, when you sad,
you can feel better, and if you make everybody in your family happy, you also
feel happy, too. Family also gives more things bigger than happiness, family
helps you when you're sick, everybody in your family do anything to make
you better, your parent lead you to hospital, take care you, your brothers,
sisters help you do houseworks . . . You can say family tries to give you the
good health. You also say family gives money for you, when you're a child,
your parent pay school fees for you, your pocket money is you parent's
money. When you get married, if you don't have enough money, your wife
can help you. And so on, family can give you many things.

My mother is the best member in my family. She works all day, she has a
shop, there, she works all day except midday. My father is the best father in
the world, he doesn't pamper his children, but he loves my sisters and me,
like my mother, he works all day, he is an engineer, he tries to earn money
for my family's life.

It is significant that in his encomium to family, Ri frames it as a supportive ideal in general that provides specific material aid. The wife in this
trope supports her husband financially and otherwise; and when Ri
describes the particularity of his life in the essay's conclusion, he begins
with his mother. He singles her out as "the best person in my family," then
adds a sentence about his father, whom he also praises but on different
grounds. Both, he avers, are dedicated and hardworking parents, with his
father trying to earn money. Ri's mother, Hiệp, confirmed this some weeks
earlier: she was continually saving up for their elder daughter's studies
abroad while Lộc's lower income supported other household expenses.

Ri's framing of his mother as the family's "best member," however,
parted ways with his broader clan's judgments. They considered Ri's father
more virtuous because Lộc's care extended beyond the nuclear circle to his
other relatives. As an outsider who had followed her husband to Đà Nẵng
years after their marriage, Hiệp was disadvantaged because she did not
have any relatives in the area to support her and had not built strong alli-
ances with Lộc's kin. Among other couples who were both locals, the person who both fulfilled their expected gender role and aided and paid visits

to a wider social network—thereby displaying broader and more far-reaching *tình cảm*—was deemed the more virtuous.

In previous chapters, we witnessed how protagonists learn and strive to embody virtuous comportment in their multiple relations with intimates. This chapter attends to the longue durée of married adult life to illuminate how the specters of war and postwar relations, together with gender, haunt present lives.[1] Vietnamese valuations of asymmetrical reciprocity, quotidian sacrifice, and *tình cảm*, I continue to show, render family life and moral personhood more complex and less amenable to reductive accounts of future-oriented motivations and monadic principle-abiding behavior. Further, Vietnamese Confucian ethics, which rely on an Aristotelian narrative logic that insists on the primacy of social context and practice-based virtue rather than resort to Kantian, utilitarian, or even Levinasian principles, can render one's status as virtuous perpetually precarious, particularly for women on the wrong side of politics.

I begin with sketches of Lộc's family in order to trace some of the contradictions entailed in gendered expectations of sacrifice and *tình cảm* while also elaborating the point made in chapter 3, that love is better understood as an entangled web of relations that include both romantic and companionate relationships between lovers, partners, or spouses *and* intergenerational relationships. To further complicate the notion of ethical personhood and to demonstrate the narrative ways by which protagonists construct morality as a fraught and contradictory assemblage, I then tell An's story about Thu's family, among whom Vietnam's three official "social evils"—prostitution, drugs, and AIDS—brought suffering and death, as well as care.[2] I end with An's reflection on her own marriage and motherhood and the ambivalences and silences that it underscores in gender and state relations.

Layer by layer, these stories indicate how social privilege translates into moral privilege. They suggest that for women, the poor, and those whose kin aligned with the South during the war it is more difficult to be recognized as virtuous and to achieve "happiness" (as defined by state discourses that link these to economic success and harmonious kin and community relations) than it is for men and for bona fide middle-class and patriotic subjects such as Hảo, discussed in chapter 3. Whereas men attain moral recognition simply by enacting filial piety to their elders and/or the nation, women must additionally display devotion to their children by uncomplainingly taking on

hardships themselves. Virtuous personhood for men thus abides less strin-
gent standards. For men, filial piety and sociality with their kin and success
in their work appear more important than suffering for their children.
Alternatively, for a woman to be considered virtuous, she must be a good
provider, a devoted mother, and genial kin: someone who financially supports and provides for her children and extended family, even if it means
willingly assuming hardships and indignities herself. Such provision is not
limited to fulfilling material needs. It also involves maintaining relations of
tình cảm with one's children and related kin and disciplining children
appropriately, so that they might cultivate a moral disposition. Women as
well as men participate in the reproduction of these gendered asymmetries
that render happiness and virtue more fraught and conflicted—and ultimately seemingly impossible—for women, as we began to see in the story of
Bà Bảy in the previous chapter.

Hierarchies of gender, class, and politics, not just age or seniority, are
reinforced through everyday narrations and interactions. These hierarchies
can cross-cut and contradict each other, resulting in tangled rather than
linear moral economies. Together, this chapter's accounts do more than
simply buttress the theoretical claim that personhood is relational in
gendered and life-course relevant ways. They also lead to an important
methodological insight developed throughout this book: to understand
personhood and ethical reasoning, psychologically oriented person-centered ethnographers ought to consider not just persons, but families, and
strive to collect and write family-centered ethnographies. Such family-centered ethnographies, I conclude, trouble both relativized cultural and total-
ized political-economic accounts, since they raise questions about the scale
of our units of analysis, for example, when considering whose suffering or
virtue is to be recognized, and how.[3] The following ethnographic sketches
illustrate these points and caution against overly agentive accounts of singular individuals, since persons are never autonomous islands but always
entangled with others. Concurrently, the ethnography also cautions against
overly homogenizing accounts of groups, as we see that even within the
small unit of a family there are multiple perspectives, judgments, and conflicts that can render accounts of social aggregates problematic. Instead,
this chapter aims to highlight the richness and nuance of ethnographic
understanding afforded by family-centered ethnographies.

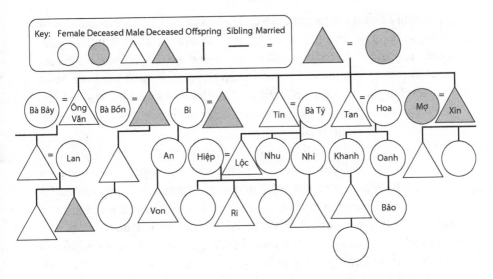

Figure 7. Kinship chart of some of the main characters in chapters 1, 4, and 5

WHO IS A VIRTUOUS VICTIM AND MORAL PAWN?

Ri's mother, Hiệp, had built up a thriving florist business in Đà Nẵng, where she felt compelled to work and capitalize on her higher earning potential than that of her husband, Lộc. She used the shop as an excuse to circumscribe the reach of her care for Lộc's broader clan, from whom she was becoming alienated. Since before my arrival at *Tết*, Lộc's sisters increasingly avoided Hiệp. Over time, they intimated that her social and geographic distance from them victimized Lộc. Hiệp's disdain for their family was forcing Lộc into mixed allegiances and depriving his children of the chance to develop *tình cảm* with them, they complained. Hiệp lacked moral virtue in their eyes, despite being such a tireless worker and high earner.

Nhu, Lộc's sister, made this explicit one day in October 2007 as we sat in her miniscule shop, idly talking while the rain drip-dropped into the green bucket she had placed in the center of the floor: "[My] poor brother" (*tội anh*), she lamented. "He barely comes to drink (*nhậu* [nosh and get drunk]) with my husband and brothers, and his kids never get to see us anymore." This was not the first time Nhu criticized Hiệp by expressing pity for her eldest brother and his children. Lộc had just stopped by to say hello, as he often did, before continuing on his route, shuttling his children back and forth to the extra lessons any student who wanted to succeed in school was obliged to take from their underpaid teachers. Hiệp was too busy to take the children to these lessons since she worked late into the evening at her shop several blocks down the street, on a busier thoroughfare that did brisker business.

Nhu's shop, which until recently she managed with her younger sister, Nhi, was a spinoff from that of their sister-in-law, Hiệp. All three women were small shopkeepers, but only Hiệp was business-savvy and successful enough to out-earn her husband. Nhi, who days earlier had given birth to her first child, was now in confinement, resting at her mother's house. Nhu continued to sell on her own, making barely enough to cover the shop's rent. She complained of her sister's lack of commitment to work and her disrespect toward her in-laws, whom Nhi had more than once declared oppressively old and dull *(chán, già quá)*.[4] Her sister Nhi, like her sister-in-law Hiệp, did not live up to appropriate Confucian standards of moral femininity and filial piety. A good daughter-in-law must always be demure and defer to her mother-in-law, Nhu explained.

As eldest daughter in her father's brood and wife of her mother-in-law's only filial son, Nhu was forever spending all her cash on the numerous feasts she organized to honor her and her husband's deceased relatives and to bless the foundations of the new house they were now building in place of their old home down the street from that of her parents. The extravagant feasts kept Nhu in perpetual debt. They also allowed her to continually affirm her *tình cảm*, or moral connection, with her relatives and to secure her place among her natal, not just affinal, kin. Nhu's efforts and generous spending of (borrowed) money burnished her own and her husband's statuses as moral beings, unlike Hiệp (and more like An, whom we encounter later in this chapter). These partially made up for the remittances Nhu might have sent home from abroad had she agreed to marry the American who had courted her a decade earlier.

Even though as a daughter Nhu did not inherit land contiguous to that of her parents, like many endogamously married women in the region, including Liên below, she was a frequent presence in her parents' home and at another brother's café, which shared walls with them.[5] The siblings all liked to congregate and sing together, swooning to numbers on the newly purchased home karaoke machine, the men often drinking to excess. Only Lộc lived farther away from the family, in cramped quarters in Đà Nẵng's city center. This allowed his wife, Hiệp, to spend nearly all her waking hours at her shop while her children, thanks to their high test scores and her earnings, attended better schools than those in Lộc's hometown.

Daily, Hiệp rose at 5 a.m. to walk to work, returned home at noon to shop at the local market and cook lunch and dinner for the day, and then returned to work until after 8 p.m. This schedule meant that Hiệp and her children spent much less time with Lộc's clan than Nhu and her siblings preferred. Hiệp said she liked this solitude. But Lộc's siblings complained. *"Vô tình cảm"* ([She] lacks *tình cảm*), they would mutter.

WEAPONIZING MORAL JUDGMENTS

Like An and Bi, who as we saw in chapter 4 subtly weaponize *tình cảm* to undercut Ông Văn's and his now-comatose wife Bà Bảy's claims to virtue by alluding to their past refusal to help siblings in need, Nhu and her siblings condemned Hiệp for her lack of *tình cảm*. A person who shared this moral feeling of love, care, and concern, ideally manifested through material support for their intimates, would not miss so many of her family's convivial get-togethers or refuse to help them out, for example, by paying for the youngest brothers' education or contributing to the siblings' various business ventures, their judgments implied. In their eyes, Hiệp was not a sufficiently virtuous person, despite embracing and embodying widely shared cultural standards of moral femininity.[6] After all, they did not dispute that just as befits a good woman, Hiệp was a consummately devoted mother and wife who kept a clean home, cooked delicious meals for her family, and earned a respectable income for her dependents through tireless work at the small shop she had built up. But she remained an outsider.

Things had not always been this way. During previous field visits, Nhu and Hiệp had been intimate friends. Years ago, Hiệp had paid for Nhu's professional education. Later, when Hiệp moved with Lộc to his natal town, they had established a household sharing walls with that of Nhu and her husband. Relations had soured only in the past year. Nhu and Nhi spent too much time and money feasting and singing at karaoke bars for Hiệp's taste instead of frugally managing the shop she had helped them establish, she told me. They also spoke poorly of their mother and disrespected her.

Hiệp intimated that Lộc's sisters were simultaneously immoral for these unfilial transgressions against their mother and for following in the elder's misguided footsteps. She elaborated, sotto voce, that her mother-in-law, Bà Tý, spent too much time playing cards and idling about instead of diligently providing for her children when they were growing up. The elder's failures now manifested in her daughters' shortcomings, Hiệp implied.

On other occasions, Nhu obliquely criticized her own mother on similar grounds as Hiệp had. Nhu explained that as the tenth child in her family, Bà Tý had never learned to work hard and provide for the clan as a good woman should. Nhu had always had to take her mother's place, cooking for her five brothers from an early age. Another sister had died of illness as a young child, and Nhi and the other brothers arrived only later, so it took years until Nhu was even partially relieved of the burden of taking care of them all. Daughters and mothers, it was clear from these and many other observations and stories, toiled more than their brothers or fathers.

Sharing the Vietnamese state's view that moral femininity should involve daily sacrifice and endurance, both Nhu and Hiệp agreed, in muted tones, that Lộc's mother was not sufficiently virtuous. Unlike themselves, she was neither a good cook nor a hard worker. She had given birth to too many children while not ensuring their well-being and success in the world. Without explicitly saying that they disagreed with Bà Tý, they discounted her usual refrain that the family's poverty was due to circumstances beyond her control, namely, Vietnam's economic depression and isolation in the years following the war. They faulted her moral character, not just environmental and structural conditions such as the war and postwar state collectivization efforts. Yet, as juniors to Bà Tý, neither Hiệp nor Nhu could confront the elder and instead resorted to barbed explanations that they confided in me. Criticism was done in relative silence, through gossip.

But this gossip did not bring them closer to each other. Instead, their gossip performed the ethical work of articulating norms and disciplining others (including the ethnographer) who might consider shirking responsibilities regarded as essential for embodying moral femininity. This form of gossip by women about other women serves to reinforce a hegemonic social order whose mores remain similar across Vietnam's changing regimes. Far from enhancing solidarity, including among feuding parties, their negative assessments of one another preclude women's joining forces, for example, to contest or subvert expectations.[7]

Further, and in contrast to their harsh judgment of Bà Tý, both Hiệp and Nhu narrated Lộc as a model figure, precisely for his care and attentiveness to his children, parents, siblings, and large extended family. He would never miss an ancestor worship (đám giỗ) or wedding ritual (đám cưới), and you could always count on his good cheer and material resources at these celebrations, they told me separately. He was always checking in on relatives and friends, showing tình cảm.

What to make of Lộc, then? Was he a virtuous victim? A moral pawn whom the women in his life could hold up against one another in judging each other's lack of tình cảm and attendant loss of family well-being? From my many exchanges with Lộc, resting after a feast, finishing a bowl of bánh canh cua (crab noodle soup) with his children between lessons, hanging the laundry on the roof, which he did to help out his wife, sipping coffee with his old schoolmates or work buddies, playing with the kids at his aunt's house, or refusing a shot at his uncle's, I concluded that Lộc did not think of or experience himself as a victim or moral pawn, nor did he ever express judgment of his mother.

He seemed to genuinely enjoy his many outings and visits, relishing the gossip exchanged and the roaring laughter of his young nieces and nephews whom he would swing in the air, planting a big kiss on their cheek as they landed on the floor. Lộc narrated himself and was described by others not as someone whose life was "difficult": this was the lot of women, though not all were recognized to the same degree. He was someone who simply enjoyed being "good." He was discursively and relationally framed as the complementary ethical second half of his wife, Hiệp, embodying outward-extended virtue while she embodied virtuous motherhood but defective kin personhood. As he told me, he would "be sad and get a headache" *(bị buồn, nhức đầu)* if he were to neglect his duties to his many relatives. Failing to visit and check up on them would burden and cause him pain. It was by fulfilling filial and familial duties that he fulfilled his desires. As for judgments of his mother, wife, or sisters, he refrained. He only criticized his brothers and son for not studying hard enough, leaving harsh judgments about each other to the women themselves.

And they, meanwhile, largely refrained from complaining about the men. Repeatedly, women insisted that while their husbands *could* help with childcare, cooking, or cleaning duties, and sometimes did, it was not their place to do so, and in fact, men's labor at home would make them feel like an incomplete woman and inadequate mother. Both Hiệp and her in-laws—like most women I knew in Vietnam—embraced prevailing "traditional" forms of femininity. They wished Vietnam were a rich country, they opined, so they "could stay at home, like women in Japan."[8] In these ways, women colluded in the reproduction of gender asymmetries, which they saw as moral and right, embedded as they were in broader webs of asymmetrical reciprocity. State projects to legislate "equality" to them seemed irrelevant at best.[9] Yet while they agreed that women's essential duties were to be caretaking, quietly sacrificing mothers who strive to bring prosperity to their family, this seemed to fuel, not abate, their negative moral judgments of one another, as exemplified in the criticisms Hiệp and Nhu lobbed at each other and at Lộc's mother, Bà Tý.

Striving to act virtuously, neither Hiệp nor Nhu could achieve the moral legitimacy in others' eyes that they sought and that they more easily conferred on men. Hiệp faltered in part because as a transplant to Đà Nẵng, she lacked supportive kin and was unwilling to consort with women she judged morally suspect, whereas Nhu struggled in part because the mandate to succeed in the new economy conflicts with equally strong norms of generosity to and conviviality with kin. Men like Lộc, on the other hand, were held to different standards. Applauded for his conviviality with kin and efforts to help at home, it did not seem to matter that both his wife and his sister might surpass him on each of these fronts. But this is not to say that men were entirely free of troubles, as I elaborate in the next section by taking up another facet of Lộc's love life, where gender asymmetries again are underscored, along with politics and class.

PINING FOR A LOST LOVE

"Have you seen Liên?" Lộc often asked me this question when we met up and had a moment in private between visiting his relatives for a death anniversary, wedding, or other worship rituals. He never tired of these events, and neither did I. They were a perfect place in which to display our *tình cảm*, or moral sentiments of care, concern, and intimacy with family members and friends. In making time for these feasts, where we would light incense, ask about guests' health and well-being, and contribute a bit of cash or food gifts, we both earned merit in the community—he as a caring and ethical relative and friend, I as the resident anthropologist. As should be clear from earlier chapters, I likely would have been expected to shoulder the much heavier burden of orchestrating and carrying out the intensive labor involved in preparing the feast and cleaning up afterward if I had been a local Vietnamese young woman preparing to marry, but as an American anthropologist, I was treated more like a man to whom others expressed gratitude simply for showing up and lending a hand, and my efforts at cooking and cleaning never equaled those of the women.

Liên and Lộc belonged to contiguous circles. They had grown up in the same small town outside Đà Nẵng, and they now still lived just blocks from each other in Đà Nẵng proper. Yet Liên was mostly outside Lộc's social orbit. He was married and had three teenage children. She, too, was now married and had a young daughter. She got married late, in her thirties, to an elderly husband who had migrated to Đà Nẵng for work.

Lộc had seen me years ago at one of Liên's family's death anniversaries, where he had stopped by to pay his respects. Her mother's house, which her brother now continued to occupy with his family, was not far from that of Lộc's parents. I often visited them both, but never with Lộc and Liên there at the same time. They did not share friends. I did not share news.

Liên's mom had lost her leg to a grenade years ago, during the war. She then lost her life to cancer in 2005. Lộc's parents, having recently sold some of their ancestral lands following Vietnam's loosening of foreign development restrictions and entry into the World Trade Organization in early 2007, seemed to have suddenly come into wealth, and new loans. They had rebuilt their own house and now had a flush toilet and a gas stove, as did their sons and one of their widowed daughters-in-law, who continued to share walls with them, despite remarrying another man. Not so Liên. She lived in her husband's modest worker's collective unit not far from Đà Nẵng's Hàn River. They had a pit toilet and washed their dishes and clothes in basins under a low faucet that one had to squat to access. Lộc's cramped home not far from there seemed luxurious by comparison, despite its patched roof and discolored walls damaged by the cyclone that had hit hard the previous year. Lộc and Hiệp's house had a proper sink, shower, flush toilet, and even a small laundry machine. They, like Lộc's parents, had achieved the status of middle-class citizens based on their material possessions.

It did not occur to me at first why Lộc often asked me about Liên and not any of her relatives. I figured they were simply old friends. But Liên told me once later on, in confidence, her eyes betraying fleeting sadness, that they had been more. Lộc had wanted to marry her years ago. Instead, he pursued his studies elsewhere and married his present wife, Hiệp.

Hiệp had earlier told me about how she and Lộc fell in love while in their early twenties, studying in Nha Trang. Upon Lộc's graduation, they established a household near her parents in the mountains of central Vietnam. They moved to Lộc's natal town only later, in the late 1990s, after her mother's death. By 2004, they purchased a house in the city center, where Hiệp could walk to her shop. She did not drive a scooter, unlike most women her age. She was too scared. But she worked tirelessly and was out-earning her husband, just like her mother had always done throughout Hiệp's childhood.

From what I could gather, Lộc was not disloyal to his wife. He was as devoted to her and to his parents, siblings, and children, as well as to his many other relatives, as any man I knew in Đà Nẵng, probably more. But, it turned out, he was not above pining, ever so subtly, for a lost love. Judging by his persistent if offhand questions, he seemed to yearn for news of Liên, which is why I eventually asked her how well she had known Lộc. Nhu and the other women in Lộc's life never talked to me about Liên. She was a silenced, secret, unrequited love.

Of all his numerous acquaintances, Liên and Hiệp were most alike. Both were great cooks, like many women in this region. Both insisted on strict discipline with their children, not unlike the others. But both were also lovers of books and had a quiet fierceness about them. Each was earning more than her husband, and saving up, always saving up. Hiệp, as a transplant from another region, was forever lonely, preferring her Alexandre Dumas and Kim Dung books (translated into Vietnamese from French and Chinese, respectively) over her husband's family's convivial get-togethers. She did not share their love of singing and had no patience for drinking and gambling. She wanted to save, just like her mother had before her, to ensure her children's prosperous future.

During the war, Hiệp recounted, her mother had run a laundromat and beer hall for American GI's at a nearby base. She used the funds to send her children to private school in Saigon and buried much of her gold shortly before the South fell. When her house was commandeered by the new, Communist regime, the family moved to one of her former workers' shabbier abodes and used the hidden gold to sponsor Hiệp's brothers on perilous (but successful) boat journeys to escape Vietnam. Hiệp now strove to work just as hard, to support her own children and guarantee their success. She intimated that she hoped her daughter studying in America would eventually sponsor the family to leave Vietnam.

Liên was no less diligent than Hiệp, always busy driving from one tween's house to another, tutoring any student who could pay. Her family had neither benefited from the Americans years ago nor ingratiated themselves with the Communists. They were caught in the middle and prospered neither before 1975 nor after. When as a teen in the 1980s she had attracted Lộc's attention, Liên had been thin. Too thin, she confided in me, for Lộc's mother's taste. Too poor. His mother, Bà Tý, rather poor herself at the time, had ruled out Liên's family. Lộc was not to marry someone from such a no-good, no-future family. Better that he devoted himself to his studies, she had insisted. And so Lộc had. As the eldest of nine children, he had to serve as a model. He worked to fund his own education and, with his new wife's help, also supported his siblings and parents.

And yet, even if ever so slightly, Lộc never stopped caring for Liên. His questions about her, his eyes longing, betrayed it. She, on the other hand, was more careful not to express this sentiment. She had moved on. She had married someone better connected to the new regime. But he turned out poorer and even less successful than Lộc. It wasn't clear if Liên had ever looked for or found love (as noted in chapter 3, both are the same in Vietnamese: *tìm người yêu*). Together with her family's questionable political background, which not unlike that of Lộc's family got in the way of freely choosing mates, her commitment to preserve her moral feminine status further precluded the possibility of even entertaining extramarital love.

Liên's sadness and hardship grew as the year progressed, her eyes brooding for a brief moment, then regaining their cheery look. She confessed only once what I had already witnessed several times, visiting and waiting for her to return. Her husband, Phụng, had lost his job in the midst of Vietnam's marketization and privatization. The collectivized, state-owned enterprise for which he had worked for years and from which he hoped to collect a small pension once he reached the age of fifty had closed its doors. By early 2007, he was drinking himself into oblivion almost nightly, ordering their young daughter to fetch him yet another beer, and another bottle, serving successive shots to himself and his friends. Liên, working around the clock, would come home to clean up.

Was her family falling apart? Could Lộc's? I sometimes wondered. Both she and Lộc lived in "modern" nuclear households. Liên, now orphaned, kept daily ties with her sisters and brother. Lộc similarly met up with his natal and extended family daily and was considered by all a paragon of virtue. Both, in local parlance, had *tình cảm*. Both made efforts to enact their "traditional" relatedness with their kin and never with each other.

Lộc and Hiệp's successful love, following his and Liên's foiled love, are just two tokens of the many class-inflected permutations of romantic relationship trajectories possible in Vietnam. Their stories, together with Hảo's, complicate Yunxiang Yan's (2016) account of wholesale domestic transformation in similarly Confucian to communist to market socialist China. They challenge the directionality he imputes to family formations, from upward-directed respect and submission in the pre–Cultural Revolution era to "descending familism" in recent years, as generations are increasingly focused on youngsters' fulfillment and happiness rather than veneration of the ancestors. In Yan's account, nuclearized units once more converge as a kin group but now with more flexibility and valuing greater "individualism" than before. In my ethnographic observations in Vietnam, a different dynamic is at play. Here, collectivization had perhaps not been so draconian and damaging to social ties as in rural China, and the logics of "modern" and "traditional" kinship structures appear to comfortably coexist, albeit inflected by class and the legacies of war.

As we saw in chapter 3, "love" in Vietnam can encompass at least two different types of intimacy: the so-called horizontal romantic modern relations between would-be spouses or lovers and the seemingly vertical traditional relations between generations such as parents and children. Whereas scholars tend to pit these against each other, my data suggest that these can intersect and converge rather than simply clash or contrast. In forgoing his attachment to Liên and bonding instead with Hiệp, Lộc may well have had his mother's concerns at heart, as well as his own, and not necessarily in fixed ranked order. A deeper ethnographic account of the characters involved would reveal that instrumental and affective motivations are entangled in ways that are both contradictory and commensurate, as we saw in chapter 3 in the case of Hảo, who disciplined her heart to fall in love, in part, perhaps, to affirm her relations with a grandmother whom she dearly cared for and loved and in part, perhaps, to secure some distance from meddling kin. Intimacy between the generations, and among lovers, can pull them apart, as in Lộc and Liên's case, or together, as in Hảo's.

Yan (2016) is correct, then, to suggest that we look beyond relations of intimacy and love between (sexual) partners to the intimate relations between generations in order to take political economy into account. But in accounting for the political and moral economies involved in relations of love, we need not necessarily privilege one vector over another, as though affect and calculation, need and desire, are opposed rather than intertwined. The cases here suggest that feelings of loyalty and care manifested through material provision entangle and extend beyond a pair of lovers to their other kith and kin, who along with the lovers play an important role in shaping what one experiences as possible, plausible, and desirable. Such feelings are rooted in a model of the self as interdependent rather than independent of others: a relational self whom Yan (and many others) likewise postulates. Indeed, along with a host of other scholars,[10] I would suggest that such a relational self is not unique to "non-Western" societies but rather is quite prevalent across communities.

Loving his children, wife, mother, and possibly Liên as well, Lộc kept in precarious balance obligations to each, to maintain closeness as well as distance, to display tình cảm by showing, and hiding, his care. Liên and Hiệp, like Lộc, engaged in similar balancing acts. Each was working, always working, arguably even harder than the men in her life, to uphold virtuous personhood; but each also worked hard to uphold specifically moral femininity. Liên did so by staying close to her natal kin and tethered to her spouse. By contrast, Hiệp, already distanced from her natal kin, also wedged a distance between herself and her affines, by encouraging her husband to remain close to them while she provided for his and her children. Not "scandalous" like D. H. Lawrence's *Sons and Lovers*, these grown children and lovers struggled, in ordinary fashion, simply to uphold and reproduce the ethical gendered forms of personhood called for in their local moral worlds.

In Vietnam, it is a relational self, embodied in characters like Liên, Lộc, and Hiệp, who acts in the social world not simply with monistic goals of upward respect or downward indulgence, as in Yan's (2016) model. This self has pluralistic, at times contradictory goals and aspirations that involve asymmetrical reciprocity, since here, neither the ancestors' nor the grand-children's generation is privileged to the exclusion of others. Instead (as elucidated in chapter 2), there is bidirectional but differentially manifested care between persons committed to disciplined hierarchical relations of interdependence—an interdependence where equality does not reign supreme. To continue this argument about intersecting gender, class, and political moral economies of virtue, love, and care and the ways that they are silenced or, in the following case, partially articulated, I turn now to another set of stories, this time narrated to me by An, whom I also inter-acted with regularly throughout the year. As in chapter 4, An formulates sideshadowing narratives that present opposing views side by side, not always with an attempt at resolution. In this muted way, her sideshadow-ing stories partially break norms of silence around conflict and actively work through ethical dilemmas.

LOVE, SIDESHADOWING THE NATION, AND THE VIOLENCE OF EQUIVALENCE

I recorded my conversation with An on a dreary, wet Friday in October 2007. It was one of many such days that I spent visiting her mother Bi's newly constructed alleyway house near the center of Đà Nẵng. Bi, a spry, toothless, and devoutly Buddhist seventy-seven-year-old, had saved up her whole adult life to be able to replace, with the aid of her grown sons and their wives' families, her dark mud shack with brightly lit, gleaming floors and sturdy walls. These now protected her three sons and their wives and children from the punishing rain that had been pouring down nearly every day for over a month, soaking you to the bone. Just the previous night, five flood-related deaths in the area were reported in the news. Every family I had been visiting that month seemed slightly on edge, sad, depleted. Nerves felt palpably raw. And today, there was a funeral proceeding in the alleyway, adding to the gloom.

An, who had resisted marriage and motherhood until she was nearly forty, was as usual sitting at her mother's ancient sewing machine, waiting for piecework to come in. Even more than before marriage, she struggled now to make ends meet and feed her toddler son, Von, from her meager earnings. Often, she relied on handouts from her brother and nieces, since her sweet but financially unsuccessful husband was chronically underemployed and had to attend to his own ailing mother. Yet, despite these hardships, An told me she was glad she had not married the American her friend tried to set her up with to leave Vietnam. She explained that by marrying her husband, who had long ago courted her and with whom she shared *tình cảm* (affection rooted in mutual understanding and support), she could still be near her mother and family. Her love for her husband, like Hảo's love discussed in chapter 3 and like Lộc's discussed above, was intimately bound up with her love for her natal family, whom she continued to visit nearly daily and on whom she was consistently able to rely. This ability to rely on her family further signaled An's own well-being, since it meant they enjoyed *tình cảm* with one another. Unlike elderly northern subjects in Vinh City, who rail against the nation's market-oriented reforms, An did not voice resentment about the lack of public support and growing inequalities resulting from Vietnam's "neoliberal" policies, as she recalled even more dire poverty under the collectivization period. Like many others in my study, she did not express nostalgia for the postwar, pre-*đổi mới* regime.[11]

On that October day, An was sad but not miserable like her mother's alleyway neighbor, Thu. Clucking her tongue with pity and repeatedly whispering the compassionate phrase, *tội họ* (poor them), An explained that Thu had just lost her drug-addicted son to AIDS. Late that morning, An had returned from a brief visit to the grieving house to pay her respects and donate a sum of money to the mourners. In this way, she and other visitors affirmed the bereaved mother's suffering and continued social belonging in the community, morally constituting themselves as people who care. For, contrary to those who theorize money as entirely separate from gifts, the former precluding while the latter enhancing social bonds, money, too, can serve as a gift in its Maussian sense: an at once interested and disinterested form of exchange that solidifies parties' social relations with each other.[12] In Vietnam as elsewhere, money is often the preferred form of gift and means of showing love,[13] for as Lynn Thomas and Jennifer Cole (2009) elucidate, the ideological separation of sentiment from material or monetized exchange may be a legacy of European colonialism and missionizing Christianity rather than a universal characteristic of human affective relations. And as we saw earlier in the case of Hiệp, this relation could spell moral hazard for women (and men), since being too well-off and not generous enough subjected them to criticism and resentment.

An's visit to Thu was ambivalent and involved a "moral breakdown," in Zigon's (2008) sense, as visitors implicitly had to assess their moral commitments and relations with the bereaved. No one, An told me, would carry the coffin, except the paid pallbearers. Neighborhood men, including her own brothers, who were normally available to do this work, all declined, fearing infection. An did not criticize them. She framed this rejection matter-of-factly, without taking a stance on its virtue or demerit. Unsure whether An might have understood AIDS to be transmitted through simple contact rather than sexual intercourse and the exchange of body fluids, I probed further by asking how HIV/AIDS is transmitted. She explained that infection only comes from the exchange of blood. Buddhist nuns and NGOs care for patients and paid men bury them, she elaborated.

In not passing judgment either on the youth or those who declined to help his bereaved mother, An equivocated: her kin and neighbors regarded AIDS as a form of moral pollution beyond the pathogenic infection. They avoided Thu, leaving her to rely on charity and hired work. Yet not helping a neighbor in need could also leave one morally compromised, since it meant rejecting relations of reciprocity and thus sociality. Money paid to pallbearers and nuns' accumulated merit, An's story implied, overcame the dangers of infection-pollution by protecting those few men and women who came into direct contact with the youth. But money and merit were not equivalent in their protection from infection and power to absolve unsavory contact or rejections. *Tình càm* bridged the two, accounting for charitable care and the ability to overcome fear.

Returning to the particularities of her neighbor's case, An next recounted how Thu's son had grown up poor and fatherless. Thu had been left to care for him and his sister, who has since married and borne children of her own. Her trajectory represents a normatively good life and implicitly suggests that improvident death was only one of a number of possible consequences following the demise of Thu's husband after he returned home from a Communist reeducation camp. Thu's daughter's fate, which is concordant with often contradictory yet also consistent Confucian, colonial, socialist, and marketizing logics that valorize motherhood across classes and political regimes, contributed to the sideshadowing quality of An's story.[14] Here, bad fates did not inevitably result from dire conditions, and dire conditions were not necessarily the punishment meted to "immoral" families. As shall become clearer below, normative linearities linking "im/moral" action and un/fortunate life paths were partially disrupted in An's tale about Thu. In communicating moral ambivalence and ambiguity about the vectors of responsibility for Thu's misfortune (losing her son and losing some of her neighbors' support), An reinforced the tale's sideshadowing quality: even as (or precisely because) she was reluctant to explicitly critique state policies, she appeared less concerned with conveying a moral teleology than with providing an account of the messiness and seeming unpredictability of life trajectories.

LOVE AND FAMILY UNHAPPINESS: "I SEE IT, AND I FEEL I PITY HER"

As the rain stopped for a while, An darkened the plot. She recounted how Thu had worked as a prostitute after her husband passed away, to support her two children. This was at a time when Vietnam was "opening up" to the nonsocialist world and its "new" forms of affliction and work. But An parted ways with Vietnam's official vilification of drug use, AIDS, and prostitution in trying to make sense of her neighbor's tragedy. Instead of condemning these "social evils" manifest in her neighbor's household, she repeatedly used the syntactically optional first-person pronoun *mình* to emphasize her personal sympathy for Thu or to invoke a nonidentified collectivity (the community in general) that, unlike the state (and her brothers), does not view the neighbor as immoral. An's meta-agentive discourse, or way of talking about her neighbor's actions,[15] constructs an account in which Thu's profession became a foregone conclusion not due to her own fault but possibly due to the lack of options for widowed women, especially those affiliated with the former South. An spoke fast here, mumbling, as though voicing an ongoing train of thought:

that situation is what seems so pitiable . . .	*cái hoàn cảnh đó thấy tội lắm . . .*
because [even if she] worked an ugly trade	*dù có làm xấu chi*
now looking at her situation	*mà chừ thấy hoàn cảnh đó*
I/we pity her/it breaks my heart	**mình** *cũng thương,*
certainly [I/we] don't hate	*chứ không có ghét*
even if her kids turned out like that	*con mà rứa rứa*
I/we don't find her contemptuous (.)	**mình** *không có ghét (.)*
I/we see it and **I/we** feel pity for her. ((pause))	**mình** *thấy* **mình** *thương.*
given that [her] husband died early	*chừ răng chồng chết sớm*
what was [she] going to do?	*thế làm chi?*
she had beauty,	*bà cũng có nhan sắc,*
she was pretty when [she was] young	*bà cũng đẹp hồi trẻ*
she was very pretty	*bà đẹp lắm*
at the time in her twenties, thirties	*hồi mà hai mấy, ba mươi tuổi*
she was pretty so she could do that work	*bà đẹp bà mới đi làm đó được*
only because she was pretty could she make money	*bà đẹp bà mới đi làm tiền được*

Women, An implied, were particularly vulnerable. With few work opportunities available to her, the neighbor had to rely on her good looks to profit from "an ugly trade."

An's mother, Bi, likewise offered an account that absolved Thu of some blame for her son's corruption and ultimate death. An had earlier suggested that the son had become profligate because he came into too much money too quickly, but, Bi added, when his mother tried to beat him for neglecting his studies, as any good parent should (deploying the adage, *thương con cho roi cho dọt ((vọt)), ghét con cho ngọt cho ngào* ["If you love your children cane and whip them, if you hate your children indulge them with sweets"]), his paternal grandmother had intervened, crying, *tại sao mày giết cháu ta, mày giết cháu ta* ("Why are you killing my grandchild? You're killing my grandchild!"). In preventing her daughter-in-law from disciplining the boy, it was the grandmother, not the devoted mother, who had set the stage for the youth to go astray but again for understandable reasons: she empathized with his loss, which was also hers.

The grandmother's (and mother's) "immoral" abandonment of discipline was in the name of moral love. Their contested actions now (as then) prompted an ethical debate, enacted through Bi's interjections. She quoted their hot words directly, as if reliving the event, turning An's story into a co-telling narration, with no easy resolution. This is paradigmatic of sideshadowing narratives, which involve multiple narrators who in dialogue invite debate over questions such as, *Who is to blame? When and how did the problem start? Why?*

Morality here is revealed to be contested and contradictory, and it is through the narrative pondering of events that An and Bi confront incommensurable goods, similar to their neighbor Thu and her mother-in-law in years past. Moral value is not to be reduced to the logic of accounting applied when assessing economic value:[16] as in other ethnographic accounts where drug addiction intersects with loving acts between spouses or parents and children, the provisioning of care can also effect moral harm, depending on the temporal scale and perspective from which events are viewed.[17] Care here is never reduced to "care of the self,"[18] for a self in these narratives is always already entangled in multiple relations and obligations to others. And unlike in Hiệp's case, where kinwomen harshly judge one another, here nonkin women instead extend compassion to their neighbors, not by lording their moral superiority over the other, but by noting mitigating circumstances that account for the other's possible moral transgressions. Empathy here is extended rather than withheld, as An imaginatively projects herself into Thu's place and suspends judgment.[19]

Repeatedly and in accruing layers that unfolded in the immediacy of their telling, An and Bi narrated their neighbor as someone who never stopped worrying about, materially caring for, and loving her son. Thu had prostituted herself and beat her son to make him study harder and cultivate an ethical character. Later, she worked for his release from jail and next sold everything and became poor again, just to buy the medicines he needed once he fell ill with AIDS. As a good mother and loyal widow, Thu had never stopped sacrificing for her son while also deferring to and supporting her late husband's mother. She stopped beating her son because of his grandmother's interdiction. And as a final act of love, Thu managed to assemble a ritually appropriate funeral, arranged despite her yet again impoverished state, to accord with local norms of respect for the dead and ensure her son's comfortable transition to the next world.[20]

ASYMMETRICALLY RECIPROCAL LOVE

In An's account, the bereaved mother is cast as embodying and remaining virtuously faithful over time to the principle of asymmetrical reciprocity that we saw socialized and inculcated in chapter 2. And just as An framed AIDS as noninfectious yet polluting, she and Bi expressed contradictory principles in telling the neighbor's sideshadowing story, where being a good mother rendered Thu a victim of circumstance. In acting as an ethical subject who continuously conformed to, reproduced, and reinforced culturally exalted norms of femininity as virtuous loving motherhood, Thu paradoxically transgressed public institutional morality. Her unhappiness and even tragedy appear spawned by a clash of sentiments, child-rearing traditions, failed reciprocity, and poor conditions. In the course of pondering her life through their joint sideshadowing narrative, An and Bi concluded that Thu deserves their care, or at least empathic acknowledgment of her grief and misfortune. As for the son and his transgressions, perhaps out of respect for his as yet-to-ascend-ghost, they remained more reticent, locating culpability in a diffuse elsewhere rather than condemn him as the conduit of "social evils."

In attending not just to the content but also to the form and moment-to-moment unfolding of the narrative as it was told, we witness the process by which moral sentiments produce and are intertwined with moral reasoning, leading subjects to "simultaneously take into account moral norms, practice ethical reflection, and consider the consequences of their acts."[21] This involves not calculative reason divorced from emotion but rather sentiment through moral reason and reason through moral sentiment, striving at normative yet contested virtues. And this is a recursive process, leading An to engage in further ethical reflection through narration, where she went on to recount her own dire circumstances, gush about her family's support, and voice her uncertainty and worry over her own son's future. As her story crescendos, it was not her son Von's material well-being that An expressed anxiety over but his moral status, as she practically cried, her voice ascending from soft whisper to voluble plea:

who can know in advance huh,
who can know in advance:
[if] the husband dies early, [or] the wife dies early
then my child here will be rotten or not
how can [we] know?
only after [he] grows up,
then if [he's] rotten or not rotten
only then can [we] know.
like now [when] he's still young::
like I'm raising little Von
I do think about whether he's rotten or not
how can [we] know?
Gradually as he grows up
I'll teach him this and that
only then will I know, right?
It's not possible to know.
Now [we] cannot confirm
if my child cannot be rotten
or my child is rotten,
I cannot know in advance.
That's why I'm afraid.

An's plea was filled with lyrical repetition characteristic of ritual oratory,[22] yet it constructed an open-ended sideshadowing future filled with uncertainty and fear. Articulating a stance that embraces doubt as an ontological condition of life, she wondered how her young child will turn out despite all her efforts. And in recounting others' beneficence, An further posited the ontology of caring kin as an anchor, but not a guarantee, for living the good life.

Care, in her accounts, was concretized in material relations, such as the supply of milk and meat for her son that she had just enumerated to me in exacting detail, fretting over how she will be able to afford feeding her son as he continues to grow. But material provisioning was not the sum total of care. As in the case of the AIDS victim, care in her account was also something less tangible, such as family love, which had also prompted the neighbor to stop short of nothing to try to save her son. Unsuccessful, and knowing full well that he had not been liked by the community, Thu had nevertheless arranged a proper burial for him. She was forever a devoted mother.

And while men refused to help carry the coffin to its final resting place, women like An did contribute money to the bereaved neighbor so that she could carry out the ritual in its proper form. These actions were directed at ensuring that after an unhappy life, the son might at least rejoin the ancestors. Or maybe less cosmologically ambitiously, the bereaved mother could rejoin the moral community of her neighbors, some of whom did take pity on her rather than shun her for her son's sins. They conveyed a stance of respect toward her for the care and sacrifice that she continued to commit to him despite his having turned "rotten."[23] Seen in this light, the money An lacked herself, yet that she still gave her neighbor, was not a way of ending the relationship, as some economists might assume, but an invitation to continue it. An's payment was not a means of discharging but affirming moral debts, through the vehicle of (modern) money.[24] This relational form of love-care contrasts markedly with the anonymous, biopolitical form of care critiqued by Lisa Stevenson (2014) and illustrates money's capacity to have diverse, not always anonymizing, uses and meanings.[25]

As An's narrations imply, love along the vertical axis of familial relations involves ethical judgments and moral choices that deeply entwine "modern" concerns related to work, livelihood, and disease. These acts of love hardly follow precisely linear or preordained rule-following obligatory acts aimed at instrumental exchange sometimes associated with "traditional" communities or a "morality of reproduction."[26] Affective bonds that entangle public prescriptions here appeared to motivate action, just as they do in what scholars typically consider romantic love relationships.[27] For An, not unlike Hảo in chapter 3 and Liên above, it was this type of public judgment—and the prodding of her mother—that eventually led her to marry, even as she (correctly) feared that life would be harder and deprive her of the freedom that she previously enjoyed:

> I didn't want to get married,
> because life would get worse.
> If I got married,
> I would . . . not have freedom.
> But the scolding.
> Everyone scolded.

In succession, An animated the aspersions and criticisms cast her way when she said she did not want to marry:

> Don't think like that,
> that's wrong.
> [You] have to get married.
> Who will take care of you when you get old?
> When you are old like your mother,
> who would care for you?

An, like Hiệp, Liên, Bà Tý, Nhu, and Nhi, was in a bind, whether in or outside marriage. For each, the critiques, even if on different premises, never abated. Just as we saw earlier in this chapter with Hiệp, Nhu, and Bà Tý, and consistent with the literature on gossip, An's narrative alludes to the ways that women's words to and about each other discipline and reinforce a hegemonic, heteronormative, pro-marriage, hierarchically gendered social order.

We might then expect An to recount a backshadowing "I told them so, I knew I was right" type of story, where she would affirm that getting married was the "wrong choice," since life has become harder and less free. But in her typical sideshadowing fashion, An instead reframes these events and allows for two contradictory realities to coexist. She narrates not just the (unwelcome) pressure she felt to marry but also an alternate reality where life is not entirely governed by bitterness or resentment against public and familial norms. Embracing sacrifice as a stance that minimizes her own hardships or suffering, she tersely summarizes the past and then immediately hastens to instead assess the present:

> [We] met.
> Got married. Uhm.
> But now . . . I think that . . . even though my life is tough,
> but it's only because [we] don't have money.
> But as for my life, family life, with my husband and child I'm happy.
> I feel happy.

Committed to this narrative frame of "happiness," which she repeats as though to convince herself of her affective state, An then elaborates on both her economic hardships and her claims that socially and affectively she is satisfied, by concluding with a list of negations:

> It's tough because . . . my job doesn't pay well.
> That's the only problem.
> I don't make money.
> But as for my family life,
> the way we live together,
> that's a happy life.
> I like it.
> **No** fighting, **nothing**.
> **No** getting mad.
> **Not** having to fight because of the money.
> **No.**

In this way, An decouples the Vietnamese state's equation of family happiness with financial security; instead, she suggests that harmony—associated with familial virtue—is also possible for those who are financially unstable, even as she continues to aspire to a state of more material comfort that might (but also might not) make the couple and their son even happier and belong more firmly to the nation's legitimated middle class. The nation's legitimated (or aspiring) middle class, we saw above, is a heterogeneous and broad category, within which conflicts arise and "happiness" is not assured.

An contrasted with people such as Tan in chapter 1, Nga in chapter 2, and Hảo in chapter 3, whose financial comfort was more or less guaranteed by their family's political standing in the community; she even contrasted with Hiệp, who had inherited her mother's business acumen and was able to succeed financially despite their postwar politically suspect status. An's extended family's previous connections to the American regime left her more vulnerable to the vicissitudes of regime changes and economic transformations. The marketization reforms left An's husband, like Liên's husband above, expendable from state enterprises and hard-pressed to find a well-paying job when competing with men half his age.

But An rejects a mood of bitterness or regret. If earlier she had refused to align with publicly promoted norms that would condemn Thu's family for their immorality, at this juncture, too, An subtly (and perhaps only partially) resisted master narratives advanced by the state about "cultured" and "happy families" as those of middle-class, docile, and compliant women who fend for their family's well-being rather than rely on social welfare for all.[28] Departing from the sideshadowing frame that might allow her to ponder past anxieties and imagine what life might have been like had she not acceded to marriage or had she embraced marriage with the American who could have taken her abroad, An instead directs her attention to present and future concerns related to raising her child. Here, she exhibits an attitude of equanimity regarding her and her husband's circumstances:

> If we have money, we eat.
> If we don't, we eat salt.
> My husband says nothing,
> I say nothing.
> We take care of Von, that's all.

Like the Yapese whom Jason Throop (2015) describes, An and other Vietnamese regard happiness as an ambivalent sentiment, since pursuing one's own happiness is supposed to go hand in hand with and achieved through virtuously suffering for the sake of others.[29] Rather than explicitly pursue individual happiness, which can be in tension with social virtue, people report it retrospectively as a state they enjoy now or in the past, or they express concern that a loved one is not happy, as Nhu did when discussing the supposed plight of her brother Lộc. Like sacrifice, happiness is less the domain of atomized individuals than a domain of social interaction and judgment that involves multiple people in webs of relationships.

The tension between feeling happy and acting virtuously, we saw, is also gendered and tied to national politics and class positions. Whereas national biopolitical campaigns aimed at developing the "quality" of the population and raising overall standards of living to render Vietnam competitive on the world stage enjoin families to be "happy" by complying with state regulations,[30] phenomenologically happiness is a more complex and morally fraught experience. And as we saw with Lộc and the women and children in his life, their stories disrupt moral linearities, showing that judgments about who is "virtuous" are perspectival, partial, and tangled with personal sentiments and familial and self-interests. Bridging chasms between ordinary ethics advocates[31] and moral assemblage theorists,[32] I suggest, in line with both streams, that ethics are encountered and grappled with less as monistic, unitary, or transcendent wholes than as ad hoc, often contradictory assemblages of public and personal commitments that can express and demand incommensurate truths and practices navigated through sideshadowing, subjunctive narratives that leave pasts, futures, and the present open-ended and tangled.

TOWARD A FAMILY-CENTERED ETHNOGRAPHY AND THICK MORAL PERSONHOOD

When studying mental illness and social abandonment, scholars point to families as both the locus of care absent in institutional settings and a source of tension and even exacerbation of some members' symptoms.[33] If social anthropologists once theorized families as the bastion of social solidarity and harmony, later theorists more often point to nuclearized units as indexing, or even causing, together with structural factors, social and moral breakdown.[34] Despite no shortage of accounts of kinship and relatedness, what needs further specification is what "families" mean to whom: whose perspective is to be taken, who counts as a member, of what configuration, and in what context? Such a level of specificity is precisely the aim of person-centered ethnography, which seeks to delineate how community members are constituted by their contexts, by focusing on respondents as objects of systematic study in themselves rather than simply as tokens of specific social types.[35]

Yet in striving at such fine-grained analysis of different family members' perspectives and delineating their moral judgments of one another in their day-to-day and longer-term dramas, we confront a quandary: Which family configuration, ethical aspirations, or set of perspectives to privilege? Who really is a virtuous victim or moral pawn? More important, who belongs in the family and on what grounds? For whom are relatives responsible, and in what ways? And whose stories might serve as templates for action or cautionary tales? As we saw in the cases of Hiệp, Nhu, Bà Tý, Liên, Thu, An, Bi, and Bà Bảy earlier, answers to such questions are not straightforward for women. They stand in precarious positions in relation to their natal and affinal kin, often subject to judgment and critique in ways different from men such as Tan, Lộc, or Xin.[36]

Indeed, one of the ironies of the cases at hand is that in their everyday struggles to ensure family well-being, the women find fault with one another, particularly on the grounds that they fail to ensure family unity and harmony. In regarding Lộc as consummately virtuous while narrating each other as problematic kin who render the family problematic, they seem myopic to the uneven burdens shouldered by women in carrying out state and cultural prescriptions to provide for, as well as sentimentally attend to, multiply configured groupings of kin. It may well be that Nhu and Hiệp, like Liên, An, and Thu, and not Lộc, are the "virtuous victims" or moral pawns of gendered practices and ideologies in these stories, raising questions about the yet to be explored gender dimensions of recent anthropological theorizing of ethics and morality, which take as their object an ethical but predominantly genderless person.

Lotte Buch Segal (2016) suggests that Palestinian detainees' wives, who struggle with the everyday burdens of carrying out life in the absence of their partners in Palestine's West Bank, have no language or legitimized avenue in which to express their hardships, loss, and grief, since this risks disaligning with dominant tropes of patriotic resistance to the Israeli state. Their struggles contrast with those of the Palestinian martyrs' wives, whose losses, suffering, and endurance are broadcast as virtuous and even heroic. Whereas for the latter the loss is final and recognized, detainees' wives can neither express their grief nor seek new partnership, even when

Israel sentences or exiles their husbands for life. For Vietnamese women living in the post–*đổi mới* era, endurance and suffering for the sake of others take on a different hue, in that they are valorized but only to the extent that they carry on silently, without complaint. For them, too, but in a less dramatic fashion than in the Palestinian case, there is no place for grief.

Under colonialism and during the war years in Vietnam, similar expectations prevailed. And as we saw in chapter 1 with Tan's story, as well as in Ri's essay here, women in Vietnam, unlike in Palestine, easily fit into narrative tropes that legitimate them as those who "suffer most" because of their "love" and "sacrifice" for natal kin, spouses, and the nation itself. This recognition, however, is contingent on their ability and willingness to *not* call attention to their suffering and to endure in accordance with nationalist and kin expectations; it also requires them to continually display *tình cảm* by cultivating both their affective and material relations with intimates.[37] These dual expectations, of recognition through silence, are perhaps what renders An's narrative of Thu paradoxically both radical and conventional, in that it both affirms and breaks with shared public ethics.

Are there then distinctions to be made in figuring ethical personhood, related, for example, to differing gender or even class and political expectations in a given community? And is there a space to talk about victimhood and inequity, or about criteria for personal, familial, or social "happiness"? If so, from whose point(s) of view? How might our theories account for plurality, disagreement, inconsistency, contradiction, and ambivalence? As I have tried to show, "thick" ethnographies[38] and attention to sideshadowing and backshadowing narratives that people like An continually tell as they carry on their lives, may begin to do this work, yet they also risk muddling dualistic categories and distinctions such as "good and bad," "right and wrong," "gift and commodity," "happy and unhappy," and so on. When studying a family, or other aggregate units in which different parties contradict one another, and where distinctions between "victims" and "perpetrators" are not so clear, ethnographers may be hard-pressed to hierarchize the perspectives of some over others, as we have come to continually witness in the foregoing two chapters.

The above vignettes of adult married life in Đà Nẵng are my attempt to refuse to reduce ethnographic insights to canned categories or a unitary argument about what constitutes "family" and "the good" or "(personal or public) morality and ethics" more generally. Instead, I attend to ethical reasoning and moral sentiment as they are revealed in the grammar of moment-by-moment narrations and over time through protagonists' longer-term experiential worlds, inflected by Vietnam's political and moral economies. The contradictory and at times disparate portraits that emerge, I hope, reveal both the complexity, ambivalence, and "messiness" of life and the patterned continuities that characters forge with their personal and nation's pasts.

Conclusion

MOURNING IN SILENT SACRIFICE

I witnessed a dramatic enactment of sustaining silent sacrifice within weeks of my visit to Loan in Saigon.[1] Forty-seven-year-old Uncle Long suffered an aneurysm while driving back from work one Saturday afternoon. Doctors could not save him. By early Sunday morning, Long's corpse was back home, naked and covered only with a white sheet, laying on a bamboo cot in the living room, three boiled eggs and an oil candle burning next to his head. Long's mother, Bà Nội, who had just traveled to Đà Nẵng the previous day to spend the summer with her grandchildren, was kneeling by his side, wailing inconsolably. She had lost her only son. Her daughters would arrive later that morning, summoned from the south, along with their children and husbands.

Long's widow, Hà, and fifteen-year-old daughter, Ria, each lay weeping on a different floor of their tall, narrow house, hugged by friends and relatives who had rushed to their aid. Long's nine-year-old son, Bin, appeared dazed and oblivious, not yet understanding the enormity of his loss. He played with his eight-year-old cousin Tin in his uncle's house next door, running back and forth through the respective kitchens' adjoining corridor. The women's faces were all tear-streaked, noses running, eyes already puffy and red. I, too, could not hold in my tears as Hà, choking with sobs, recounted how she had been with her husband at the hospital but he could not speak, could not say a thing; he had no parting words. I felt paralyzed by pain and sorrow for my hosts.

Long's loss resonated all too strongly with that of my fiancé's father, who died of an aneurysm in Boston years earlier, when Huy and I were just getting to know each other. I had not understood the family's elaborate rituals and mode of coping with grief then. In my effort to make sense of the aftermath of mourning, I began to read about Vietnam and soon found myself in an anthropology graduate program. During the course of fieldwork, I observed funerary mourning among more distantly related households. But Long's death was too raw, and it now baffled me. I did not know what to do or say and could barely stop shedding tears. His death was a major rupture. But not quite so for my hosts.

Like other Vietnamese, Long's mourners considered death a dangerous time-space for both the deceased and themselves, since those not properly buried and worshipped can turn into malevolent, angry ghosts.[2] Because Long died close to home and left surviving children behind, his death was not as morally dangerous as others'. Still, the family did not want to risk (as they told me while carrying out other worship rites) making the ancestors "sad" (*buồn*) by skimping on their spiritual obligations and failing to display *tình cảm*. Even Long's brother-in-law, a seasoned navy veteran who usually scoffed at "superstitious" rites, agreed that they now were required to properly display piety and familial loyalty to guarantee Long's soul a safe passage to the otherworld, in case it existed. As the brother-in-law explained, Long's death was "bad" (*xấu*) because he was still in the prime of life when he died suddenly and unexpectedly. For these reasons, there was no time for family members to wallow in grief. To ensure that Long could become a venerated ancestor and benevolent spirit to guard their home, they needed to fashion a cohesive narrative about the righteous life Long had lived and the "good death" he had suffered. Dying a "good" death, I learned, (re)casts people in backshadowing ways as having led a good life, which is morally and socially important for the deceased as well as the bereaved.[3]

Elsewhere,[4] I describe in detail the elaborate ritual process that Long's extended family immediately undertook to convert the space of the living into a sacred space for the dead and ensure Long's gradual and safe passage to the otherworld. To cope with the grief, kin and friends used a range of objects, including mass-produced, sold and gifted commodified funerary text artifacts such as embroidered banners and printed placards. These inscribed artifacts' placement (indoors or outdoors), materiality (cloth or paper), scripts (traditional Chinese or Romanized Vietnamese), and semantic content recalled and collectively prescribed appropriate forms of grieving. Along with other ritual practices, the material objects were intended to delimit mourners' affective expression to specific spaces and their associated temporal scales, as elaborated by Shohet (2018b). For the most part, this process was successful: ritual acts and artifacts served as ethical affordances[5] that mediated and helped contain feelings and expressions of loss by the bereaved. They constituted the worlds of those who produced, viewed, and displayed them, mobilizing inchoate feelings of loss by providing templates for mourners to frame, manage, and channel their *tình cảm* (material provisioning motivated by love and care) for the deceased and for each other and so comport themselves in culturally appropriate ways.

Once Long was buried, grief was not to be explicitly and loudly expressed. To do so would interfere with his ascent to the otherworld. Pain had to be borne in silence. The bereaved now had to continually tend to Long's newly erected altar and carry out periodic commemorative feasts to feed his spirit (and also the bellies of his mourners, who lit incense and prayed at his altar and grave).[6] By carrying out the rituals without devolving into disputes or contestations,[7] mourners displayed care and respect for Long and for one another: they strove to avoid unduly burdening each other with contagious, overwhelming, and unsanctioned expressions of loss that could lead to fatigue, headaches, and the inability to carry out daily tasks, including taking care of loved ones. Sacrifice, I was reminded, is silent and secretive.

Both Long's widow and mother, however, struggled with these mandates. Ritual had only temporarily transformed their world to allow them to share and thereby alleviate their grief *(chia buồn)*. Hà returned to work soon after her husband's death, but each night she wept bitterly. Day after day and week by week, she found it difficult to eat, cook, clean her house, drive to work, or drive to Long's grave. Her sisters acknowledged her pain but increasingly admonished Hà. They insisted that the time for expressing grief had passed. Before the burial, placards and banners had announced the death and associated sentiments of loss, enumerated plans and the dignitaries responsible for the funeral, and publicly pleaded for forbearance for any "mistakes" that might occur.[8] Once the musicians were disbanded and the text artifacts were immolated as Long's body was transported on its last journey away from home, however, the carefully orchestrated mourning space had disappeared and, with it, the warrant to transgress norms. "It's done" *(xong rồi)*, they said. "To go on grieving is just self-tormenting because the dead cannot rise again" *(buồn rầu mãi chỉ khổ thân mà người chết cũng không sống lại được)*, they reasoned.

Long's mother fared even worse. Her sense of bereavement continued to fester, even after returning to her home in Nha Trang after the large ritual feasts marking the forty-ninth and hundredth days of Long's death. Barely consolable, she lamented that there was nothing more to live for. And then, ten days before *Tết*, while standing in front of her house alongside her daughter, Bà Nội was struck by an errant motorist who jumped the curb. The fall killed her. This time, the family in Đà Nẵng was not so forgiving. They rushed to Bà Nội's funeral to carry it out according to ritual prescriptions; but they now also grumbled under their breath that Bà had not comported herself with virtue ever since Long's death.

Upon hearing of her fatal fall, Hà's kin re-narrated Bà's wails. At the time of Long's death, they had borne her despair without complaint; but now they recounted it as a failure on Bà's part to show *tình cảm*. Ever since the burial, they said, Bà had not returned to the ordinary rhythms of life. The effects of her transgressions cascaded.

Adding misfortune to an already stricken family, the second death further burdened everyone both materially, by requiring the travel and financing of the funeral, and cosmologically, by marking the associated households as polluted with death. Hà and her children, like Long's sisters and their families, were now doubly barred from visiting others during the upcoming holiday and from commencing new celebrations, such as betrothals and weddings. Their misfortune was conceived of as contagious, liable to displease the deceased and bring ill fortune to those whom they visited.

Family members explained that despite their status as modern Communist Party members or affiliates, they were under the thrall of "superstition." Even if they did not personally believe in "such matters" (spiritual contagion), out of respect for others, including sometimes their own wife or mother-in-law, they would abide ritual customs.[9] Accordingly, upon their return from Đà Nẵng, Hà's siblings arranged for a ritual specialist to cleanse and bless her home, having already consulted with a feng shui *(phong thuỷ)* specialist on how to ward off malevolent spirits who could be behind this succession of ill luck. Karma and personal responsibility intermixed with "bad luck" and "fate" in their explanations. Rejecting purist explanatory models in favor of syncretic and seemingly contradictory ones,[10] the family took a pragmatic stance in trying to prevent further misfortune.

STORIES OF SILENCE AND SACRIFICE REVERBERATE

The disciplinary and cautionary tales told to Hà or about Bà resonate with those recounted in the previous two chapters, where we witnessed how women and men participate in disciplining one another. Implicitly through gossip and the telling of usually unsanctioned tales, as well as explicitly through direct admonishments, they enjoin each other to strive to enact what at times seem like impossible standards of gendered ethical personhood. As idealized caretakers, wives and mothers are expected to control their desires, emotions, and actions and to embody social virtue. The boundaries designating who is included in the family shift in sometimes unnerving ways for women, as they navigate the demands of natal and affinal kin, as we saw in chapters 3, 4, and 5 and again glimpsed here with the relations between Bà Nội, Hà, and Hà's siblings and other relatives. Respecting those above and yielding to those below is shorthand for a complex and at times contradictory set of relationships that constitutes the boundaries of relatedness, not just among those bonded through blood or marriage.[11]

More specific to Vietnam is the demand that people act with *tình cảm*, which, we have repeatedly witnessed, is a value that everyone subscribes and aspires to, despite historical (political and regional), class, age, and gender cleavages that otherwise divide and differentiate people. Acting morally with *tình cảm* involves displaying care and concern through material and affective signs, as was described in each of the chapters. It is coded as "sacrifice" *(hy sinh)* when one's actions are understood to benefit another, without one calling attention to or demanding recognition for the personal hardship involved. In chapter 1, Tan highlighted this with his stories of the pervasive suffering of war. There, he deflected his own individual role in favor of recounting a publicly sanctioned collective tale of patriotism and bearing of hardship, where he emphasized especially the anguish endured by his mother and wife. Yet, parting with authoritative remembrance practices that erase from official state memory the suffering of those Vietnamese who fought on the Americans' side, Tan also even lamented their losses.[12]

In chapter 2, Bà Hai's, Nga's, Mom's, and Em's actions illustrated these points about sacrifice, care, and hierarchy less with stories than through their embodied comportment in greeting and ritual actions. We witnessed in chapter 2 how adults and children continually apprentice one another to behave as sacrificing beings who are entangled with intimates in relations of discipline-as-care, reproducing a commitment to asymmetrical reciprocity across generations. Similar themes about continuity, discipline, and love were repeated in different variations in chapters 3 and 4. In chapter 4, we saw how Lan and Ông provided care for Bà Bảy, refusing to let her body relax even when comatose. In that same chapter, An's and Bi's sideshadowing accounts next troubled any linear and easy connections we might draw between waiting and care.

Actions that appear as virtuous from one vantage point can take a different hue from another. Motives that appear directed toward the benefit of others can actually benefit oneself, or vice versa, as we saw both in the case of Hảo in chapter 3 and in Hiệp's and Thu's stories in chapter 5. Hảo, for example, strove to find love to comply with familial demands, but in embracing "traditional" norms, she married someone who afforded her distance from watchful kin. Conversely, Thu and Hiệp, who each abided by cultural mandates to care and sacrifice for their children, risked social opprobrium for engaging in socially "immoral" behaviors, ranging from prostitution to refusal to pay for kin's businesses and education.

Benefits and hardships, I have further shown, are not symmetrical across participants. Notions of asymmetrical reciprocity govern the different feelings of debt and obligation between beings who are entangled in multiparty and multigenerational relationships, including with those already buried and continually venerated. The ideal is that these asymmetrically reciprocal relations mutually benefit both status superiors and inferiors. But this takes a lot of effort and work, and the burdens of care are not distributed evenly.

Women, the poor, and those who had not sided with the victorious North are not afforded the same freedoms, benefits, or opportunities accorded to men, the well-to-do, or those affiliated with the winning side. Hierarchies of moral and social worth may appear in this system as "natural" and even "essential," yet they are produced, reinforced, and renewed through the microdynamics of daily conversation and interaction, as well as through more entrenched political and economic forces that structure daily relations. Whereas for some, such as Hảo and her boss in chapter 3, circumstances align to lead "traditional" values and motives to result in "modern" self-serving configurations, women like Bi in chapter 4 and Hiệp, Liên, Thu, and An in chapter 5 are caught in fraught moral binds. They are subjected, in various ways, to anger and criticism by women or men, kin and nonkin.

Women's attempts to abide by societal and familial norms of virtue leave them vulnerable to critique and moral or social solitude, trapped in existential dilemmas not unlike Sophocles's *Antigone*. Unlike Antigone, however, they do not rail against their fates, nor (among my sample) do they find escape in death. Instead, for the most part, they endure and submit and subject to silence or criticism those who protest or act against inequities. But they do not necessarily narrate themselves as victims in light of such submission. Hiệp, for example, relied on her husband Lộc's filial virtue to absolve her of the need to maintain close ties with his kin, negotiating for herself a life of solitude where she embodied motherly if not filial virtue. An reluctantly submitted to marriage despite the hardships that she knew it would bring but narrated herself not as wronged or misguided but "happy," even though she was left hard-pressed to achieve state-valorized middle-class prosperity.[13] And Bi, caught between feuding brothers and caring for her children, remained loyal to all, silently bitter and liable to scold anyone who dared speak ill of the brothers by whom she felt wronged.

The moral and causal lines in the foregoing stories are not so clear-cut. Contexts fold onto one another, and like the sideshadowing narratives of characters like An, they underscore aporia as an existential condition, leaving lives and tales unfinished. Sideshadowing stories, again, are ones that articulate multiple, at times incommensurate, truths, or that high-light ambiguity, ambivalence, and contradiction. They engage hypotheti-cal possibilities that extend beyond the future or present to the past to ponder not only what could still be but also what might have been other-wise, even when deeds are already done. In contrast to foreshadowing and backshadowing narratives, which frame the future and past as inevitable, sideshadowing stories are open-ended and often are co-narrated by mul-tiple speakers who may debate possibilities rather than advance a unitary, constant, and consistent moral stance and a linear temporal trajectory.

Earlier ethnographies have beautifully highlighted the aporias of life, often in dire circumstances where worlds crumble and have to be remade in the face of "natural" disasters exacerbated by human deeds and iniqui-tous structural distributions of resources and care.[14] The present ethnog-raphy, in focusing on ordinary family life and on the multiple perspectives within a family, takes these insights a step further by showing that it is not just in the face of crisis but also when life is at its most ordinary that drama and inconsistency characterize it. And at the same time, in this seeming chaos, we see patterns emerge and continuities achieved—ones that are not inevitable but crafted in the face of Vietnam's broad-scale massive changes over the past century and recent decades.

Striving to enact quotidian sacrifice, family members in unison and also in opposition orient to particular modes of care, love, relationality, and reciprocity in remarkably similar ways, despite the social upheaval that had gripped them and that would continue to send tentacles into the present and future, leaving accounts, as shifting parts of a family-centered ethnography, inherently incomplete. In these accounts, we also see how people's lives are not all their own, even as Vietnam continues to under-take neoliberal reforms. In their efforts to achieve middle-class respecta-bility, individuals rely on and maintain family ties that enable as well as entangle their practices, aspirations, and identities. These practices, aspi-rations, and identities, I hope to have shown, remain deeply gendered and engendering, as well as organized by generational, class, and political cleavages that are sometimes articulated but often remain naturalized and submerged. While cultural patterns, discerned through attention to the minutiae of language and interaction, color and even constitute the ways in which families and communities struggle to cohere, an old feminist insight is also revealed: "public ethics" are to be found in the after-all-not-so-private domain of families' always already political home lives.[15]

ORDINARY ENTANGLEMENT, ETHICS, AND CONTINUITY IN TIMES OF CHANGE

I left Vietnam with the project unfinished (as projects and life itself always are),[16] and it has taken many years to write this book. Most of the family members I had come to know and miss continue to live in Đà Nẵng, aging, raising children and grandchildren, waiting for, with, and sometimes to care. Hảo lives in Europe with her husband and growing son, visited by her parents or visiting them every several years. Bà Bảy died several months after I left, and Lộc, too, passed away after succumbing to illness. His widow, Hiệp, remains in Đà Nẵng, estranged from Lộc's sisters but continuing to attend the most important of his relatives' death anniversaries and Tết celebrations. No longer able to afford rent on the busiest thoroughfare where her shop used to stand, she now sells out of her house. Her business savvy allows her to continue to prosper, and she relies on invitations from her siblings abroad to travel across and beyond Vietnam. She lives with her youngest daughter, who is unmarried; our occasional chats reassure me that even if Hiệp remains mostly alone, she is not always lonely. Sometimes she prefers solitude, she says.

Liên moved away from the small apartment in the center of Đà Nẵng to a larger house on the outskirts, where her husband can walk to her brothers-in-law and drink with them while her daughter plays with her cousins. I have not heard from Liên in years. Bi moved with her sons to a different part of town when their house was taken by eminent domain. She has lost a daughter to cancer and another daughter's children were sent to study abroad. They and another granddaughter who married a Vietnamese American and converted to his Catholic faith rarely visit. But An still visits her mother nearly daily, shuttling Bi to her brothers' houses, including Ông Văn's, to socialize and to mark important occasions.

Em is now a precocious teenager with a winsome smile. Tan has grown quite old and weak. He no longer plays badminton or even drives since his eyesight and legs are too weak. He continues to live with his wife, Hoa, and daughter, Oanh, and her husband and two children. Oanh's elder sister, Khanh, now a grandmother herself, visits with Hans every few years and has several times sponsored Oanh to visit her in Europe. They enjoy posting about their consumerist wealth on Facebook, just like Loan's son, who also lives abroad.

Huân has married his longtime girlfriend in Saigon. His mother now prepares feasts for the spirits to bless not just her business, as she did on the day we arrived, but also the health and fertility of her children. She keeps asking why Huân still has no children of his own and encourages her little granddaughter Hạ, who now stands tall above her, to study harder to be able to support Hạ's widowed mother in old age. Hà, like Hiệp, recovered from her husband's loss. She says she still misses Long sometimes, but she enjoys grandmothering Ria's new baby, and she has several times traveled to sightsee across Vietnam with her sisters and close friends. Life was less tragic than it had first seemed. Mourning did not turn into endless melancholia for her. For everyone, as for us all, life went on.

Why do these stories matter? For Vietnam and Asia scholars, the vignettes from Đà Nẵng provide a corrective against overly totalizing accounts that assume the new market conditions represent a rupture from or a linear continuation of the socialist revolution or colonial and feudal regimes that preceded. Families torn by war did not permanently split, siding either with the North or the South. Nostalgic for neither the distant nor the more recent past,[17] family members reconstituted themselves as at times internally conflicted, yet nonetheless effortfully cohesive units. They draw on cultural, social, and political tropes that demand and extol "sacrifice" and *tình cảm*, especially for women. These engender significant continuities in modes of acting, feeling, and thinking, despite the seismic changes that gripped Vietnam over the past century. The ethnography presented in this book thus supports accounts of thick subjectivity, where gender and other essentialisms are indicative neither of false consciousness nor of entirely instrumental machinations, and where state and social groups entangle in complex ways.[18] Such accounts are part of a contentious and ongoing (feminist) anthropological project aimed at understanding kinship and gendered ethics, among other facets of social life.

More broadly for feminist, cultural, psychological, and linguistic anthropologists, as for a generalist, curious public, we learn from the stories in

Vietnam about how it is that families hold themselves together and how "family" itself remains a contested category where the boundaries of insiders and outsiders are fluid and yet not so porous. Belonging is at once taken for granted and an achievement. Attention to narrative structure and form, to the pragmatics of silence and speech, and to the content of stories as they unfold in moment-by-moment utterances, as well as over longer spans of time, can be revealing of the richness and nonreducibility of characters' subjectivities and the ways they are embedded and entangled in their sociocultural, including linguistic, worlds.

Entanglement becomes even more readily visible by attending in person-centered ways to the multiple protagonists who make up a family[19] and by undertaking a *family*-centered ethnography, instead of stopping at the level of individuals.[20] In line with earlier works,[21] the stories here reveal that multivocality characterizes not only multiple people, but even a singular being such as An, Liên, or Lộc. Again, humans are ambivalent and have multiple, conflicting attachments; they are not rational self-maximizing or self-minimizing machines, nor are they driven by transcendent instincts.[22] Entering the home and training a microscopic lens on family interactions, contestations, and orchestrations of even fleeting harmony was my means in this endeavor. It led me to the insight that person-centered ethnographies are not always sufficient: we need family-centered ethnographies to more fully fathom the complexity and contested, yet continuous, nature of ordinary life and the ways that gendered ideologies and practices shape what counts as "ordinary."

It is my hope that readers come to see how ordinary lives are filled with drama and intrigue, even if these lower- to middle-class subjects are not the most marginalized or the most advantaged. Studying neither up[23] nor down[24] is surprisingly uncommon, particularly when the ethnographic object is not the *making* of a middle class but simply its diverse denizens, ones not confined to a single institution or predefined problem.[25] Training our eyes on the messy yet patterned nature of quotidian life may renew respect for how continuity is not the opposite of change but another of its facets.

To paraphrase Karl Marx's (2001) truism, lives are not preordained or predetermined: people make up their lives in relation with others, even as history makes them. History and the people who live it remain unfinished.

If in Vietnam the forces that pull families together, like the tensions that they spawn, are condensed by the terms *hy sinh* (sacrifice) and *tình cảm*, the form of relationality that undergirds them—which I have dubbed asymmetrical reciprocity—is not unique to this ethnographic context. Adding nuance to conventional understandings of hierarchy and power, it helps us see when and how social ties unravel, loosen, or become reinforced within particular moral worlds and how continuity is sometimes achieved.

Following Ernst Bloch (1995, 343), Cheryl Mattingly has argued that "*only* when the past can be seen in its contingency (from the perspective of what might have been otherwise) can it provide a ground for action directed to *change* rather than repetition of the past."[26] Though sympathetic to this view in light of the moral ambiguity and emergent narrative possibilities that Mattingly advocates, I wonder if this view may also overly valorize change in place of a repetition of the past. As the stories from my ethnography suggest, repetition itself is a form of change, since stasis is not inherent but achieved: again, there is continuity in change.

Gender and class, generational and even love asymmetries are but some of the vectors where continuity appears to inhere but in fact is produced and reproduced in the daily and more wide-ranging rhythms of life in Đà Nẵng and beyond. These rhythms, produced through articulations and enactments of sacrifice, asymmetrical reciprocity, and *tình cảm*, structure but do not fully encompass the (mini-)dramas that I witnessed and attempt to document in this book. Sometimes, sideshadowing narratives can challenge seemingly intractable continuities by exposing the contradictions that inhere in them, to privilege life in the subjunctive mode. And yet, while seeing the sideshadowed past—the what might have been—can be liberating, it is also constraining, as I imagine it was for Bà Nội. She died hurt and with a broken heart, having witnessed the aneurysm that killed her husband also take away her only son. Repetition, like change, does not always beget futurity or natality,[27] even in Vietnamese, where *hy sinh* signals life . . . and suffering in silence for the sake of love.

Notes

1. Consistent with anthropological research conventions, to protect their confidentiality, I use pseudonyms and change some identifying information for all persons other than my partner and public figures.

2. For a collection of some of their stories and the policies that shaped their trajectories, see Freeman 1989; Lipman 2020.

3. See Small 2018 on the affective and material importance of remittance gifts in Vietnam.

4. Vietnamese typically use honorifics such as Aunt or Doctor, and preferably those connoting (fictive) kinship, when talking with and about their interlocutors (Luong 1990; Shohet 2010; Sidnell and Shohet 2013). These continually create and reinforce relations of hierarchy and intimacy among speakers, but I omit them here in deference to most English speakers' general lack of familiarity with a linguistic convention that could require a book of its own to fully convey; I partially explain the system in chapter 2 and make references to specific instances, as well as use the honorifics *Ông* and *Bà* (elder Grandfather and Grandmother, respectively) throughout the book.

5. Audiovisual ethnographic methods were crucial to my research, and I was glad to see that as in previous pilot studies in Hanoi and Đà Nẵng, these methods continued to be readily accepted within multigenerational family homes.

6. See Arnold et al. 2012; Ochs and Kremer-Sadlik 2013; Ochs et al. 2010.

7. On life after the massacre, see Kwon 2006.

INTRODUCTION

1. As I elaborate below, I give varying translations of this concept because its cultural thickness does not allow a more parsimonious and consistent use of a single term.

2. See e.g., Nguyễn Du 1983; Gammeltoft 1999; Malarney 2001; Pettus 2003; Rydstrøm 2003a; Shohet 2017.

3. For classic and contemporary anthropological accounts of sacrifice as a violence-filled ritual event or patriotic act, see Evans-Pritchard 1954; Hubert and Mauss 1964; Hoskins 1993; Keane 2018; Lambek 2007; Valeri 1985; Weiss 2011.

4. This domain has grown exponentially over the past decade; see Mattingly and Throop 2018 for a concise review. Following Didier Fassin (2012), Michael Lambek (2015), and Cheryl Mattingly (2014a), I use "ethics" and "morality" relatively interchangeably rather than distinguish morality as the "local context" and ethics as universalized general principles (Kleinman 1999) or morality as the range of prescriptive (articulated and nonconscious) possibilities and ethics as intentional, reflexive, and reflective tactics and practices used in moments of moral breakdown (Zigon 2011). Like Keane (2016), I highlight the ways in which ethics pervade those language and interaction practices that constitute subjects' moral worlds.

5. See Gammeltoft 2014; Nguyễn-võ 2008; Wahlberg 2006 for discussions of the Vietnamese state's biopolitical goals and practices.

6. For erudite meditations on neoliberalism in Vietnam, see the collection of essays edited by Ann Marie Leshkowich and Christina Schwenkel (2012).

7. For excellent studies of postwar and late-socialist development and their uneven impacts on Vietnam's residents in Ho Chi Minh City, see Harms 2011, 2016; Leshkowich 2014a; Nguyễn-võ 2008; for the role of remittances and other forms of "foreign" and local money and their role in forging relationships, desires, and anxieties, see Hoang 2015; Lainez 2018; Small 2018.

8. For moving literary accounts of ambivalence and division, see, e.g., Hayslip 1990; Nguyen 2015; Ninh 1995.

9. See Antze and Lambek 1996; Cole 2001; Hacking 1995; Langer 1991.

10. For another plea to study sacrifice beyond its ritual context, see Mayblin 2014 and Mayblin and Course 2014, where Maya Mayblin examines the ways in which Catholic women's laments about their daily sacrifices in Northeast Brazil helps frame their hardships as not mere banal suffering but rather virtuous, if unremarkable, action.

11. Durkheim 1995; Hubert and Mauss 1964.

12. As theorized from the early inception of anthropology, sacrifice is enacted through intentional, violent killing, followed by a communal feast (see Tylor [1871] 2009; Robertson Smith [1889] 1969; Frazer [1890] 1948; Hubert and Mauss [1913] 1964). Sacrifice is consummated through the slaughter of a human or animal offered to a deity or deities or other higher power, or the killing of soldiers in war, and their lionization. Such sacrifice is performed in the name and for the benefit of a higher cause, which in recent centuries has been framed as the nation-state (Keane 2018; Lincoln 1991; Mosse 1990; Valeri 1985). In reality, actual soldiers often go to their deaths for the benefit of their buddies as brothers-in-arms rather than strictly in the name of the nationalist ideologies that place them in harm's way. And there can be a series of substitutions that render the act of sacrifice less violent and highly dramatic in other contexts, such as the metaphoric substitution of a bloody ox by a cucumber made famous by Edward E. Evans-Pritchard (1956). Yet the centerpiece of sacrifice is nearly always death rather than birth or life. Thus sacrifice is significant because it acts both as a ritual and as an act of initiation, a beginning that is irreversible because it involves death, even if only symbolic (Lambek 2007). Sacrifice can initiate relations of the gift and reciprocity as theorized by Marcel Mauss ([1925] 1990), a theme to which I return later.

13. The term for ritual slaughter is usually *hiến tế*.

14. Tai 2001.

15. Malarney 2002, 48; Schwenkel 2009.

16. Pettus 2003.

17. See also Lambek 2014.

18. See Abramowitz 2014; Das et al. 2001; Pinto 2014; Samuels 2019a.

19. This insight became ever more viscerally clear in the wake of COVID-19, as families around the world have had to create (new) routines to manage living under state-mandated or self-imposed physical isolation to maintain "social distancing."

20. See Murphy 2015 for a masterful account that attends to both scales and, e.g., Abramowitz 2014; Jenkins 2015; and Wool 2015 for interesting meditations on what is meant by terms such as "normal" or "ordinary" in extraordinary situations. In Vietnam, one such achieved (if puzzling) teleology was the state's framing of its present "market economy with a socialist orientation," instituted since the 1980s *đổi mới* (Renovation) reforms, as a natural and beneficial outcome and progression from its former Communist mode of governance, which in turn succeeded years of anticolonial and anti-imperial struggle.

21. See Mayblin 2014 for another argument regarding the continuous, monotonous, largely unrecognized sacrifices of Catholics in Brazil's interior Northeast and the challenges of rendering these visible.

22. Bernstein 1994; Morson 1994; Ochs and Capps 2001; Shohet 2017.

23. This is akin to the work Lisa Stevenson (2014) attributes to images, which like sideshadowing narratives foster uncertainty as an ontological, not just epistemological, condition of life.

24. See Bruner 1986; Good and Del Vecchio Good 1994; Mattingly 1998, 2010; Samuels 2018. Sideshadowing narratives can foreground ambivalence and ambiguity by giving voice to contradictory realities, such as when a struggling anorexic asserts, "I was *dumped* into treatment [. . .] it was such a lucky chance" (Shohet 2007, 361), or by contemplating plausible scenarios, as when a self-starving woman muses, "If I were transplanted somewhere where no one knew me, [. . .] I just might completely relax and eat whatever I want" (Shohet 2018b, 506).

25. E.g., Fassin 2012; Keane 2016; Zigon 2011.

26. Cf. Hollan and Wellenkamp 1994; Levy 1973; Throop 2010.

27. See Duranti, Ochs, and Schieffelin 2012; Kulick and Schieffelin 2006; Schieffelin and Ochs 1986.

28. E.g., Das 2007; Gammeltoft 2014; Pinto 2014.

29. E.g., Leshkowich 2014a; Pettus 2003; Zigon 2011.

30. For a thoughtful critique of our assumptions of continuity or discontinuity of persons and personhood, see Lambek 2013. Stevenson (2014) makes similar claims but limits the scope to Inuit ontologies.

31. Ebrey 1991; Jamieson 1995; McHale 2004; Slote and De Vos 1998; Tu 1986.

32. Sahlins 1974.

33. Graeber 2001.

34. Cf. Kipnis 1997; Yan 1996; Yang 1994.

35. Cf. Graeber 2001; Gregory 2015; Sahlins 1974.

36. Cf. Beidelman 1989; Bourdieu 1977; Singh 2011.

37. E.g., Aulino 2019; Buch 2014; Garcia 2010; Han 2012; Pinto 2014; Stevenson 2014.

38. This is akin to the moral laboratories described by Cheryl Mattingly (2014a), where both at home and in hospital settings caregivers struggle to transform, in seemingly small, mundane ways, circumstances or personal orientations, to make life tolerable for seriously ill children.

39. There is also a growing segment of Vietnamese who are turning to Protestantism and a variety of other religious practices (see Ngo 2016), but I did not encounter or focus on them in this study.

40. Taylor 1983.

41. Dutton, Werner, and Whitmore 2012; Tai 1992.

42. Taylor 2013.

43. Dutton 2006; Taylor 2013.

44. Goscha 2016; Taylor 2013.

45. Goscha 2016.

46. Lentz 2019.

47. For historiographical and ethnographic affirmation of Vietnamese syncretic traditions, see, e.g., Dutton, Werner, and Whitmore 2012; Goscha 2016; Hoskins 2015.

48. Goscha 2016; Nguyen 2012.

49. Đà Nẵng-Quảng Nam had been one administrative unit until 1997, and the two are still thought of together, which is why I designed the study to involve and compare urban, urbanizing, and rural families in these two contiguous regions.

50. See Earl 2014; Harms 2011, 2016; Nguyen-Marshall 2012; Nguyễn-võ 2008; Schwenkel and Leshkowich 2012; Small 2018 for anthropological and historical portraits of this diverse population sector and their cross-cutting interests.

51. The study received IRB approval from UCLA as well as from relevant research centers and institutes of higher learning in Đà Nẵng and Hanoi; I omit their names to protect subjects' confidentiality. I met some of the initial families through Huy's connections and others through the local university that officially hosted my research.

52. E.g., Abu-Lughod 1999; Garcia 2010; Pinto 2008.

53. See Schielke 2009 for a similar approach to the piety Islamic movement in Egypt, as he calls on theorists to attend to those people who are not the most devout and active members of the movement.

CHAPTER 1. "NOT ONLY THOSE ON THE BATTLEFIELD"

1. For more on Vietnam's rising middle class, see, e.g., Earl 2014; Harms 2016; Leshkowich 2014a; Nguyen 2020; Nguyen-Marshall et al. 2012.

2. In both cities, friends had introduced me to relatives from whom I could learn about the war and postwar eras. I eventually chose Đà Nẵng because here the families whom I had come to know were less directly connected to the local university, and the city itself had a larger population, which allowed for greater anonymity and freedom for us to get to know one another.

3. Former anthropology PhD candidate Narquis Barak, who had set out to study trauma and discovered the "absence of PTSD in Vietnam" in the 1990s, first alerted me to this possibility in a private conversation in 2002. See Allan Young (1995) for a history of PTSD in the United States and Didier Fassin and Richard Rechtman (2009) for a global history and contemporary analysis of the invention and increasing utilization of the psychological category of trauma as the basis on which to make rights claims to compensation. Working in central Vietnam, Heonik Kwon (2006, 2008) has suggested that Vietnamese survivors of the war use the idiom of haunting ghosts to contend with their suffering.

4. Foucault 1988a, 1988b.

5. Levy and Hollan (1998, 336) suggest that this is the difference between ethnographic interviews that attend to people as specific tokens of a generalized type, and hence treat them as "informants" from whom to learn about the type in question, and person-centered ethnographic interviews that treat people as "respondents": unique individuals from whom we learn about the contours of their specific phenomenological being-in-the-world.

6. Cf. Burns et al. 2017; Goscha 2016; Marr 1981; Tai 1992.

7. After a long siege and fierce battles in this strategic hilly northwestern region bordering Laos, France was officially defeated on May 7, 1954, and agreed, under the leadership of a new premier, to withdraw its forces from French Indochina (what eventually became Vietnam, Cambodia, and Laos). For more on this battle and its significance in Vietnamese historiography and nation-making, see Lentz 2019.

8. Cf. Asselin 2018; Nguyen 2012.

9. Leshkowich 2014b, 143.

10. Cf. Duiker 1995; Hayslip 1990; Jamieson 1995; Trương 1986.

11. See Bruner 1986, 1990, 2003; Garro and Mattingly 2001; Jackson 2002; Ochs and Capps 2001; Ricoeur 1980.

12. Austin 1975; Butler 1999; Goffman 1959.

13. On the power of narrative to craft selves and moral moods, see, e.g., Ochs 2007, 2012; Samuels 2018, 2019b; Shohet 2007, 2018a; Throop 2010, 2014, 2015, 2017.

14. Subsequent research has linked the chemical herbicide to cancer and birth defects in future generations, in addition to incinerating those in its immediate path, yet to date the United States has not taken responsibility or compensated its Vietnamese victims for these enduring harms (see, e.g., D. Fox 2013; Gammeltoft 2014; Martini 2012; Uesugi 2016; Zierler 2011).

15. Cf. Đặng 2005; Turner-Gottschang 1998.

16. For a forceful argument asserting Vietnam's historic division rather than unity, see Goscha 2016.

17. E.g., Tai 1992, 2001; Turner-Gottschang 1998.

18. Karen Turner-Gottschang (1998) and Hue-Tam Ho Tai (2001) argue that in Vietnam, patriotic sacrifice was never the sole domain of men.

19. Gammeltoft 2019.

20. In 1987, under the *đổi mới* reforms, the government instituted a family planning policy that mandated that (urban, Kinh-majority) couples limit themselves to having just one or two children (Goodkind 1995). Tan and Hoa had become the government's model "cultured family" ahead of their time.

21. In response to Pol Pot's encroachment on its border, Vietnam had first invaded Cambodia in late December 1978 to overthrow the genocidal leader and

became embroiled in what came to be seen as an unpopular invasion for over a decade. China in turn invaded Vietnam in 1979, resulting in border clashes that would last until 1989, adding to the already hefty casualty count that Vietnam suffered throughout the twentieth century.

22. I elaborate on this theme in chapter 5.

23. Agamben 1998.

24. Cf. Malarney 2001.

25. Ochs 2007; Ochs and Capps 2001.

26. See Ochs 2007 for a delineation of the typological features that distinguish narratives that strive for "coherence" from those that favor "authenticity"; and Burke 1945 for the constitutive role of "trouble" in all narrative forms.

27. See Shohet (2018b) on the different usages of these scripts in contemporary Vietnamese families' ritual life, particularly at funerals, and Marr (1981) and McHale (2004) for historical accounts of the growth and expansion of literacy in Vietnam under French colonial rule.

28. Gammeltoft (2016, 2018) and Rydstrøm (2003b), among others, would counter that domestic violence against women continues to be a problem in contemporary Vietnam.

29. This is in sharp contrast to many Ho Chi Minh City residents, for whom the postwar, pre-đổi mới period looms quite large as a bitter time of harassment and loss at the hands of Northern victors (cf. Harms 2016; Leshkowich 2014a; Tran pers. comm.).

30. Weller 2017, 12.

CHAPTER 2. RITUALS AND ROUTINES OF SACRIFICE

1. On the social organization of death anniversary feasts, see Avieli 2007, 2012; on the use of terms of reference and address to index (point to) social hierarchies in everyday interaction in Vietnam, see Luong 1984, 1990; Shohet 2010; Sidnell and Shohet 2013. At nonritual meals the seating is less rigidly organized, but younger members typically invite the elder ones to eat first. Honorifics are titles or terms of respect, such as "Grandpa/Mr." (ông) or "Auntie/Ms/Mrs./Teacher" (cô).

2. As noted in the introduction and elaborated in subsequent chapters and by Shohet (2017, 2018a), tình cảm is not simply an emotion internal to individuals: it is an eminently social, intersubjective matrix that connects persons to their sociomoral and material worlds.

3. In canonical Confucianism, relations of hierarchy and piety included those between a ruler and his subjects; father and son; husband and wife; and elder brother and younger brother; only friend-friend relations approximated equality rather than upward-directed piety.

4. Cf. Ikels 2004; Slote and De Vos 1998; Yan 2003, 2009. Charlotte Ikels (2004) and Yunxiang Yan (2009), in particular, decry younger generations' lack of deference to their elders in China.

5. In Vietnam, these sets of social connections and responsibilities are situated within a field of hierarchical relations where there is no one supreme being whose status is elevated above all others. Relations extend both far into the past and into the future, and they can cross-cut one another laterally, as I discuss in the following chapters.

6. Ochs and Kremer-Sadlik 2015.

7. Yan 2016.

8. A similar point is made in Graeber 2012.

9. Nicolas Lainez (2012) writes of the troubling ways in which ideas of sacrifice and unrepayable debt can turn into "blackmail," wherein young women are forced to enter the sex work industry by their parents or other kin, using a discursive trope quite similar to Vietnam's nineteenth-century lyrical saga, *The Tale of Kiều*, by the poet Nguyễn Du.

10. I use "subjectivation" in Saba Mahmood's (2005) and Ayala Fader's (2009) senses, where they appropriate Michel Foucault's (1988) notion of technologies of the self. Through repetition, subjects cultivate habits that are intended to orient novices and experts to adopt particular moral dispositions that come to form their subjectivity: their ethical sense of self in interaction with their world.

11. Language socialization research shows that in the process of acquiring language novices become competent members of their culture and that cultural practices and values are learned, perpetuated, or challenged through communicative routines (Duranti, Ochs, and Schieffelin 2012; Kulick and Schieffelin 2006; Schieffelin and Ochs 1986).

12. See Mauss 1973 and Csordas 1990 and the vast literature that emerged in their wake on the ways in which humans' experience of the world and of relationships with others is always embodied, hence the importance of examining the body not simply as an object in relation to culture, but as the subject of culture.

13. E.g., Evans-Pritchard 1956; Firth 1963; Valeri 1985.

14. E.g., Cole 2001; Keane 2018; Lambek 2007; Lincoln 1991; Shipton 2014; Weiss 2014; Willerslev 2009; Zerubavel 2006.

15. Lambek 2007, 27.

16. See also Mayblin and Course 2014.

17. Thúy uses the generic pronoun *mình*, which can mean the first-person singular (I) or plural (we) or the generic "one" (line 3). In the next breath, as if to signal that she is now reporting her *own* opinion, she refers to herself as "cô Thúy" (teacher Thúy, line 8), which is the more common way of referring to oneself in this situation of a teacher-student dyad.

18. The Vietnamese term for sacrifice, *hy sinh*, contains within it the term commonly used to denote *life, living,* and *giving birth;* it is also part of other com-

pounds, including the science of biology (*sinh học*, literally, "life studies"). One of my pilot fieldwork visits had coincided with the publication of Đặng Thùy Trâm's diary, published in Vietnamese as *Nhật ký Đặng Thùy Trâm* (Đặng 2005) and in English as *Last Night I Dreamed of Peace: The Diary of Dang Thuy Tram* (Đặng 2007). By 2007, the diary had become a best-seller in Vietnam, embraced as evidence of Vietnamese women's suffering-laced heroism and sacrifice. Written by a young doctor who had left her comfortable home in Hanoi to join the war effort shortly after graduating from medical school, the diary was taken by an American soldier, Fred Whitehurst, after Đặng Thùy Trâm was killed in action in 1970. Despite instructions to destroy it, Whitehurst kept the diary for thirty-five years. When in 2005 he found Trâm's mother and returned the diary to her, he, too, was regarded as a sacrificing hero and a sign of increasingly warm relations between the former foes.

19. Shohet 2018b.

20. See Hubert and Mauss 1964; Lambek 2007.

21. See, e.g., Hollan and Wellenkamp 1994; Weiss 2014; and Willerslev 2009, which describe how sacrificers (those who perform the ritual slaughter or send their victims to die) may identify with and experience themselves as suffering along with their victims.

22. Mahmood 2005; Mattingly 2012.

23. Cf. Bourdieu 1977.

24. By this same logic, not showing up or arriving too late can be a powerful way to express one's disaffiliation with the kin group (Avieli 2007).

25. Correctly addressing kin whom one sees regularly is easy, but it is more challenging to greet those whom one meets only rarely.

26. See Lamb 2000 for a description of similar dynamics in India.

27. E.g., Goffman 1959; 1981; Goodwin 2007; Goodwin and Goodwin 2004.

28. See more on this in chapter 4.

29. See also Kwon 2007, 2008.

30. See Seligman et al. 2008 on how ritual creates an "as-if" world that provides participants with a subjunctive frame in which to enact reinforcing or subversive alternate realities.

31. Schutz 1967, 181.

32. Goffman 1959.

33. As Elinor Ochs (1988) and Bambi Schieffelin (1990) show, children need not be those whom a speaker addresses directly to learn the language, communicative conventions, and cultural values associated with these communicative acts; thus, even "bystanders," who are not attentively interested in an event, but witness it, participate in it. This may be another reason it is important for the children to be present at the worship event, constituting it as an affair that affirms generational continuity. Toddlers display their knowledge of expected embodied practices (albeit in the wrong context) on other occasions where bowing and showing respect are called for, as evidenced in the following pages.

34. Schutz 1967, 170–72.

35. Duranti 2010.

36. Brenneis 1986.

37. This is further elaborated in chapter 4. Unlike the pious subjects in Ayala Fader's (2009) and Saba Mahmood's (2005) ethnographies, my interlocutors focused on their relationship with the ancestor and the lineage rather than describe acts of piety as helping set them apart from other groups (e.g., Gentiles or other Muslims, respectively).

38. A register is a variety of speech associated with a particular use within a community (e.g., lawyers use legalese). Baby talk, or the language directed at babies and young children, is not universal (Ochs 1988; Ochs and Schieffelin 1984; Schieffelin 1990), but in English and other languages that use it, the register typically includes high-pitched intonation, diminutives such as *itty-bitty* and *tummy*, specialized words and reduplications such as *boo-boo* and *choo-choo*, and simplified grammar (Ferguson 1964).

39. Em's family belonged to the region's large lower-middle-class population, earning just over US$100 per month.

40. Thompson 1965.

41. This expresses the language ideology, or belief about a feature of language and its speakers, that q is "easier" than dq and therefore a form of yielding to help babies learn; for more on language ideologies, see Schieffelin, Woolard, and Kroskrity 1998; Woolard and Schieffelin 1994.

42. Caregivers did, however, sometimes express approval for girls being *ngoàn* and *hiền* (compliant and gentle) or comment with delight that a boy was *nghịch* (active or "naughty within bounds"), which carried a positive connotation for boys (see also Fung and Thu 2019; Rydstrøm 2003a).

43. Not obeying would signal lack of respect by the child for the intended addressee and the caregiver initiating the prompt, as well as reflect poorly on the child's caregivers, who may be blamed for not having properly trained the child to respond respectfully.

44. The RAZR2 flip phone I used at the time did not support emojis or even Vietnamese diacritics; in Facebook and WhatsApp messages that we have since exchanged, I continue to be addressed with *dạ* and the appropriate honorific, *cô* or *chị* (auntie or elder sister, respectively).

45. E.g., Burdelski 2010; Cook and Burdelski 2017; Clancy 1986.

46. Howard 2012.

47. E.g., Blum 1997; Fung 1999.

48. Closing sequences are those exchanges aimed at ending a particular interaction, for example, ending a visit or phone conversation (Schegloff and Sacks 1973; Sidnell and Stivers 2012). As evidenced in what follows, Em's (in)ability to respond appropriately and her mother's and neighbor's jovial insistence are critical, for as suggested in Duranti and Brenneis's (1986) *Text* special issue, *The*

Audience as Coauthor, audiences' uptake of utterances plays a crucial part in the (co-)construction of their significance and meanings.

49. Duranti 1997.

50. Goffman 1959.

51. See Schieffelin and Ochs 1986; Paugh 2012. Nguyễn Thị Thanh Bình's (2002) sociolinguistic study in rural North Vietnam also documents this combination of both child-oriented and situation-oriented interaction patterns.

52. Please see "Notes on Vietnamese and Transcription Conventions" at the beginning of this book.

53. Craven and Potter (2010) note that it is precisely this lack of space for negotiations that distinguishes directives from (even forceful) requests.

54. Bald imperatives are unmitigated directives (orders), such as "Close the window," which contrast with those framed as questions, such as "Could you close the window please?" (Ervin-Tripp 1976; Goodwin 1990).

55. An honorific is a part of speech such as a title or other expression that conveys respect (Agha 1994).

56. See also Cowell 2007.

57. See also Cook and Burdelski 2017 for a review of "(im)politeness" in language socialization situations; and Berman 2019 on the strategies by which communities "produce" age by linguistically encoding children's specially marked moral status. I first proposed the notion of asymmetrical reciprocity in Shohet 2010, 2013.

58. Geertz 1973, 89.

59. Patricia Clancy (1986) and Matthew Burdelski (2010) document similar strategies between parents or teachers and young children in Japan to teach them to be attentive to their social surroundings.

60. See Shohet 2010; Sidnell and Shohet 2013.

61. Among the Ifaluk (Lutz 1987) and Gusii (LeVine 1994), extensive praise similarly is discouraged to avoid giving children the (culturally) misguided sense that they are special. In Vietnam's Mekong Delta, however, Fung and Thu (2019) find that young children related to Vietnamese migrant mothers married to Taiwanese men *are* extensively praised for their correct productions of similar displays of respect.

62. Cf. Harms 2011, 2016; Hoang 2015; Leshkowich 2014b, 2017; Leshkowich and Schwenkel 2012; Nguyen-Marshall, Drummond, and Bélanger 2012; Tran 2015, 2017.

63. See, e.g., Gammeltoft 1999; 2016; 2018; Hong 2004; Horton and Rydstrom 2019; Lainez 2018; Rydstrøm 2003b; Tran 2017.

64. Although they do not use the term *sacrifice*, contributors to Drummond and Rydstrøm (2004) indict this tendency to perpetuate the social order through related gender (and iniquitous class) practices in Vietnam—a tendency that my

Hanoi-based language tutor, Thúy, also alluded to in noting that "women sacrifice more." In his work with sex workers, Lainez (2018) similarly indicts this underbelly of the logic of sacrifice in Vietnam.

65. For reviews, see, e.g., Li 2017; Ochs and Schieffelin 2017; Ochs and Shohet 2006.

66. See also Chapin 2014 on the dynamics of child socialization in Sri Lanka.

67. Cf. Paugh 2012.

68. See Luong 1990; Shohet 2010; Sidnell and Shohet 2013.

69. Husserl 2013.

70. Bourdieu 1990.

CHAPTER 3. TROUBLING LOVE

1. Among the families I studied, Hảo was the only person with whom I could converse in English on occasion.

2. Pronounced like "Yoom" in the local dialect and "Dzung" (long u) in the northern dialect. Cô is an honorific that means both "teacher" and "aunt," as well as "Ms. / Mrs." for someone about one's mother's age, all depending on the interactional context, and which Hảo—like others—always used when referring to her status superiors, thereby indexing deference to them, even in their absence.

3. Ngo Thi Ngan Binh 2004, 47.

4. Zigon 2013, 201.

5. Zigon does not make claims about the "modernity" or "individuality" of subjects who love, and I think we both agree about the texture of moral subjectivity; we part ways in where we locate ethics, however: as experiences of simultaneous sensation, reflection, and action in my case; and as more discrete eventlike "breakdowns" that allow subjects to work through dilemmas in his accounts (e.g., Zigon 2008, 2011, 2019).

6. Das 2012.

7. See also Bruner 1986; Good and Del Vecchio Good 1994; Samuels 2018.

8. Catherine Lutz (1988) describes a similar type of love that foregrounds status asymmetries and the affects and obligations entailed therein among the Ifaluk.

9. See Schwenkel and Leshkowich 2012.

10. E.g., Abu-Lughod 2008; Clifford and Marcus 1986; Kuper 1973.

11. Whether "liberal" is a cohesive enough construct against which to contrast the type of subjectivity these scholars highlight is a question that Laidlaw (2014) convincingly raises but that I skirt here since it does not alter the substance of the argument I seek to advance and since I do not place reflective freedom at the center of ethics, as Laidlaw does. For an additional critique of Mahmood's framing of "liberalism," see also Hefner 2019.

12. Nguyen Hong Son and Dao Thai Thi Xuan 2008; UNICEF 2015. Scholars attribute this to nationalist mass literacy campaigns that promoted and were aided by the adoption of a Romanized script, itself developed centuries earlier but which did not enjoy wide circulation until the twentieth century (Bianco 2001; Hannas 1997; Marr 1981; McHale 2004).

13. Gammeltoft 2014; Nguyen Thanh Binh 2011; World Bank 2020.

14. Wisensale 1999.

15. Wisensale 1999, 604. Similar laws are advocated by ethics of care feminists to counter the excesses of "development" in other parts of the world, but in Vietnam they were supposed to make the nation *more* "modern" and "developed." Far from presenting a unified theory, ethics of care theorists like Joan Tronto (1993), Nel Noddings (2002), and Virginia Held (2006) differ on the legislative measures and grounds underpinning them, leaving it an open question whether to advocate for "difference" or "equality" to advance women's status in society.

16. See Gammeltoft 2016; Lainez 2012; Rydstrøm 2003b; Tran 2004.

17. It is based on this logic that posits women's "natural," biologically given difference from men that Sherry Ortner (1974) explained the persistent and arguably universal subordination of women to men across cultures and societies. Ortner (1996) has long since distanced herself from her original postulated dichotomy and its universalist claims. Nevertheless, her early formulation of this "(sadly) efficient feedback system" (1974, 87) whereby physical, social, and psychological aspects in every society lead to women being seen as closer to nature than men, and as mediating or ambiguously standing in between nature and culture, remains useful for understanding how seemingly "empowering" ideologies and practices can also devalue and demean women. Her theory in turn helps explain why real social change would not take place unless and until both social institutions and cultural ideologies were to change substantially and simultaneously.

18. See also Pashigian 2002, 2009 on women's struggles with infertility; and Bélanger 2002, Rydstrøm 2003b, and Gammeltoft 2018 on the persistent preference for sons in northern Vietnam that continues to lead to women's disproportionate suffering.

19. Phinney 2008.

20. Lê Thị Thu 2004, 4, quoted in Gammeltoft 2014, 62.

21. By contrast, Yunxiang Yan (2003, 2009) provides scathing accounts of "individualism" as a product of state socialism in China. A key difference between Vietnam and China is that it is the family, rather than the individual, who is the target of reform in Vietnam, leaving relatively intact the value of "familism" in this context (see Lainez 2020 and Leshkowich 2014a on the economic implications of familism in Vietnam; and León and Migliavacca 2013 on familism in relation to the welfare state in southern Europe). Yan suggests that in China the family was dismantled as an institution after the 1949 Revolution, giving rise to a toxic "incomplete and uncivil individual" in the decollectivization and following

marketization eras, leading to rampant self-interest, isolation, and anomie reminiscent of Durkheim's and Weber's characterization of Europe's industrializing populations a century earlier (Yan 2009, 224).

22. Phinney 2008.

23. Cole and Thomas 2009; Hirsch and Wardlow 2006; Padilla, Hirsch, and Munoz-Laboy 2007.

24. While romantic love is typically represented as "conquering all" and potentially dangerous because one might love a "wrong" (socially inappropriate) partner (Lindholm 2006), community members' interventions to help place would-be lovers in situations where they might encounter and fall in love with one another is hardly unique to Vietnam, as attested by the plethora of matchmaking websites such as Tinder, OKCupid, J-Date, and Matchmaker.com.

25. Cf. Giddens 1992. Oscar Salemink and Nguyễn Tuấn Anh (2019) add that for many in Vietnam hạnh phúc (happiness) remains intimately tied to bearing children.

26. Michael Lambek (2010c, 60) explains that moral personhood involves being always already entangled in relationships that make up our being, as he elaborates: "We come to be persons 'under a description,' hence ethical subjects, precisely by means of such nominations or interpellations, performative acts that begin even before we are born." In short, persons find themselves born into roles and in relationships, which they actively work to maintain and care for by caring (or not, or not adequately caring) for others (see also Garcia 2010, 2014; Pinto 2014; Willen 2014). Responding to Clifford Geertz's (1984) claims about culturally distinctive selves, Douglas Hollan (1992) similarly suggests that this version of a relational self is not unique to so-called sociocentric societies. In Vietnam, see also Gammeltoft 2014, 2018 for the ways in which women's reproductive decisions reflect their efforts to secure belonging within their families.

27. As we shall see in subsequent chapters, this is not to say that all families always are harmonious and happy or that all members uniformly enjoy tình cảm and hy sinh relations among them.

28. Sarah Ahmed (2010) and Lauren Berlant (2011) critique such equations that harness people's "private" affects to exert disciplinary power in the name of "public" good, a "good" that suppresses and mandates against tolerance for difference. Under high socialism, similar equations were made when valorizing the egalitarian justness of patriotic fervor over feudalistic adherence to lineage and hierarchy, or selfish, bourgeois capitalist individualism (Nguyen 1998; Pettus 2003). James Laidlaw (2014) characterizes this mode of ethical reasoning as a type of "positive freedom" that justifies authoritarian regimes in the name of a public, higher good.

29. See, e.g., Gammeltoft 2002; Nguyễn-võ 2008; Rydstrøm 2006. Kimberly Hoang (2015) adds that recent years have witnessed high-end sex work in Ho Chi Minh City being used to help facilitate and cement development projects and

foreign investment deals that the Vietnamese state and local elites see as key for Vietnam's prosperity and global ascendance. This has led to the decriminalization of sex work in high-end and mid-tier bars, even as street work remains stigmatized and subject to police sweeps and prosecution. Bribes to the police by lower-tier bar owners who cater to Western businessmen or to budget travelers (Western backpackers), respectively, in turn allow Vietnamese sex workers to attract smaller amounts of capital in the form of "remittances" from men moved not by stories of Vietnam's modernization, development, and success, as at the upper-tier bars, but by maintaining their fantasy of Vietnam as a poor, third world country with destitute women in need of saving.

30. Foucault 1979, 13.

31. Jarrett Zigon (2010, 2011, 2014) suggests that ethical life in a given community is not unitary but made up of a patchwork or assemblage of partially overlapping and at times contradictory and conflicting moral commitments.

32. See Sidnell and Shohet 2013 for an analysis of the challenges (linguistic and normative) posed for Vietnamese who might want to minimize the hierarchies of age or rank between them.

33. On changing attitudes toward marriage, divorce, and sexuality in Vietnam, see, e.g., Hoang 2015; Hoang and Yeoh 2015; Nguyen 2007.

34. Charles Lindholm (2006) suggests that the linking of romance with marriage and sexual relations is a relative anomaly when considered across documented cases in the anthropological record over time, as also corroborated by recent scholarship on sex work (e.g., Hoang 2015; Wardlow 2004).

35. Talk of ghosts was quite common among my interlocutors, including both rural family members and the educated elite, among them the local university president; on the ongoing haunting by ghosts of war in the province, see Kwon 2008.

36. Gammeltoft 1999, 2014; Hirschman and Minh 2002; Rydstrøm 2003a. Hy Van Luong (1989) convincingly contests the characterization of Vietnam as strictly patrilocal and instead proposes that it may be more accurately described as bilateral. Some of my data support these conclusions, even as the *ideal*—if not always the practice—remains to reside patrilocally upon marriage.

37. As Maya Mayblin (2012) and Heather Paxson (2007) elucidate, "agape" refers to the ontological principle of love, whereas eros refers more to personal sentiments and pursuits; see also Singer 2009.

38. As I discuss in subsequent chapters, such interdependencies can also introduce conflict and feelings of ambivalence and even resentment—but such negative sentiments were never labeled *tình cảm* but rather indicated its absence.

39. Allen Tran (2018), however, recounts the suffering of dejected lovers in Ho Chi Minh City, some of whom claim, unlike the people I knew, that *tình cảm* is increasingly a "traditional" sentiment of the past; yet others of Tran's interlocutors consider *tình cảm* a traditional but not obsolete and, in fact, continually relevant sentiment guiding moral behavior.

40. Cf. Horton and Rydstrom 2019; Newton 2015.

41. E.g., Garro 2003; Mattingly 2010, 2014a; Throop 2015.

42. Jarrett Zigon disputes equating morality with actors' "aims at 'the good' or attempts 'to do right'" and suggests that we instead locate morality "in the social world" through a phenomenological situating of subjects in relation to "the various aspects of . . . institutional and public discourses, as well as embodied moralities," that "emerge in moments of breakdown" (2014, 17–18). The story presented here may be described precisely as involving such a "breakdown" that nevertheless reveals the pursuit of rather monistic goals of affirming "fidelity" to being in and forging relationships with others. In this way, it aligns rather well with what Cheryl Mattingly (2014a) describes as pursuing the "best good": this is a striving that points not toward an acontexual ideal or principle, but that is attentive to personal, societal, and structural constraints.

43. E.g., Jankowiak 1995, 2008.

44. E.g., Lindholm 1998, 2006; Zigon 2013.

45. E.g., Giddens 1992; Illouz 2012; Yan 2003.

46. E.g., Ahearn 2001; Cole and Thomas 2009; Hirsch and Wardlow 2006; Povinelli 2006; Rebhun 1999; Venkatesan et al. 2011.

CHAPTER 4. WAITING AS CARE?

1. See Shohet 2018b.

2. As Stalford (2019) documents, hospitalized patients in Vietnam are expected to provide their own nourishment and care, placing added burdens on their families to travel with and attend their sick.

3. See also Gammeltoft (1999, 2018), who writes of women's hardships and the moral mandate to "endure" (chịu).

4. Samuels 2019b, 117; Vigh 2009.

5. See Mattingly 2010 and Ochs and Capps 2001 for the ways in which narrative is a form of life achieved in the ongoing flux of interaction; and, despite their differences, Keane 2016; Lambek 2015; Zigon 2019 on the ontological qualities of humans as both evaluative and relational.

6. Bruner 1986; Good and Del Vecchio Good 1994; Mattingly 2010; Samuels 2018.

7. Han 2012, 52.

8. Aulino 2016, 99; for further elaboration on these themes, see also Aulino 2019.

9. Aulino 2016, 96.

10. Buch 2015, 279.

11. Stevenson 2014.

12. Pinto 2014.

13. Garcia 2010.

14. Merleau-Ponty 2008.

15. See also Das 2007; Han 2011.

16. Desjarlais 2016, 12.

17. Proust 1993, 689, in Desjarlais 2016, 18.

18. See, e.g., Kwon 2008; Malarney 2001.

19. *Cô* literally means "aunt," but people typically use it to address kin and nonkin women of roughly their mother's age; children and their spouses typically address their mother(-in-law) as "mother" *(mẹ).*

20. Sidnell and Shohet 2013.

21. Goodwin and Goodwin 2004, 225; Csordas 1994.

22. Goodwin and Goodwin 2004, 229.

23. This is consistent with how ancestors are treated: as discussed in chapter 2, people often address them directly, as present, sentient beings who are capable of a response. Personhood here extends beyond death and also into the liminal space of near-death illness, as from before birth to beyond death, humans evidently are entangled in and attuned to their relationships with others (see also Lambek 2010c, 2013; Zigon 2014).

24. Following Bernard Williams (1981) and Martha Nussbaum (1986), Cheryl Mattingly uses this term to characterize dilemmatic situations. When there are no unequivocally good choices, protagonists are forced to "choose" among less than ideal, even undesirable courses of action, yet they strive to pursue those ends that seem worth acting upon as they "continue to care about and struggle to obtain some version of a good life" (Mattingly 2014a, 5).

25. See Das 2012; Lambek 2010a; and Mattingly 2014a on the ways in which ethical deliberation is a feature of everyday, daily interaction. Writing of mental health institutions in India, Sarah Pinto (2014) further elucidates the entanglement of love and violence, care and pain, and the troubled ways in which suffering women are treated as responsible for their afflictions and relational dissolutions or reconstitution.

26. Tran 2017.

27. Vietnam scholars attribute this mantra to Buddhist, not Confucian, teachings but note that the two were often intermingled rather than clearly distinguished in the minds of laypeople (see, e.g., Jamieson 1995; McHale 2004).

28. Another brother, Bà Bốn's husband, had later died due to a mechanical failure in some machinery during the war, but the family rarely spoke of him.

29. The term for "reeducation," *học tập,* literally means "learn collectivism" but was experienced by many as cruel imprisonment.

30. These themes are echoed in Thi Bui's (2017) critically acclaimed illustrated memoir of the same era, *The Best We Could Do.*

31. This is to be contrasted with Ho Chi Minh City residents who were being displaced for similar development projects in the south (cf. Harms 2016).

32. Cf. Crapanzano 1985; Haas 2017; Timmermans and Buchbinder 2010. The latter type of affect-laden waiting is more akin to the type of precarious hope theorized by Ayşe Parla (2019).

33. *Bên ngoại* literally means the "outside side," which is the Vietnamese way of referring to one's maternal relatives (as distinct from one's paternal relatives, *bên nội*, the "inside side").

34. Mauss 1990.

35. The term *mợ* literally means "wife of one's maternal uncle" but is typically used in place of that female relative's name.

36. As Annemarie Samuels (2019b) illustrates, such navigation is made possible through acts of narration.

37. See https://2001-2009.state.gov/r/pa/prs/ps/2005/56936.htm, accessed June 4, 2017.

38. As Lauren Berlant (2011) writes, optimism, which breeds hope and anticipation for a future yet to come, can be cruel if those optimistic expectations are not materialized.

39. Traditionally, such land was guarded by the eldest son, whose responsibility it was to worship the ancestors and maintain their altar in good condition (Jamieson 1995).

40. Erving Goffman (1981) explains that principals are those whom speakers frame as responsible for a segment of talk, whereas animators are those who utter it.

41. See Marjorie Harness Goodwin (1990) on this type of back-and-forth mode of reporting conflict.

42. Adding the *hỏi (?)* diacritic to a kin term, e.g., *ông → ổng* performs the same function as adding the determiner *ấy* after the kin term (e.g., *ông ấy*): it grammatically and unambiguously encodes third-person reference (grandfather → he/that grandfather). As noted earlier, it is the eldest son's responsibility to maintain the family altar.

43. See Crapanzano 1985; Haas 2017; Timmermans and Buchbinder 2010.

44. Jarrett Zigon (2008) suggests that it is precisely at such moments of breakdown, when moral agents are called on to reflect on their actions in light of a situation that does not accord with their taken-for-granted world, that ethics emerge.

45. See also Das (2012), Keane (2016), Lambek (2015), Mattingly (2014), who describe ethics as achieved in the course of ordinary interaction rather than solely a moment of transcendent reflection.

46. Emmanuel Levinas (1985, 86–87, 98–100) concurs that a condition of our being is to be entangled with the other but adds:

> The Other, in the rectitude of his face, is not a character within a context. Ordinarily one is a "character." . . . And all signification in the usual sense of the term is relative to such a context: the meaning of something is in its relation to another

thing. Here, to the contrary, the face is meaning all by itself. You are you. In this sense one can say that the face is not "seen." It is what cannot become a content, which your thought would embrace; it is uncontainable, it leads you beyond. It is in this that the signification of the face makes it escape from being, as a correlate of a knowing. Vision, on the contrary, is a search for adequation; it is what par excellence absorbs being. But the relation to the face is straightaway ethical. . . . The tie with the Other is knotted only as responsibility. . . . I am responsible for the other without waiting for reciprocity. . . . My responsibility is untransferable, no one could replace me.

47. Cf. Das 2012; Keane 2016; Lambek 2015; Mahmood 2005.

48. Cf. Faubion 2011; Laidlaw 2014; Robbins 2016; Zigon 2008.

49. E.g., Aulino 2019; Das 2007; Pinto 2014; Stevenson 2014; Samuels 2019a.

CHAPTER 5. CHILDREN AND LOVERS

1. Family members did not criticize one another (to me) for siding with the North or South, but dominant state discourses that frame the victorious Democratic Republic of Vietnam (the North) as ethical and the American-collaborating Republic of Vietnam (the South) as morally bankrupt differentially shaped their postwar opportunities. Sides taken during the war were narrated as beyond relatives' individual control and assessments of character related instead to their sacrifice, devotion, and *tình cảm* to the family during and since those trying times.

2. See Nguyễn-võ 2008 on the campaign against social evils.

3. Kinship and family have shifting, contentious meanings in anthropological theorizing (e.g., Bamford 2019; Carsten 2000; Fox 1983; Franklin and McKinnon 2002; Sahlins 2013; Schneider 1984). In Vietnam, where kinship is reckoned bilaterally and heteronormatively (Barbiéri and Bélanger 2009; Earl 2014; Luong 1989) and is preferentially patrilocal (Hirschman and Minh 2002), "family" refers to both the nuclear unit and relatives and ancestors on both parents' sides with whom one was expected to maintain long-lasting relationships.

4. See Gammeltoft 2018 on women's pregnancy and postbirth troubles and moods of depression in their in-laws' houses in northern Vietnam.

5. Endogamous marriages are between partners within the same community and social group, whereas exogamous marriages are those between partners from different communities or social groups.

6. See, e.g., Leshkowich 2014a; Earl 2014; Ngo 2004; Rydstrøm 2003a on moral femininity for middle-aged women, young women, and girls in contemporary Vietnam, respectively; and Pettus 2003 on changing twentieth-century norms for idealized femininity articulated by state organs.

7. Anthropologists have written extensively about the disciplinary social control work that gossip and similar assessment activities perform, and their

micro-interactional as well as broader political effects (e.g., Besnier 2009; Brenneis 1988; Gluckman 1963; Goodwin 2006; Merry 1984).

8. Exceptions included some women researchers in Hanoi at the Institute for Family and Gender Studies *(Viện Gia Đình và Giới)*, whose mission was explicitly to produce research and policy promoting gender equality, and one working mother in Đà Nẵng who joked that she wished she had an *"ô sin"*: a house helper based on the 1980s Japanese serial *Oshin*.

9. As discussed in chapter 3, the Women's Union has been an active governmental organ since the 1930 inception of the Communist Party and 1945 declaration of a free state in the North (Democratic Republic of Vietnam), and in addition to laws revolutionizing what was allowed and forbidden (e.g., abolishing child marriage and wife-beating), campaigns continue to promote gender equality as constitutive of the "happy" and normatively shrinking family (see figure 5 above). Government-sponsored institutes and publications committed to gender research likewise continue to identify barriers and solutions to promoting gender equality (but for a critical assessment of the state of gender research in Vietnam, see Scott and Truong Thi Kim 2007). Even in Hanoi, seat of the revolution, I observed women of all social strata shoulder a larger portion of the "second shift" than did men, despite their being less suspicious and more supportive of state policies venerating family, women, and gender equality.

10. E.g., Butler 2020; Ewing 1990; Hollan 1992; 2000; Lambek 2010c; 2013; Zigon 2014.

11. See Schwenkel and Leshkowich 2012 for a critical examination of "neoliberalism" in Vietnam; and Schwenkel 2013, 2015 on the contrasting disillusionment experienced by elder revolutionaries living in Vinh City in northern Vietnam.

12. For more on the relation between gifts and money, see, e.g., Parry and Bloch 1989; Graeber 2001; Hart 1986; Small 2018.

13. Small 2018; Yan 1996.

14. As we saw in chapters 1 and 3, socialism was officially set against the iniquitous gender relations of the other regimes, but it valorizes women's difference from men no less than the others.

15. Ahearn 2010, 41.

16. Lambek 2008.

17. See Garcia 2010, 2014; Han 2011, where parents, children, or spouses support their loved one's drug habit out of a sense of loyalty, love, and duty to each other.

18. Foucault 1988b.

19. Following Alessandro Duranti's (2010) Husserlian explication of intersubjectivity as being not primarily about enjoying mutual understanding but an effort to trade places with the Other, Jason Throop (2012, 412) suggests that empathy, as a form of this version of intersubjectivity, only becomes possible

when one is in the midst of imagining the self in the Other's position and bodily experiencing another's lived experience through time. This becomes increasingly evident below, as An's narrative progresses.

20. For accounts of the ritual management of death in Vietnam's changing political economy, see Malarney 1996, 2002; Kwon 2007; Shohet 2018b. The mother and daughter's co-narrated accounts also resemble the moral tragedy and conflicted care that Garcia (2010, 2014) highlights in her accounts of kinship and drug addiction in New Mexico.

21. Fassin 2014, 433.

22. Keane 2004.

23. Parents frequently used this idiom of the threat of being "rotten" or "spoiled" *(hư)* when disciplining their children.

24. By the same logic, Hiệp's refusal to spend on Lộc's kin was read by them as her rejection of relatedness, care, and intimacy *(tình cảm)* with them.

25. Anthropologists continue to debate the extent to which commodity markets based on money, which allow for dissimilar types of services and relationships to be rendered equivalent in their exchange, preclude presumably earlier, precapitalist forms of reciprocity based on Marcel Mauss's (1990) theory of the gift as an all-encompassing form of exchange where such reductions would not be possible. Some question strictly opposing gifts to money, since money can also function as a gift. They worry, however, that the logic of the gift as rooted in sentiment and (erroneously) premised, in many Christian contexts, on selfless generosity can be used as an excuse for states to encourage "fellow-feelings," which in turn substitute for more robust social provisioning by the state itself. When states expect citizens to contribute charitably based on relations of sentiment between givers and receivers, rather than see such giving as an obligation on the part of states and entitlement on the part of its recipient people, they inequitably discharge their responsibilities and reinforce as "moral" power differentials between givers and receivers (for further discussion of these themes, see, e.g., Bloch and Parry 1989; Derrida 1992; Graeber 2001, 2012; Kenworthy 2014; Muehlebach 2012; Schrift 1997).

26. Cf. Robbins 2007a.

27. E.g., Illouz 2012; Jankowiak 2008; Lindholm 2006.

28. For more on this campaign, see, e.g., Gammeltoft 2014; Leshkowich 2014a; Nguyễn-võ 2008.

29. Jason Throop (2015, 64–65) draws on Levinas's (1998) distinction between suffering *for*, which "open[s] up orientations to alternate ways of being," and *mere* (useless) suffering; see also Tran 2015, 2017, 2018 on changing orientations to sentiment and self in Ho Chi Minh City.

30. Gammeltoft 2014; Nguyễn-võ 2008.

31. E.g., Das 2012; Lambek 2010b; Mattingly 2014a.

32. E.g., Zigon 2010, 2014.

33. E.g., Edington 2019; Garcia 2010; Han 2012; Jenkins 2015; Pinto 2014.

34. See, e.g., Carsten 2004; Levine 2008; Peletz 1995 for reviews of twenti-eth-century theories of kinship; Sahlins 2013 for a renewed discussion of kinship as mutuality; and, e.g., Biehl 2013; Yan 2009 for situated accounts of familial breakdown and the abandonment of mutuality and care in neoliberaliz-ing contexts.

35. Levy and Hollan 1998, 333, 335; Hollan 2000.

36. This is consistent with classic accounts of patrilineal kinship (cf. Wolf 1968, 1972).

37. Such silent forms of suffering are of course not only the lot of women. As I have suggested, even if subtly, An's husband, like Liên's husband, Phụng, suffered other types of indignities related to their inabilities to provide for their families, just like Lộc and like Hiệp's father before him, though only Phụng seemed both-ered enough to drink away his shame. Lộc, meanwhile, preserved his virtuous status in part by sufficiently disguising remnant love for Liên and continually cultivating *tình cảm* with the rest of his kin. Asymmetries are further compli-cated when we consider how, in chapter 3, Hảo's boss, who was a man of political stature and means, was able to preserve his moral status while maintaining both a wife and Mai as his loving female companion.

38. Geertz 1973.

CONCLUSION

1. The visit to Loan is described in the introduction.

2. See Kwon 2008; Malarney 1996; Bảo Ninh 1995. In light of families' strug-gles to reckon with the many never-recovered bodies left in the wake of its wars, Vietnam is a landscape "teeming with wandering ghosts, spirits of the dead whose lack of filial descendants leaves them suspended between this world and the next" (Leshkowich 2014a, 127).

3. For similar ideologies in Nepal and Aceh, Indonesia, see Desjarlais 2016 and Samuels 2019a, respectively.

4. Shohet 2010, 2018b.

5. As Webb Keane (2016, 27) explains, ethical affordances are those "aspects of people's experiences and perceptions that they might draw on in the process of making ethical evaluations and decisions, whether consciously or not." Ethical affordances do not determine a given course of action but rather facilitate its possibility in particular circumstances.

6. In accordance with custom, feasts were organized weekly during the first 49 days of death, followed by a large ceremony marking the first 100 days and the first lunar year of death, after which the *đám giỗ* was to be held yearly.

7. Cf. Geertz 1957.

8. Shohet 2018b, 63–64.

9. In light of previous research on gender practices and ideologies in Vietnam (e.g., Drummond and Rydstrøm 2004; Gammeltoft 2014; Leshkowich 2014a; Rydstrøm 2003a; Werner 2009), it should not be surprising that women were marked as more "backward" and "superstitious," even when they were themselves cadre servants of the state or Communist Party members.

10. Cf. Hefner 1998; Weller and Wu 2017.

11. Cf. Schneider 1984.

12. Cf. Kwon 2006; Schwenkel 2009; Tai 2001.

13. As suggested in earlier chapters and also elucidated by Salemink and Nguyễn Tuấn Anh (2019), happiness *(hạnh phúc)* in Vietnam is not primarily conceptualized as a quality enjoyed by a bounded, autonomous individual; instead, happiness is intimately tied to bearing children and maintaining asymmetrically reciprocal ties of *tình cảm* with a dense social network of social inferiors and superiors in one's family, community, and nation.

14. See, e.g., Biehl 2013; Biehl and Locke 2017; Garcia 2010; Han 2012; Mattingly 2010, 2014a; Pinto 2014; Samuels 2019a; Stevenson 2014.

15. Strathern 2016.

16. Biehl and Locke 2017.

17. Cf. Schwenkel 2015; Small 2018.

18. In Vietnam, such accounts include, e.g., Gammeltoft 2014; Leshkowich 2014a; Schwenkel 2018; Tran 2018. In anthropology more broadly, see also, e.g., Abu-Lughod 1999; Antze and Lambek 1996; Davidson 2016; Han 2012; Lamb 2000; Mattingly 2010; 2014a; McIntosh 2009, 2016; Millar 2018; Ortner 1996, 2005; Samuels 2019a; Trawick 1990; Willen 2019.

19. Hollan 2000; Levy and Hollan 1998; Mattingly 2010.

20. See also Jenkins 2015 for a similar effort.

21. E.g., Briggs 1998; Pinto 2014; Trawick 1990.

22. The literature on this is too vast to enumerate here; I take inspiration from Mattingly (2010, 2014a) in focusing on the ordinary trials and tribulations of specific characters as they unfold over time and in interaction, but I have intentionally chosen to focus not on those in the clinic or other bounded institutions but those who lead seemingly "boring" family lives.

23. Cf. Nader 1972; Gusterson 1997; Ortner 2010.

24. Cf. Bourgois 1990; Farmer 2009; Scheper-Hughes 1995.

25. See Donner 2017 for a review of "global middle-class" ethnographies.

26. Mattingly 2014a, 207; emphasis in the original.

27. Arendt 1958.

Bibliography

Abramowitz, Sharon Alane. 2014. *Searching for Normal in the Wake of the Liberian War*. Philadelphia: University of Pennsylvania Press.

Abu-Lughod, Lila. 1999. *Veiled Sentiments: Honor and Poetry in a Bedouin Society*. Berkeley: University of California Press.

———. 2008. *Writing Women's Worlds: Bedouin Stories*. 15th anniversary ed. Berkeley: University of California Press.

Agamben, Giorgio. 1998. *Homo Sacer: Sovereign Power and Bare Life*. Stanford, CA: Stanford University Press.

Agha, Asif. 1994. "Honorification." *Annual Review of Anthropology* 23: 277–302.

Ahearn, Laura M. 2001. *Invitations to Love: Literacy, Love Letters, and Social Change in Nepal*. Ann Arbor: University of Michigan Press.

———. 2010. "Agency and Language." In *Society and Language Use*, edited by Jürgen Jaspers, Jan-Ola Östman, and Jef Verschueren, 28–48. Philadelphia, PA: John Benjamins.

Ahmed, Sara. 2010. *The Promise of Happiness*. Durham, NC: Duke University Press.

Antze, Paul, and Michael Lambek. 1996. *Tense Past: Cultural Essays in Trauma and Memory*. New York: Routledge.

Arendt, Hannah. 1958. *The Human Condition*. Chicago: University of Chicago Press.

Arnold, Jeanne E., Anthony P. Graesch, Elinor Ochs, and Enzo Ragazzini. 2012. *Life at Home in the Twenty-First Century: 32 Families Open Their*

Doors. Los Angeles: Cotsen Institute of Archaeology, University of California, Los Angeles.

Asselin, Pierre. 2018. *Vietnam's American War: A History.* Cambridge: Cambridge University Press.

Aulino, Felicity. 2016. "Rituals of Care for the Elderly in Northern Thailand: Merit, Morality, and the Everyday of Long-Term Care." *American Ethnologist* 43 (1): 91–102. https://doi.org/10.1111/amet.12265.

———. 2019. *Rituals of Care: Karmic Politics in an Aging Thailand.* Ithaca, NY: Cornell University Press.

Austin, John L. 1975. *How to Do Things with Words.* 2nd ed. Cambridge, MA: Harvard University Press.

Avieli, Nir. 2007. "Feasting with the Living and the Dead: Food and Eating in Ancestor Worship Rituals in Hoi An." In *Modernity and Re-Enchantment: Religion in Post-Revolutionary Vietnam.* Lanham, MD: Lexington Books.

———. 2012. *Rice Talks: Food and Community in a Vietnamese Town.* Bloomington: Indiana University Press.

Bakhtin, Mikhail M. 1981. *The Dialogic Imagination: Four Essays.* Austin: University of Texas Press.

Bamford, Sandra. 2019. *The Cambridge Handbook of Kinship.* Cambridge: Cambridge University Press.

Bảo Ninh. 1995. *The Sorrow of War: A Novel of North Vietnam.* New York: Pantheon Books.

Barbiéri, Magali, and Danièle Bélanger. 2009. *Reconfiguring Families in Contemporary Vietnam.* Stanford, CA: Stanford University Press.

Beidelman, T. O. 1989. "Agonistic Exchange: Homeric Reciprocity and the Heritage of Simmel and Mauss." *Cultural Anthropology* 4 (3): 227–59. https://doi.org/10.1525/can.1989.4.3.02a00010.

Bélanger, Danièle. 2002. "Son Preference in a Rural Village in North Vietnam." *Studies in Family Planning* 33 (4): 321–34. https://doi.org/10.1111/j.1728-4465.2002.00321.x.

Berlant, Lauren Gail. 2011. *Cruel Optimism.* Durham, NC: Duke University Press.

Berman, Elise. 2019. *Talking like Children: Language and the Production of Age in the Marshall Islands.* New York: Oxford University Press.

Bernstein, Michael André. 1994. *Foregone Conclusions: Against Apocalyptic History.* Berkeley: University of California Press.

Besnier, Niko. 2009. *Gossip and the Everyday Production of Politics.* Honolulu: University of Hawaii Press.

Bianco, Joseph. 2001. "Viet Nam: Quoc Ngu, Colonialism and Language Policy." In *Language Planning and Language Policy: East Asian Perspectives,* edited by Nanette Gottlieb and Ping Chen, 159–205. Richmond, Surrey: Curzon Press.

Biehl, João Guilherme. 2013. *Vita: Life in a Zone of Social Abandonment.* Berkeley: University of California Press.

Biehl, João Guilherme, and Peter Andrew Locke. 2017. *Unfinished: The Anthropology of Becoming.* Durham, NC: Duke University Press.

Bloch, Ernst. 1995. *The Principle of Hope.* Vol. 2. Cambridge, MA: MIT Press.

Bloch, Maurice, and Jonathan P. Parry, eds. 1989. *Money and the Morality of Exchange.* Cambridge: Cambridge University Press.

Blum, Susan D. 1997. "Naming Practices and the Power of Words in China." *Language in Society* 26 (3): 357–79. https://doi.org/10.1017/S0047404500019503.

Borneman, John. 1997. "Caring and Being Cared For: Displacing Marriage, Kinship, Gender and Sexuality." *International Social Science Journal* 49 (154): 573–84.

Bourdieu, Pierre. 1977. *Outline of a Theory of Practice.* Cambridge: Cambridge University Press.

———. 1990. *The Logic of Practice.* Stanford, CA: Stanford University Press.

Bourgois, Philippe. 1990. "Confronting Anthropological Ethics: Ethnographic Lessons from Central America." *Journal of Peace Research* 27 (1): 43–54. https://doi.org/10.1177/0022343390027001005.

Brenneis, Donald. 1986. "Shared Territory: Audience, Indirection and Meaning." *Text* 6 (3): 339–47. https://doi.org/10.1515/text.1.1986.6.3.339.

———. 1988. "Telling Troubles: Narrative, Conflict and Experience." *Anthropological Linguistics* 30 (3–4): 279–91.

Briggs, Jean L. 1998. *Inuit Morality Play: The Emotional Education of a Three-Year-Old.* New Haven, CT: Yale University Press.

Brown, Penelope, and Stephen C. Levinson. 1987. *Politeness: Some Universals in Language Usage.* Cambridge: Cambridge University Press.

Bruner, Jerome S. 1986. *Actual Minds, Possible Worlds.* Cambridge, MA: Harvard University Press.

———. 1990. *Acts of Meaning.* Cambridge, MA: Harvard University Press.

———. 2003. *Making Stories: Law, Literature, Life.* Cambridge, MA: Harvard University Press.

Buch, Elana D. 2014. "Troubling Gifts of Care: Vulnerable Persons and Threatening Exchanges in Chicago's Home Care Industry." *Medical Anthropology Quarterly* 28 (4): 599–615. https://doi.org/10.1111/maq.12126.

———. 2015. "Anthropology of Aging and Care." *Annual Review of Anthropology* 44 (1): 277–93. https://doi.org/10.1146/annurev-anthro-102214-014254.

Buch Segal, Lotte. 2016. *No Place for Grief: Martyrs, Prisoners, and Mourning in Contemporary Palestine.* Philadelphia: University of Pennsylvania Press.

Bui, Thi. 2017. *The Best We Could Do: An Illustrated Memoir.* New York: Abrams ComicArts.

Burdelski, Matthew. 2010. "Socializing Politeness Routines: Action, Other-Orientation, and Embodiment in a Japanese Preschool." *Journal of Pragmatics* 42 (6): 1606–21. https://doi.org/10.1016/j.pragma.2009.11.007.

Burns, Ken, Lynn Novick, Paul Barnes, Peter Coyote, Erik Ewers, Craig Mellish, Sarah Botstein, et al. 2017. *The Vietnam War. Volume One (Episodes 1–5)*. Arlington, VA: PBS Distribution.

Butler, Judith. 1999. *Gender Trouble: Feminism and the Subversion of Identity*. New York: Routledge.

———. 2020. *The Force of Nonviolence: An Ethico-Political Bind*. London: Verso.

Carsten, Janet. 2000. *Cultures of Relatedness: New Approaches to the Study of Kinship*. Cambridge: Cambridge University Press.

———. 2004. *After Kinship*. Cambridge: Cambridge University Press.

Chapin, Bambi L. 2014. *Childhood in a Sri Lankan Village: Shaping Hierarchy and Desire*. New Brunswick, NJ: Rutgers University Press.

Clancy, Patricia M. 1986. "The Acquisition of Communicative Style in Japanese." In *Language Socialization across Cultures*, edited by Bambi B. Schieffelin and Elinor Ochs, 213–50. Cambridge: Cambridge University Press.

Clifford, James, and George E. Marcus. 1986. *Writing Culture: The Poetics and Politics of Ethnography*. Berkeley: University of California Press.

Cole, Jennifer. 2001. *Forget Colonialism? Sacrifice and the Art of Memory in Madagascar*. Berkeley: University of California Press.

Cole, Jennifer, and Lynn M. Thomas. 2009. *Love in Africa*. Chicago: University of Chicago Press.

Cook, Haruko M., and Matthew Burdelski. 2017. "(Im)Politeness: Language Socialization." In *The Palgrave Handbook of Linguistic (Im)Politeness*, edited by Jonathan Culpeper, Michael Haugh, and Dániel Z. Kádár, 461–88. London: Palgrave Macmillan.

Cowell, Andrew. 2007. "Arapaho Imperatives: Indirectness, Politeness and Communal 'Face.'" *Journal of Linguistic Anthropology* 17 (1): 44–60. https://doi.org/10.1525/jlin.2007.17.1.44.

Crapanzano, Vincent. 1985. *Waiting: The Whites of South Africa*. New York: Random House.

Craven, Alexandra, and Jonathan Potter. 2010. "Directives: Entitlement and Contingency in Action." *Discourse Studies* 12 (4): 419–42. https://doi.org/10.1177/1461445610370126.

Csordas, Thomas J. 1990. "Embodiment as a Paradigm for Anthropology." *Ethos* 18 (1): 5–47.

———. 1994. *Embodiment and Experience: The Existential Ground of Culture and Self*. Cambridge: Cambridge University Press.

Đặng, Thùy Trâm. 2005. *Nhật ký Đang Thùy Trâm*. Hà Nội: Hội Nhà Văn.

———. 2007. *Last Night I Dreamed of Peace: The Diary of Dang Thuy Tram*. 1st American ed. New York: Harmony Books.

Das, Veena. 2007. *Life and Words: Violence and the Descent into the Ordinary.* Berkeley: University of California Press.

———. 2012. "Ordinary Ethics." In *A Companion to Moral Anthropology,* edited by Didier Fassin, 133–49. New York: John Wiley & Sons.

Das, Veena, Pamela Reynolds, Memphela Ramphele, Arthur Kleinman, and Margaret Lock. 2001. *Remaking a World: Violence, Social Suffering, and Recovery.* Berkeley: University of California Press.

Davidson, Joanna. 2016. *Sacred Rice: An Ethnography of Identity, Environment, and Development in Rural West Africa.* New York: Oxford University Press.

Deeb, Lara. 2006. *An Enchanted Modern: Gender and Public Piety in Shi'i Lebanon.* Princeton, NJ: Princeton University Press.

Derrida, Jacques. 1992. *Given Time. I, Counterfeit Money.* Chicago: University of Chicago Press.

Desjarlais, Robert R. 2016. *Subject to Death: Life and Loss in a Buddhist World.* Chicago: University of Chicago Press.

Donner, Henrike. 2017. "The Anthropology of the Middle Class across the Globe." *Anthropology of This Century.* http://aotcpress.com/articles/anthropology-middle-class-globe/.

Drummond, Lisa B. W., and Helle Rydstrøm. 2004. *Gender Practices in Contemporary Vietnam.* Singapore: Singapore University Press.

Duiker, William J. 1995. *Vietnam: Revolution in Transition.* 2nd ed. Boulder, CO: Westview.

Duranti, Alessandro. 1986. "The Audience as Co-Author: An Introduction." *Text* 6 (3): 239–47. https://doi.org/10.1515/text.1.1986.6.3.239.

———. 1997. "Universal and Culture-Specific Properties of Greetings." *Journal of Linguistic Anthropology* 7 (1): 63–97. https://doi.org/10.1525/jlin.1997.7.1.63.

———. 2010. "Husserl, Intersubjectivity and Anthropology." *Anthropological Theory* 10 (1–2): 16–35. https://doi.org/10.1177/1463499610370517.

Duranti, Alessandro, Elinor Ochs, and Bambi B. Schieffelin. 2012. *The Handbook of Language Socialization.* Malden, MA: Wiley-Blackwell.

Durkheim, Émile. 1995. *The Elementary Forms of Religious Life.* New York: Free Press.

Dutton, George Edson. 2006. *The Tây Son Uprising: Society and Rebellion in Eighteenth-Century Vietnam.* Honolulu: University of Hawaii Press.

Dutton, George Edson, Jayne Susan Werner, and John K. Whitmore. 2012. *Sources of Vietnamese Tradition.* New York: Columbia University Press.

Earl, Catherine. 2014. *Vietnam's New Middle Classes: Gender, Career, City.* Copenhagen: NIAS Press.

Ebrey, Patricia Buckley. 1991. *Confucianism and Family Rituals in Imperial China: A Social History of Writing about Rites.* Princeton, NJ: Princeton University Press.

Edington, Claire E. 2019. *Beyond the Asylum: Mental Illness in French Colonial Vietnam*. Ithaca, NY: Cornell University Press.

Ervin-Tripp, Susan. 1976. "Is Sybil There? The Structure of Some American English Directives." *Language in Society* 5 (1): 25–66. https://doi.org/10.1017/S0047404500006849.

Evans-Pritchard, Edward E. 1956. *Nuer Religion*. Oxford: Clarendon Press.

Ewing, Katherine P. 1990. "The Illusion of Wholeness: Culture, Self, and the Experience of Inconsistency." *Ethos* 18 (3): 251–78.

Fader, Ayala. 2009. *Mitzvah Girls: Bringing up the next Generation of Hasidic Jews in Brooklyn*. Princeton, NJ: Princeton University Press.

Farmer, Paul. 2009. "On Suffering and Structural Violence: A View from Below." *Race/Ethnicity: Multidisciplinary Global Contexts* 3 (1): 11–28.

Fassin, Didier. 2012. *A Companion to Moral Anthropology*. Chichester, UK: Wiley-Blackwell.

———. 2014. "The Ethical Turn in Anthropology." *HAU: Journal of Ethnographic Theory* 4 (1): 429–35. https://doi.org/10.14318/hau4.1.025.

Fassin, Didier, and Richard Rechtman. 2009. *The Empire of Trauma: An Inquiry into the Condition of Victimhood*. Princeton, NJ: Princeton University Press.

Faubion, James D. 2011. *An Anthropology of Ethics*. Cambridge: Cambridge University Press.

Ferguson, Charles A. 1964. "Baby Talk in Six Languages." *American Anthropologist* 66 (6): 103–14. https://doi.org/10.1525/aa.1964.66.suppl_3.02a00060.

Firth, Raymond. 1963. "Offering and Sacrifice: Problems of Organization." *Journal of the Royal Anthropological Institute of Great Britain and Ireland* 93 (1): 12–24. https://doi.org/10.2307/2844331.

Foucault, Michel. 1979. *Discipline and Punish: The Birth of the Prison*. New York: Vintage Books.

———. 1988a. *The History of Sexuality*. Vol. 3: *The Care of the Self*. New York: Vintage Books.

———. 1988b. *Technologies of the Self: A Seminar with Michel Foucault*. Amherst: University of Massachusetts Press.

Fox, Diane. 2013. "Chemical Politics and the Hazards of Modern Warfare Agent Orange." *Vietnamese Studies* 187 (1): 5–40.

Fox, Robin. 1983. *Kinship and Marriage: An Anthropological Perspective*. Cambridge: Cambridge University Press.

Franklin, Sarah, and Susan McKinnon. 2002. *Relative Values: Reconfiguring Kinship Studies*. Durham, NC: Duke University Press.

Frazer, James George. [1890] 1948. *The Golden Bough: A Study in Magic and Religion*. Abridged ed. New York: Macmillan.

Freeman, James M. 1989. *Hearts of Sorrow: Vietnamese-American Lives*. Stanford, CA: Stanford University Press.

Fung, Heidi. 1999. "Becoming a Moral Child: The Socialization of Shame among Young Chinese Children." *Ethos* 27 (2): 180–209. https://doi.org/10.1525 /eth.1999.27.2.180.

Fung, Heidi, and Mai Thị Thu. 2019. "Cultivating Affection-Laden Hierarchy: Embodied Moral Socialization of Vòng Tay (Khoanh Tay) with Children in Southern Vietnam." *Ethos* 47 (3): 281–306. https://doi.org/10.1111/etho.12247.

Gammeltoft, Tine M. 1999. *Women's Bodies, Women's Worries: Health and Family Planning in a Vietnamese Rural Community*. Richmond, Surrey: Curzon Press.

———. 2002. "Seeking Trust and Transcendence: Sexual Risk-Taking among Vietnamese Youth." *Social Science & Medicine* 55 (3): 483–96. https://doi .org/10.1016/S0277-9536(01)00182-4.

———. 2014. *Haunting Images: A Cultural Account of Selective Reproduction in Vietnam*. Berkeley: University of California Press.

———. 2016. "Silence as a Response to Everyday Violence: Understanding Domination and Distress through the Lens of Fantasy." *Ethos* 44 (4): 427–47. https://doi.org/10.1111/etho.12140.

———. 2018. "Domestic Moods: Maternal Mental Health in Northern Vietnam." *Medical Anthropology* 37 (7): 582–96. https://doi.org/10.1080/01459 740.2018.1444612.

———. 2019. "Selecting for Sons: Kinship as a Product of Desire." In *Cambridge Handbook of Kinship*, edited by Sandra Bamford, 344–68. Cambridge: Cambridge University Press.

Garcia, Angela. 2010. *The Pastoral Clinic: Addiction and Dispossession along the Rio Grande*. Berkeley: University of California Press.

———. 2014. "The Promise: On the Morality of the Marginal and the Illicit." *Ethos* 42 (1): 51–64. https://doi.org/10.1111/etho.12038.

Garro, Linda C. 2003. "Narrating Troubling Experiences." *Transcultural Psychiatry* 40 (1): 5–43. https://doi.org/10.1177/1363461503040001001.

Garro, Linda C., and Cheryl Mattingly. 2001. "Narrative as Construct and Construction." In *Narrative and the Cultural Construction of Illness and Healing*, edited by Cheryl Mattingly and Linda C. Garro, 1–49. Berkeley: University of California Press.

Geertz, Clifford. 1957. "Ritual and Social Change: A Javanese Example." *American Anthropologist* 59 (1): 32–54. https://doi.org/10.1525/aa.1957 .59.1.02a00040.

———. 1973. *The Interpretation of Cultures: Selected Essays*. New York: Basic Books.

———. 1984. "From the Native's Point of View: On the Nature of Anthropological Understanding." In *Culture Theory: Essays on Mind, Self, and Emotion*, edited by Richard A. Shweder and Robert A. LeVine, 123–36. Cambridge: Cambridge University Press.

Giddens, Anthony. 1992. *The Transformation of Intimacy: Sexuality, Love, and Eroticism in Modern Societies.* Stanford, CA: Stanford University Press.

Gluckman, Max. 1963. "Papers in Honor of Melville J. Herskovits: Gossip and Scandal." *Current Anthropology* 4 (3): 307–16. https://doi.org/10.1086/200378.

Goffman, Erving. 1959. *The Presentation of Self in Everyday Life.* Garden City, NY: Doubleday.

———. 1981. *Forms of Talk.* Philadelphia: University of Pennsylvania Press.

Good, Byron J., and Mary-Jo Del Vecchio Good. 1994. "In the Subjunctive Mode: Epilepsy Narratives in Turkey." *Social Science and Medicine* 38 (6): 835–42. https://doi.org/10.1016/0277-9536(94)90155-4.

Goodkind, Daniel. 1995. "Vietnam's One-or-Two-Child Policy in Action." *Population and Development Review* 21 (1): 85–111.

Goodwin, Charles. 2007. "Participation, Stance and Affect in the Organization of Activities." *Discourse & Society* 18: 53–73.

Goodwin, Charles, and Marjorie Harness Goodwin. 2004. "Participation." In *A Companion to Linguistic Anthropology,* edited by Alessandro Duranti, 222–44. Malden, MA: Blackwell.

Goodwin, Marjorie Harness. 1990. *He-Said-She-Said: Talk as Social Organization among Black Children.* Bloomington: Indiana University Press.

———. 2006. *The Hidden Life of Girls: Games of Stance, Status, and Exclusion.* Malden, MA: Blackwell.

Goscha, Christopher. 2016. *Vietnam: A New History.* Boulder, CO: Basic Books.

Graeber, David. 2001. *Toward an Anthropological Theory of Value: The False Coin of Our Own Dreams.* New York: Palgrave.

———. 2012. *Debt: The First 5,000 Years.* Brooklyn, NY: Melville House.

Gregory, Christopher A. 2015. *Gifts and Commodities.* 2nd ed. Chicago: HAU Books.

Gusterson, Hugh. 1997. "Studying Up Revisited." *PoLAR: Political and Legal Anthropology Review* 20 (1): 114–19. https://doi.org/10.1525/pol.1997.20.1.114.

Haas, Bridget M. 2017. "Citizens-in-Waiting, Deportees-in-Waiting: Power, Temporality, and Suffering in the U.S. Asylum System." *Ethos* 45 (1): 75–97. https://doi.org/10.1111/etho.12150.

Hacking, Ian. 1995. *Rewriting the Soul: Multiple Personality and the Sciences of Memory.* Princeton, NJ: Princeton University Press.

Han, Clara. 2011. "Symptoms of Another Life: Time, Possibility, and Domestic Relations in Chile's Credit Economy." *Cultural Anthropology: Journal of the Society for Cultural Anthropology* 26 (1): 7–32. https://doi.org/10.1111/j.1548-1360.2010.01078.x.

———. 2012. *Life in Debt: Times of Care and Violence in Neoliberal Chile.* Berkeley: University of California Press.

Hannas, William C. 1997. *Asia's Orthographic Dilemma*. Honolulu: University of Hawaii Press.

Harms, Erik. 2011. *Saigon's Edge: On the Margins of Ho Chi Minh City*. Minneapolis: University of Minnesota Press.

———. 2016. *Luxury and Rubble: Civility and Dispossession in the New Saigon*. Oakland: University of California Press.

Hart, Keith. 1986. "Heads or Tails? Two Sides of the Coin." *Man* 21 (4): 637–56. https://doi.org/10.2307/2802901.

Hashimoto, Akiko. 2004. "Culture, Power, and the Discourse of Filial Piety in Japan: The Disempowerment of Youth and Its Social Consequences." In *Filial Piety: Practice and Discourse in Contemporary East Asia*, edited by Charlotte Ikels, 182–97. Stanford, CA: Stanford University Press.

Hayslip, Le Ly. 1990. *When Heaven and Earth Changed Places: A Vietnamese Woman's Journey from War to Peace*. New York: Plume.

Hefner, Robert W. 1998. "Multiple Modernities: Christianity, Islam, and Hinduism in a Globalizing Age." *Annual Review of Anthropology* 27: 83–104.

———. 2019. "Reading and Remembering Saba Mahmood: Islam, Ethics, and the Hermeneutics of Tradition." *Contemporary Islam* 13 (2): 139–53. https://doi.org/10.1007/s11562-018-424-z.

Held, Virginia. 2006. *The Ethics of Care: Personal, Political, and Global*. Oxford: University Press.

Hirsch, Jennifer S., and Holly Wardlow. 2006. *Modern Loves: The Anthropology of Romantic Courtship and Companionate Marriage*. Ann Arbor: University of Michigan Press.

Hirschman, Charles, and Nguyen Huu Minh. 2002. "Tradition and Change in Vietnamese Family Structure in the Red River Delta." *Journal of Marriage and Family* 64 (4): 1063–79.

Hoang, Kimberly Kay. 2015. *Dealing in Desire: Asian Ascendancy, Western Decline, and the Hidden Currencies of Global Sex Work*. Oakland: University of California Press.

Hoang, Lan Anh, and Brenda S. A. Yeoh. 2015. "'I'd Do It for Love or for Money': Vietnamese Women in Taiwan and the Social Construction of Female Migrant Sexuality." *Gender, Place and Culture* 22 (5): 591–607. https://doi.org/10.1080/0966369X.2014.885892.

Hollan, Douglas W. 1992. "Cross-Cultural Differences in the Self." *Journal of Anthropological Research* 48 (4): 283–300. https://doi.org/10.1086/jar.48.4.3630440.

———. 2000. "Constructivist Models of Mind, Contemporary Psychoanalysis, and the Development of Culture Theory." *American Anthropologist* 102 (3): 538–50. https://doi.org/10.1525/aa.2000.102.3.538.

Hollan, Douglas W., and Jane C. Wellenkamp. 1994. *Contentment and Suffering: Culture and Experience in Toraja*. New York: Columbia University Press.

Hong, Khuat Thu. 2004. "Sexual Harassment in Vietnam: A New Term for an Old Phenomenon." In *Gender Practices in Contemporary Vietnam*, edited by Lisa B. W. Drummond and Helle Rydstrøm, 117–36. Singapore: Singapore University Press.

Horton, Paul, and Helle Rydstrom. 2019. "Reshaping Boundaries: Family Politics and GLBTQ Resistance in Urban Vietnam." *Journal of GLBT Family Studies* 15 (3): 290–305. https://doi.org/10.1080/1550428X.2018.1518739.

Hoskins, Janet. 1993. "Violence, Sacrifice, and Divination: Giving and Taking Life in Eastern Indonesia." *American Ethnologist* 20 (1): 159–78. https://doi.org/10.1525/ae.1993.20.1.02a00080.

———. 2015. *The Divine Eye and the Diaspora: Vietnamese Syncretism Becomes Transpacific Caodaism*. Honolulu: University of Hawaii Press.

Howard, Kathryn. 2007. "Kinterm Usage and Hierarchy in Thai Children's Peer Groups." *Journal of Linguistic Anthropology* 17 (2): 204–30. https://doi.org/10.1525/jlin.2007.17.2.204.

———. 2012. "Language Socialization and Hierarchy." In *The Handbook of Language Socialization*, edited by Alessandro Duranti, Elinor Ochs, and Bambi B. Schieffelin, 341–64. Malden, MA: Wiley-Blackwell.

Hubert, Henri, and Marcel Mauss. [1913] 1964. *Sacrifice: Its Nature and Function*. Midway Reprints. Chicago: University of Chicago Press.

Husserl, Edmund. 2013. *Ideas: General Introduction to Pure Phenomenology*. New York: Routledge.

Ikels, Charlotte. 2004. *Filial Piety: Practice and Discourse in Contemporary East Asia*. Stanford, CA: Stanford University Press.

Illouz, Eva. 2012. *Why Love Hurts: A Sociological Explanation*. Malden, MA: Polity Press.

Jackson, Michael. 2002. *The Politics of Storytelling: Violence, Transgression, and Intersubjectivity*. Copenhagen: Museum Tusculanum Press.

Jamieson, Neil L. 1995. *Understanding Vietnam*. Berkeley: University of California Press.

Jankowiak, William R. 1995. *Romantic Passion: A Universal Experience?* New York: Columbia University Press.

———. 2008. *Intimacies: Love and Sex across Cultures*. New York: Columbia University Press.

Jenkins, Janis H. 2015. *Extraordinary Conditions: Culture and Experience in Mental Illness*. Oakland: University of California Press.

Keane, Webb. 2004. "Language and Religion." In *A Companion to Linguistic Anthropology*, edited by Alessandro Duranti, 431–48. Malden, MA: Blackwell.

———. 2016. *Ethical Life: Its Natural and Social Histories*. Princeton, NJ: Princeton University Press.

———. 2018. "Killing Animals: On the Violence of Sacrifice, the Hunt and the Butcher." *Anthropology of This Century* 22. http://aotcpress.com/articles /killing-animals-violence-sacrifice-hunt-butcher/.

Kenworthy, Nora J. 2014. "Global Health: The Debts of Gratitude." *Women's Studies Quarterly* 42 (1–2): 69–85. https://doi.org/10.1353/wsq.2014.0026.

Kipnis, Andrew B. 1997. *Producing Guanxi: Sentiment, Self, and Subculture in a North China Village*. Durham, NC: Duke University Press.

Kleinman, Arthur. 1999. "Experience and Its Moral Modes: Culture, Human Conditions, and Disorder." In *Tanner Lectures on Human Values*, 355–420. Salt Lake City: University of Utah Press.

Kulick, Don, and Bambi B. Schieffelin. 2006. "Language Socialization." In *A Companion to Linguistic Anthropology*, edited by Alessandro Duranti, 349–68. Malden, MA: Blackwell.

Kuper, Adam. 1973. *Anthropologists and Anthropology: The British School, 1922–1972*. New York: Pica Press.

———. 2018. "We Need to Talk about Kinship." *Anthropology of This Century* 23. http://aotcpress.com/articles/talk-kinship/.

Kwon, Heonik. 2006. *After the Massacre: Commemoration and Consolation in Ha My and My Lai*. Berkeley: University of California Press.

———. 2007. "The Dollarization of Vietnamese Ghost Money." *Journal of the Royal Anthropological Institute* 13 (1): 73–90. https://doi.org/10.1111/j.1467-9655.2007.00414.x.

———. 2008. *Ghosts of War in Vietnam*. Cambridge: Cambridge University Press.

Laidlaw, James. 2014. *The Subject of Virtue: An Anthropology of Ethics and Freedom*. Cambridge: Cambridge University Press.

Lainez, Nicolas. 2012. "Commodified Sexuality and Mother-Daughter Power Dynamics in the Mekong Delta." *Journal of Vietnamese Studies* 7 (1): 149–80. https://doi.org/10.1525/vs.2012.7.1.149.

———. 2018. "The Contested Legacies of Indigenous Debt Bondage in Southeast Asia: Indebtedness in the Vietnamese Sex Sector." *American Anthropologist* 120 (4): 671–83. https://doi.org/10.1111/aman.13105.

———. 2020. "Relational Work and Careers of Intimacy: Rethinking the Cultural Interpretation of the Sex Trade in Vietnam." *Sociological Review* (February): 1–15. https://doi.org/10.1177/0038026120903949.

Lamb, Sarah. 1997. "The Making and Unmaking of Persons: Notes on Aging and Gender in North India." *Ethos* 25 (3): 279–302.

———. 2000. *White Saris and Sweet Mangoes: Aging, Gender, and Body in North India*. Berkeley: University of California Press.

Lambek, Michael. 2007. "Sacrifice and the Problem of Beginning: Meditations from Sakalava Mythopraxis." *Journal of the Royal Anthropological Institute* 13 (1): 19–38. https://doi.org/10.1111/j.1467-9655.2007.00411.x.

———. 2008. "Value and Virtue." *Anthropological Theory* 8 (2): 133–57. https://doi.org/10.1177/1463499608090788.

———. 2010a. Introduction to *Ordinary Ethics: Anthropology, Language, and Action*, edited by Michael Lambek, 1–36. New York: Fordham University Press.

———, ed. 2010b. *Ordinary Ethics: Anthropology, Language, and Action*. New York: Fordham University Press.

———. 2010c. "Toward an Ethics of the Act." In *Ordinary Ethics: Anthropology, Language, and Action*, edited by Michael Lambek, 39–63. New York: Fordham University Press.

———. 2013. "The Continuous and Discontinuous Person: Two Dimensions of Ethical Life." *Journal of the Royal Anthropological Institute* 19 (4): 837–58. https://doi.org/10.1111/1467-9655.12073.

———. 2014. "Afterthoughts on Sacrifice." *Ethnos: Journal of Anthropology* 79 (3): 430–37. https://doi.org/10.1080/00141844.2012.747552.

———. 2015. *The Ethical Condition: Essays on Action, Person, and Value.* Chicago: University of Chicago Press.

Langer, Lawrence L. 1991. *Holocaust Testimonies: The Ruins of Memory.* New Haven, CT: Yale University Press.

Lentz, Christian C. 2019. *Contested Territory: Điện Biên Phủ and the Making of Northwest Vietnam.* Yale Agrarian Studies. New Haven, CT: Yale University Press.

León, Margarita, and Mauro Migliavacca. 2013. "Italy and Spain: Still the Case of Familistic Welfare Models?" *Population Review* 52 (1): 46–59. https://doi.org/10.1353/prv.2013.0001.

Leshkowich, Ann Marie. 2014a. *Essential Trade: Vietnamese Women in a Changing Marketplace.* Honolulu: University of Hawaii Press.

———. 2014b. "Standardized Forms of Vietnamese Selfhood: An Ethnographic Genealogy of Documentation." *American Ethnologist* 41 (1): 143–62. https://doi.org/10.1111/amet.12065.

———. 2017. "Kinship Secrets and Narrative Work: The Shifting Political Economy of Adoption in Vietnam." *Sojourn: Journal of Social Issues in Southeast Asia* 32 (2): 260–90.

Leshkowich, Ann Marie, and Christina Schwenkel. 2012. "Neoliberalism in Vietnam." *Positions: Asia Critique* 22: 379–667.

Lê Thị Thu. 2004. "The Vietnamese Family in the Cause of National Industrialization and Modernization." *Population, Family and Children* (September–October): 4–5.

Levinas, Emmanuel. 1985. *Ethics and Infinity: Conversations with Philippe Nemo.* Translated by Richard A. Cohen. Pittsburgh, PA: Duquesne University Press.

———. 1998. *Entre Nous: On Thinking-of-the-Other.* New York: Columbia University Press.

Levine, Nancy E. 2008. "Alternative Kinship, Marriage, and Reproduction." *Annual Review of Anthropology* 37 (1): 375–89. https://doi.org/10.1146 /annurev.anthro.37.081407.085120.

LeVine, Robert A. 1994. *Child Care and Culture: Lessons from Africa.* Cambridge: Cambridge University Press.

Levy, Robert I. 1973. *Tahitians: Mind and Experience in the Society Islands.* Chicago: University of Chicago Press.

Levy, Robert I., and Douglas W. Hollan. 1998. "Person-Centered Interviewing and Observation." In *Handbook of Methods in Cultural Anthropology,* 333–64. Walnut Creek, CA: AltaMira Press.

Li, Duanduan. 2017. "Pragmatic Socialization." In *Language Socialization,* edited by Patricia A. Duff and Stephen May, 1–14. Cham: Springer International Publishing.

Lincoln, Bruce. 1991. *Death, War, and Sacrifice: Studies in Ideology and Practice.* Chicago: University of Chicago Press.

Lindholm, Charles. 1998. "Love and Structure." *Theory, Culture & Society* 15: 243–63.

———. 2006. "Romantic Love and Anthropology." *Etnofoor* 19 (1): 5–21.

Lipman, Jana K. 2020. *In Camps: Vietnamese Refugees, Asylum Seekers, and Repatriates.* Oakland: University of California Press.

Luong, Hy Van. 1984. "'Brother' and 'Uncle': An Analysis of Rules, Structural Contradictions, and Meaning in Vietnamese Kinship." *American Anthropologist* 86 (2): 290–315. https://doi.org/10.1525/aa.1984.86.2.02a00050.

———. 1989. "Vietnamese Kinship: Structural Principles and the Socialist Transformation in Northern Vietnam." *Journal of Asian Studies* 48 (4): 741–56. https://doi.org/10.2307/2058112.

———. 1990. *Discursive Practices and Linguistic Meanings: The Vietnamese System of Person Reference.* Amsterdam: John Benjamins.

Lutz, Catherine. 1987. "Goals, Events, and Understanding in Ifaluk Emotion Theory." In *Cultural Models in Language and Thought,* edited by Dorothy Holland and Naomi Quinn, 290–312. Cambridge: Cambridge University Press.

———. 1988. *Unnatural Emotions: Everyday Sentiments on a Micronesian Atoll and Their Challenge to Western Theory.* Chicago: University of Chicago Press.

Mahmood, Saba. 2005. *Politics of Piety: The Islamic Revival and the Feminist Subject.* Princeton, NJ: Princeton University Press.

Malarney, Shaun Kingsley. 1996. "The Limits of 'State Functionalism' and the Reconstruction of Funerary Ritual in Contemporary Northern Vietnam." *American Ethnologist* 23 (3): 540–60.

———. 2001. "'The Fatherland Remembers Your Sacrifice': Commemorating War Dead in North Vietnam." In *The Country of Memory: Remaking the Past in Late Socialist Vietnam*, edited by Hue-Tam Ho Tai, 46–76. Berkeley: University of California Press.

———. 2002. *Culture, Ritual, and Revolution in Vietnam*. Honolulu: University of Hawaii Press.

Malinowski, Bronislaw. [1922] 2014. *Argonauts of the Western Pacific: An Account of Native Enterprise and Adventure in the Archipelagos of Melanesian New Guinea*. Routledge Classics. London: Routledge.

Marr, David G. 1981. *Vietnamese Tradition on Trial, 1920–1945*. Berkeley: University of California Press.

Martini, Edwin A. 2012. *Agent Orange: History, Science, and the Politics of Uncertainty*. Amherst: University of Massachusetts Press.

Marx, Karl. 2001. *The 18th Brumaire of Louis Bonaparte*. London: Electric Book Co.

Marx, Karl, and Friedrich Engels. 1978a. "The German Ideology: Part I." In *The Marx-Engels Reader*, 2nd ed., edited by Robert C. Tucker, 147–200. New York: Norton.

———. 1978b. "Manifesto of the Communist Party." In *The Marx-Engels Reader*, 2nd ed., edited by Robert C. Tucker, 473–500. New York: Norton.

Matsumoto, Yoshiko. 1989. "Politeness and Conversational Universals—Observations from Japanese." *Multilingua* 8 (2–3): 207–22. https://doi .org/10.1515/mult.1989.8.2–3.207.

Mattingly, Cheryl. 1998. *Healing Dramas and Clinical Plots: The Narrative Structure of Experience*. Cambridge: Cambridge University Press.

———. 2010. *The Paradox of Hope: Journeys through a Clinical Borderland*. Berkeley: University of California Press.

———. 2012. "Two Virtue Ethics and the Anthropology of Morality." *Anthropological Theory* 12 (2): 161–84. https://doi.org/10.1177/1463499612455284.

———. 2014a. *Moral Laboratories*. Berkeley: University of California Press.

———. 2014b. "The Moral Perils of a Superstrong Black Mother." *Ethos* 42 (1): 119–38. https://doi.org/10.1111/etho.12042.

Mattingly, Cheryl, and Jason Throop. 2018. "The Anthropology of Ethics and Morality." *Annual Review of Anthropology* 47: 475–92.

Mauss, Marcel. 1973. "Techniques of the Body." *Economy and Society* 2 (1): 70–88. https://doi.org/10.1080/03085147300000003.

———. [1925] 1990. *The Gift: The Form and Reason for Exchange in Archaic Societies*. London: Routledge.

Mayblin, Maya. 2012. "The Madness of Mothers: Agape Love and the Maternal Myth in Northeast Brazil." *American Anthropologist* 114 (2): 240–52. https://doi.org/10.1111/j.1548-1433.2012.01422.x.

————. 2014. "The Untold Sacrifice: The Monotony and Incompleteness of Self-Sacrifice in Northeast Brazil." *Ethnos* 79 (3): 342–64. https://doi.org/10.1080/00141844.2013.821513.

Mayblin, Maya, and Magnus Course. 2014. "The Other Side of Sacrifice: Introduction." *Ethnos* 79 (3): 307–19. https://doi.org/10.1080/00141844.2013.841720.

McHale, Shawn Frederick. 2004. *Print and Power: Confucianism, Communism, and Buddhism in the Making of Modern Vietnam.* Honolulu: University of Hawaii Press.

McIntosh, Janet. 2009. *The Edge of Islam: Power, Personhood, and Ethnoreligious Boundaries on the Kenya Coast.* Durham, NC: Duke University Press.

————. 2016. *Unsettled: Denial and Belonging among White Kenyans.* Oakland: University of California Press.

Merleau-Ponty, Maurice. 2008. *Phenomenology of Perception.* Translated by Colin Smith. Routledge Classics. London: Taylor and Francis.

Merry, Sally Engle. 1984. "Rethinking Gossip and Scandal." In *Toward a General Theory of Social Control,* edited by Donald Black, 271–302. New York: Academic Press.

Millar, Kathleen M. 2018. *Reclaiming the Discarded: Life and Labor on Rio's Garbage Dump.* Durham, NC: Duke University Press.

Morson, Gary Saul. 1994. *Narrative and Freedom: The Shadows of Time.* New Haven, CT: Yale University Press.

Mosse, George L. 1990. *Fallen Soldiers: Reshaping the Memory of the World Wars.* New York: Oxford University Press.

Muehlebach, Andrea Karin. 2012. *The Moral Neoliberal: Welfare and Citizenship in Italy.* Chicago: University of Chicago Press.

Murphy, Keith M. 2015. *Swedish Design: An Ethnography.* Ithaca, NY: Cornell University Press.

Nader, Laura. 1972. "Up the Anthropologist: Perspectives Gained from Studying Up." In *Reinventing Anthropology,* edited by Dell Hymes, 284–311. New York: Vintage Books.

Newton, Natalie. 2015. "Homosexuality and Transgenderism in Vietnam." In *Routledge Handbook of Sexuality Studies in East Asia,* edited by Mark McLelland and Vera Mackie, 255–67. New York: Routledge.

Ngo, Tam T. T. 2016. *The New Way: Protestantism and the Hmong in Vietnam.* Seattle: University of Washington Press.

Ngo Thi Ngan Binh. 2004. "The Confucian Four Feminine Virtues (Tu Duc): The Old versus the New—Ke Thua Versus Phat Huy." In *Gender Practices in Contemporary Vietnam,* edited by Lisa B. W. Drummond and Helle Rydstrøm, 47–73. Singapore: Singapore University Press.

Nguyen, Dat Manh. 2020. "Crafting a Buddhist Public: Urban Buddhism and Youth Aspirations in Late-Socialist Vietnam." PhD dissertation, Boston University.

Nguyễn, Du. 1983. *The Tale of Kiều: A Bilingual Edition of Truyện Kiều*. New Haven, CT: Yale University Press.

Nguyen Hong Son and Dao Thai Thi Xuan. 2008. "National Report of Vietnam: The Development and State of the Art of Adult Learning and Education." Ministry of Education and Training (MOET), Vietnam.

Nguyen, Lien-Hang T. 2012. *Hanoi's War: An International History of the War for Peace in Vietnam*. New Cold War History. Chapel Hill: University of North Carolina Press.

Nguyen, Ngoc Huy. 1998. "The Confucian Incursion into Vietnam." In *Confucianism and the Family*, edited by Walter H. Slote and George A. De Vos, 91–103. Albany: State University of New York Press.

Nguyen, Phuong An. 2007. "Relationships Based on Love and Relationships Based on Needs: Emerging Trends in Youth Sex Culture in Contemporary Urban Vietnam." *Modern Asian Studies* 41 (2): 287–313. https://doi.org/10.1017/S0026749X05002258.

Nguyen Thanh Binh. 2011. "Birth Rate and the Proportion of Vietnamese Women Having a Third Child in the Period 1999–2009." *International Journal of Social Sciences and Humanity* 1 (4): 256–60.

Nguyễn, Thị Thanh Bình. 2002. "The Diversity in Language Socialization: Gender and Social Strata in a North Vietnamese Village." PhD dissertation, University of Toronto.

Nguyen, Viet Thanh. 2015. *The Sympathizer*. New York: Grove Press.

Nguyen-Marshall, Van, Lisa B. Welch Drummond, and Danièle Bélanger, eds. 2012. *The Reinvention of Distinction: Modernity and the Middle Class in Urban Vietnam*. Dordrecht: Springer Netherlands.

Nguyễn-võ, Thu-Hương. 2008. *The Ironies of Freedom: Sex, Culture, and Neoliberal Governance in Vietnam*. Seattle: University of Washington Press.

Noddings, Nel. 2002. *Starting at Home: Caring and Social Policy*. Berkeley: University of California Press.

Nussbaum, Martha C. 1986. *The Fragility of Goodness: Luck and Ethics in Greek Tragedy and Philosophy*. Cambridge: Cambridge University Press.

Ochs, Elinor. 1988. *Culture and Language Development: Language Acquisition and Language Socialization in a Samoan Village*. Cambridge: Cambridge University Press.

———. 2007. "Narrative Lessons." In *A Companion to Linguistic Anthropology*, edited by Alessandro Duranti, 269–89. Malden, MA: Wiley.

———. 2012. "Experiencing Language." *Anthropological Theory* 12 (2): 142–60. https://doi.org/10.1177/1463499612454088.

Ochs, Elinor, and Lisa Capps. 2001. *Living Narrative: Creating Lives in Everyday Storytelling*. Cambridge, MA: Harvard University Press.

Ochs, Elinor, and Tamar Kremer-Sadlik. 2013. *Fast-Forward Family: Home, Work, and Relationships in Middle-Class America*. Berkeley: University of California Press.

———. 2015. "How Postindustrial Families Talk." *Annual Review of Anthropology* 44 (1): 87–103. https://doi.org/10.1146/annurev-anthro-102214-014027.

Ochs, Elinor, and Bambi B. Schieffelin. 1984. "Language Acquisition and Socialization: Three Developmental Stories and Their Implications." In *Culture Theory: Essays on Mind, Self, and Emotion*, edited by Robert A. LeVine and Richard A. Shweder, 276–320. Cambridge: Cambridge University Press.

———. 2017. "Language Socialization: An Historical Overview." In *Language Socialization*, edited by Patricia A. Duff and Stephen May. Encyclopedia of Language and Education. Cham: Springer International Publishing.

Ochs, Elinor, and Merav Shohet. 2006. "The Cultural Structuring of Mealtime Socialization." *New Directions for Child and Adolescent Development*, no. 111: 35–49.

Ochs, Elinor, Merav Shohet, Belinda Campos, and Margaret Beck. 2010. "Coming Together at Dinner." In *Workplace Flexibility: Realigning 20th-Century Jobs for a 21st-Century Workforce*, edited by Kathleen Christensen and Barbara Schneider, 57–70. Ithaca, NY: Cornell University Press.

Ortner, Sherry B. 1974. "Is Female to Male as Nature Is to Culture?" In *Woman, Culture, and Society*, edited by Michelle Zimbalist Rosaldo and Louise Lamphere, 67–87. Stanford, CA: Stanford University Press.

———. 1996. *Making Gender: The Politics and Erotics of Culture*. Boston: Beacon Press.

———. 2005. "Subjectivity and Cultural Critique." *Anthropological Theory* 5 (1): 31–52. https://doi.org/10.1177/1463499605050867.

———. 2010. "Access: Reflections on Studying up in Hollywood." *Ethnography* 11 (2): 211–33. https://doi.org/10.1177/1466138110362006.

Padilla, Mark B., Jennifer S. Hirsch, and Miguel Munoz-Laboy, eds. 2007. *Love and Globalization: Transformations of Intimacy in the Contemporary World*. Nashville, TN: Vanderbilt University Press.

Parla, Ayşe. 2019. *Precarious Hope: Migration and the Limits of Belonging in Turkey*. Stanford, CA: Stanford University Press.

Parry, Jonathan P., and Maurice Bloch. 1989. "Introduction: Money and the Morality of Exchange." In *Money and the Morality of Exchange*, edited by Maurice Bloch and Jonathan P. Parry, 1–32. Cambridge: Cambridge University Press.

Pashigian, Melissa J. 2002. "Conceiving the 'Happy Family': Infertility, Gender and Reproductive Experience in Northern Vietnam." PhD dissertation, University of California, Los Angeles.

———. 2009. "The Womb, Infertility, and the Vicissitudes of Kin-Relatedness in Vietnam." *Journal of Vietnamese Studies* 4 (2): 34–68. https://doi.org/10.1525/vs.2009.4.2.34.

Paugh, Amy. 2012. "Local Theories of Child Rearing." In *The Handbook of Language Socialization*, edited by Alessandro Duranti, Elinor Ochs, and Bambi B. Schieffelin, 150–68. Malden, MA: Wiley-Blackwell.

Paxson, Heather. 2007. "A Fluid Mechanics of Erotas and Aghape: Family Planning and Maternal Consumption in Contemporary Greece." In *Love and Globalization: Transformations of Intimacy in the Contemporary World*, edited by Mark Padilla, Jennifer S. Hirsch, and Miguel Munoz-Laboy, 120–38. Nashville, TN: Vanderbilt University Press.

Peletz, Michael. 1995. "Kinship Studies in Late Twentieth-Century Anthropology." *Annual Review of Anthropology* 24: 343–72.

Pettus, Ashley. 2003. *Between Sacrifice and Desire: National Identity and the Governing of Femininity in Vietnam*. New York: Routledge.

Phinney, Harriet M. 2008. "Objects of Affection: Vietnamese Discourses on Love and Emancipation." *Positions: East Asia Cultures Critique* 16 (2): 329–58.

Pinto, Sarah. 2008. *Where There Is No Midwife: Birth and Loss in Rural India*. New York: Berghahn Books.

———. 2014. *Daughters of Parvati: Women and Madness in Contemporary India*. Philadelphia: University of Pennsylvania Press.

Povinelli, Elizabeth A. 2006. *The Empire of Love: Toward a Theory of Intimacy, Genealogy, and Carnality*. Public Planet Books. Durham, NC: Duke University Press.

Rebhun, Linda-Anne. 1999. *The Heart Is Unknown Country: Love in the Changing Economy of Northeast Brazil*. Stanford, CA: Stanford University Press.

Ricoeur, Paul. 1980. "Narrative Time." *Critical Inquiry* 7 (1): 169–90.

———. 1990. *Time and Narrative*. Vol. 3. Translated by Kathleen Blamey and David Pellauer. Chicago: University of Chicago Press.

Robbins, Joel. 2007a. "Between Reproduction and Freedom: Morality, Value, and Radical Cultural Change." *Ethnos* 72 (3): 293–314. https://doi.org/10.1080/00141840701576919.

———. 2007b. "Continuity Thinking and the Problem of Christian Culture: Belief, Time, and the Anthropology of Christianity." *Current Anthropology* 48 (1): 5–38. https://doi.org/10.1086/508690.

———. 2016. "What Is the Matter with Transcendence? On the Place of Religion in the New Anthropology of Ethics." *Journal of the Royal Anthropological Institute* 22 (4): 767–81. https://doi.org/10.1111/1467-9655.12494_1.

Robertson Smith, William. [1889] 1969. *Lectures on the Religion of the Semites: The Fundamental Institutions*. 3rd ed. New York: Ktav Publishing House.

Rosaldo, Renato. 1989. *Culture and Truth: The Remaking of Social Analysis.* Boston: Beacon Press.

Rydstrøm, Helle. 2003a. *Embodying Morality: Growing up in Rural Northern Vietnam.* Honolulu: University of Hawaii Press.

———. 2003b. "Encountering 'Hot' Anger: Domestic Violence in Contemporary Vietnam." *Violence Against Women* 9 (6): 676–97. https://doi.org/10.1177 /1077801203009006004.

———. 2006. "Sexual Desires and 'Social Evils': Young Women in Rural Vietnam." *Gender, Place and Culture* 13 (3): 283–302. https://doi.org/10.1080 /09663690600701053.

Sahlins, Marshall. 1974. *Stone Age Economics.* London: Tavistock Publications.

———. 2013. *What Kinship Is—And Is Not.* Chicago: University of Chicago Press.

Salemink, Oscar, and Nguyễn Tuấn Anh. 2019. "The Pursuit of Happiness in Vietnam." In *Regimes of Happiness: Comparative and Historical Studies,* edited by Yuri Contreras-Vejar, Joanna Tice Jen, and Brian S. Turner, 201–18. London: Anthem Press.

Samuels, Annemarie. 2018. "'This Path Is Full of Thorns': Narrative, Subjunctivity, and HIV in Indonesia." *Ethos* 46 (1): 95–114. https://doi.org/10.1111 /etho.12194.

———. 2019a. *After the Tsunami: Disaster Narratives and the Remaking of Everyday Life in Aceh.* Honolulu: University of Hawaii Press.

———. 2019b. "Narrative Navigation: HIV and (Good) Care in Aceh, Indonesia." *Culture, Medicine, and Psychiatry* 43 (1): 116–33. https://doi.org/10.1007 /s11013-018-9602-y.

Schegloff, Emanuel A. 1986. "The Routine as Achievement." *Human Studies* 9 (2): 111–151. https://doi.org/10.1007/BF00148124.

Schegloff, Emanuel A., and Harvey Sacks. 1973. "Opening up Closings." *Semiotica* 8 (4): 289–327. https://doi.org/10.1515/semi.1973.8.4.289.

Scheper-Hughes, Nancy. 1995. "The Primacy of the Ethical: Propositions for a Militant Anthropology." *Current Anthropology* 36 (3): 409–40. https://doi .org/10.1086/204378.

Schieffelin, Bambi B. 1990. *The Give and Take of Everyday Life: Language Socialization of Kaluli Children.* Cambridge: Cambridge University Press.

Schieffelin, Bambi B., and Elinor Ochs. 1986. "Language Socialization." *Annual Review of Anthropology* 15: 163–91.

Schieffelin, Bambi B., Kathryn Ann Woolard, and Paul V. Kroskrity. 1998. *Language Ideologies: Practice and Theory.* Oxford Studies in Anthropological Linguistics 16. New York: Oxford University Press.

Schielke, Samuli. 2009. "Ambivalent Commitments: Troubles of Morality, Religiosity and Aspiration among Young Egyptians." *Journal of Religion in Africa* 39 (2): 158–85. https://doi.org/10.1163/157006609X427814.

Schneider, David M. 1984. *A Critique of the Study of Kinship*. Ann Arbor: University of Michigan Press.

Schrift, Alan D. 1997. *The Logic of the Gift: Toward an Ethic of Generosity*. New York: Routledge.

Schutz, Alfred. 1967. *The Phenomenology of the Social World*. Evanston, IL: Northwestern University Press.

Schwenkel, Christina. 2009. *The American War in Contemporary Vietnam: Transnational Remembrance and Representation*. Bloomington: Indiana University Press.

———. 2013. "Post / Socialist Affect: Ruination and Reconstruction of the Nation in Urban Vietnam." *Cultural Anthropology* 28 (2): 252–77. https://doi.org/10.1111/cuan.12003.

———. 2015. "Spectacular Infrastructure and Its Breakdown in Socialist Vietnam." *American Ethnologist* 42 (3): 520–34. https://doi.org/10.1111/amet.12145.

———. 2018. "Religious Reassemblage and Late Socialist Planning in Urban Vietnam." *Journal of the American Academy of Religion* 86 (2): 526–53. https://doi.org/10.1093/jaarel/lfx067.

Schwenkel, Christina, and Ann Marie Leshkowich. 2012. "How Is Neoliberalism Good to Think Vietnam? How Is Vietnam Good to Think Neoliberalism?" *Positions: East Asia Cultures Critique* 20 (2): 379–401.

Scott, Steffanie, and Thi Kim Chuyen Truong. 2007. "Gender Research in Vietnam: Traditional Approaches and Emerging Trajectories." *Women's Studies International Forum* 30 (3): 243–53. https://doi.org/10.1016/j.wsif.2007.03.006.

Seligman, Adam B., Robert P. Weller, Michael J. Puett, and Bennett Simon. 2008. *Ritual and Its Consequences: An Essay on the Limits of Sincerity*. Oxford: Oxford University Press.

Shipton, Parker. 2014. "Trusting and Transcending." *Current Anthropology* 55 (S9): S51–S61. https://doi.org/10.1086/676593.

Shohet, Merav. 2007. "Narrating Anorexia: 'Full' and 'Struggling' Genres of Recovery." *Ethos* 35 (3): 344–82.

———. 2010. "Silence and Sacrifice: Intergenerational Displays of Virtue and Devotion in Central Vietnam." PhD dissertation, University of California, Los Angeles.

———. 2013. "Everyday Sacrifice and Language Socialization in Vietnam: The Power of a Respect Particle." *American Anthropologist* 115 (2): 203–17. https://doi.org/10.1111/aman.12004.

———. 2017. "Troubling Love: Gender, Class, and Sideshadowing the 'Happy Family' in Vietnam." *Ethos* 45 (4): 555–76. https://doi.org/10.1111/etho.12177.

———. 2018a. "Beyond the Clinic? Eluding a Medical Diagnosis of Anorexia through Narrative." *Transcultural Psychiatry* 55 (4): 495–515. https://doi .org/10.1177/1363461517722467.

———. 2018b. "Two Deaths and a Funeral: Ritual Inscriptions' Affordances for Mourning and Moral Personhood in Vietnam." *American Ethnologist* 45 (1): 60–73. https://doi.org/10.1111/amet.12599.

Sidnell, Jack, and Merav Shohet. 2013. "The Problem of Peers in Vietnamese Interaction." *Journal of the Royal Anthropological Institute* 19 (3): 618–38. https://doi.org/10.1111/1467-9655.12053.

Sidnell, Jack, and Tanya Stivers. 2012. *The Handbook of Conversation Analysis*. Malden, MA: Wiley-Blackwell.

Singer, Irving. 2009. *Philosophy of Love: A Partial Summing-Up*. Cambridge, MA: MIT Press.

Singh, Bhrigupati. 2011. "Agonistic Intimacy and Moral Aspiration in Popular Hinduism: A Study in the Political Theology of the Neighbor." *American Ethnologist* 38 (3): 430–50. https://doi.org/10.1111/j.1548-1425.2011 .01315.x.

Slote, Walter H., and George A. De Vos. 1998. *Confucianism and the Family*. Albany: State University of New York Press.

Small, Ivan V. 2018. *Currencies of Imagination: Channeling Money and Chasing Mobility in Vietnam*. Ithaca, NY: Cornell University Press.

Stalford, Maria. 2019. "Connecting Rural Patients with Urban Hospitals across the Cancer Care Continuum: A View from Vietnam on a Global Problem." In *Negotiating Structural Vulnerability in Cancer Control*, edited by Julie Armin, Nancy J. Burke, and Laura Eichelberger, 117–40. Albuquerque: University of New Mexico Press.

Stevenson, Lisa. 2014. *Life Beside Itself: Imagining Care in the Canadian Arctic*. Oakland: University of California Press.

Stonington, Scott D. 2011. "Facing Death, Gazing Inward: End-of-Life and the Transformation of Clinical Subjectivity in Thailand." *Culture, Medicine, and Psychiatry* 35 (2): 113–33. https://doi.org/10.1007/s11013-011-9210-6.

———. 2012. "On Ethical Locations: The Good Death in Thailand, Where Ethics Sit in Places." *Social Science & Medicine* 75 (5): 836–44. https://doi .org/10.1016/j.socscimed.2012.03.045.

Strathern, Marilyn. 2016. *Before and after Gender*. Chicago: HAU Books.

Tai, Hue-Tam Ho. 1992. *Radicalism and the Origins of the Vietnamese Revolution*. Cambridge, MA: Harvard University Press.

———. 2001. *The Country of Memory: Remaking the Past in Late Socialist Vietnam*. Berkeley: University of California Press.

Taylor, Keith Weller. 1983. *The Birth of Vietnam*. Berkeley: University of California Press.

———. 2013. *A History of the Vietnamese*. Cambridge: Cambridge University Press.

Thomas, Lynn M., and Jennifer Cole. 2009. "Thinking through Love in Africa." In *Love in Africa*, edited by Jennifer Cole and Lynn M. Thomas, 1–30. Chicago: University of Chicago Press.

Thompson, Laurence C. 1965. *A Vietnamese Grammar*. Seattle: University of Washington Press.

Throop, C. Jason. 2010. *Suffering and Sentiment: Exploring the Vicissitudes of Experience and Pain in Yap*. Berkeley: University of California Press.

———. 2012. "On the Varieties of Empathic Experience: Tactility, Mental Opacity, and Pain in Yap." *Medical Anthropology Quarterly* 26 (3): 408–30. https://doi.org/10.1111/j.1548-1387.2012.01225.x.

———. 2014. "Moral Moods." *Ethos* 42 (1): 65–83. https://doi.org/10.1111/etho.12039.

———. 2015. "Ambivalent Happiness and Virtuous Suffering." *HAU: Journal of Ethnographic Theory* 5 (3): 45–68. https://doi.org/10.14318/hau5.3.004.

———. 2017. "Despairing Moods: Worldly Attunements and Permeable Personhood in Yap." *Ethos* 45 (2): 199–215. https://doi.org/10.1111/etho.12163.

Timmermans, Stefan, and Mara Buchbinder. 2010. "Patients-in-Waiting: Living between Sickness and Health in the Genomics Era." *Journal of Health and Social Behavior* 51 (4): 408–23. https://doi.org/10.1177/0022146510386794.

Tolstoy, Leo. 2014. *Anna Karenina*. New Haven, CT: Yale University Press.

Tran, Allen L. 2015. "Rich Sentiments and the Cultural Politics of Emotion in Postreform Ho Chi Minh City, Vietnam." *American Anthropologist* 117 (3): 480–92. https://doi.org/10.1111/aman.12291.

———. 2017. "Neurasthenia, Generalized Anxiety Disorder, and the Medicalization of Worry in a Vietnamese Psychiatric Hospital." *Medical Anthropology Quarterly* 31 (2): 198–217. https://doi.org/10.1111/maq.12297.

———. 2018. "The Anxiety of Romantic Love in Ho Chi Minh City, Vietnam." *Journal of the Royal Anthropological Institute* 24 (3): 512–31. https://doi.org/10.1111/1467-9655.12858.

Tran, Ngoc Angie. 2004. "What's Women's Work? Male Negotiations and Gender Reproduction in the Vietnamese Garment Industry." In *Gender Practices in Contemporary Vietnam*, edited by Lisa B. W. Drummond and Helle Rydstrøm, 210–35. Singapore: Singapore University Press.

Trawick, Margaret. 1990. *Notes on Love in a Tamil Family*. Berkeley: University of California Press.

Tronto, Joan C. 1993. *Moral Boundaries: A Political Argument for an Ethic of Care*. New York: Routledge.

Trương, Như Tảng. 1986. *A Vietcong Memoir*. New York: Vintage Books.

Tu, Wei-ming. 1986. "On Neo-Confucianism and Human Relatedness." In *Religion and the Family in East Asia*, edited by George A. De Vos and Takao Sofue, 111–25. Berkeley: University of California Press.

Turner-Gottschang, Karen. 1998. *Even the Women Must Fight: Memories of War from North Vietnam*. New York: Wiley.

Tylor, Edward Burnett. [1871] 2009. *Primitive Culture: Researches into the Development of Mythology, Philosophy, Religion, Language, Art, and Custom*. Whitefish, MT: Kessinger Publications.

Uesugi, Tak. 2016. "Toxic Epidemics: Agent Orange Sickness in Vietnam and the United States." *Medical Anthropology* 35 (6): 464–76. https://doi.org/10.1080/01459740.2015.1089438.

Valeri, Valerio. 1985. *Kingship and Sacrifice: Ritual and Society in Ancient Hawaii*. Chicago: University of Chicago Press.

Venkatesan, Soumhya, Jeanette Edwards, Rane Willerslev, Elizabeth Povinelli, and Perveez Mody. 2011. "The Anthropological Fixation with Reciprocity Leaves No Room for Love: 2009 Meeting of the Group for Debates in Anthropological Theory." *Critique of Anthropology* 31 (3): 210–50. https://doi.org/10.1177/0308275X11409732.

Vigh, Henrik. 2009. "Motion Squared: A Second Look at the Concept of Social Navigation." *Anthropological Theory* 9 (4): 419–38. https://doi.org/10.1177/1463499609356044.

Wahlberg, Ayo. 2006. "Bio-Politics and the Promotion of Traditional Herbal Medicine in Vietnam." *Health* 10 (2): 123–47. https://doi.org/10.1177/1363459306061784.

Wardlow, Holly. 2004. "Anger, Economy, and Female Agency: Problematizing 'Prostitution' and 'Sex Work' among the Huli of Papua New Guinea." *Signs* 29 (4): 1017–40. https://doi.org/10.1086/382628.

Wardlow, Holly, and Jennifer S. Hirsch. 2006. Introduction to *Modern Loves: The Anthropology of Romantic Courtship and Companionate Marriage*, edited by Jennifer S. Hirsch and Holly Wardlow, 1–31. Ann Arbor: University of Michigan Press.

Weiss, Erica. 2014. *Conscientious Objectors in Israel: Citizenship, Sacrifice, Trials of Fealty*. Philadelphia: University of Pennsylvania Press.

Weller, Robert P. 2017. "Salvaging Silence: Exile, Death and the Anthropology of the Unknowable." *Anthropology of This Century* 19. http://aotcpress.com/articles/salvaging-silence/.

Weller, Robert P., and Keping Wu. 2017. "On the Boundaries between Good and Evil: Constructing Multiple Moralities in China." *Journal of Asian Studies* 76 (1): 47–67. https://doi.org/10.1017/S0021911816001182.

Werner, Jayne. 2009. *Gender, Household and State in Post-Revolutionary Vietnam*. London: Routledge.

Willen, Sarah S. 2014. "Plotting a Moral Trajectory, Sans Papiers: Outlaw Motherhood as Inhabitable Space of Welcome." *Ethos* 42 (1): 84–100. https://doi.org /10.1111/etho.12040.

———. 2019. *Fighting for Dignity: Migrant Lives at Israel's Margins*. Philadelphia: University of Pennsylvania Press.

Willerslev, Rane. 2009. "The Optimal Sacrifice: A Study of Voluntary Death among the Siberian Chukchi." *American Ethnologist* 36 (4): 693–704. https://doi.org/10.1111/j.1548-1425.2009.01204.x.

Williams, Bernard A. O. 1981. *Moral Luck: Philosophical Papers, 1973–1980*. Cambridge: Cambridge University Press.

Wisensale, Steven K. 1999. "Marriage and Family Law in a Changing Vietnam." *Journal of Family Issues* 20 (5): 602–16. https://doi.org/10.1177 /019251399020005002.

Wolf, Margery. 1968. *The House of Lim: A Study of a Chinese Farm Family*. New York: Appleton-Century-Crofts.

———. 1972. *Women and the Family in Rural Taiwan*. Stanford, CA: Stanford University Press.

Wool, Zoë H. 2015. *After War: The Weight of Life at Walter Reed*. Durham, NC: Duke University Press.

Woolard, Kathryn A., and Bambi B. Schieffelin. 1994. "Language Ideology." *Annual Review of Anthropology* 23: 55–82.

World Bank. 2020. "Fertility Rate, Total (Births per Woman) | Data." https://data.worldbank.org/indicator/SP.DYN.TFRT.IN.

Yan, Yunxiang. 1996. *The Flow of Gifts: Reciprocity and Social Networks in a Chinese Village*. Stanford, CA: Stanford University Press.

———. 2003. *Private Life under Socialism: Love, Intimacy, and Family Change in a Chinese Village, 1949–1999*. Stanford, CA: Stanford University Press.

———. 2009. *The Individualization of Chinese Society*. Oxford: Berg.

———. 2016. "Intergenerational Intimacy and Descending Familism in Rural North China." *American Anthropologist* 118 (2): 244–57. https://doi .org/10.1111/aman.12527.

Yang, Mayfair Mei-Hui. 1994. *Gifts, Favors, and Banquets: The Art of Social Relationships in China*. Ithaca, NY: Cornell University Press.

Young, Allan. 1995. *The Harmony of Illusions: Inventing Post-Traumatic Stress Disorder*. Princeton, NJ: Princeton University Press.

Zerubavel, Yael. 2006. "Patriotic Sacrifice and the Burden of Memory in Israeli Secular National Hebrew Culture." In *Memory and Violence in the Middle East and North Africa*, edited by S. Makdisi and Paul A. Silverstein, 77–100. Bloomington: University of Indiana Press.

Zierler, David. 2011. *The Invention of Ecocide: Agent Orange, Vietnam, and the Scientists Who Changed the Way We Think about the Environment*. Athens: University of Georgia Press.

Zigon, Jarrett. 2008. *Morality: An Anthropological Perspective*. Oxford: Berg.

———. 2010. "Moral and Ethical Assemblages." *Anthropological Theory* 10 (1-2): 3-15. https://doi.org/10.1177/1463499610370520.

———. 2011. *HIV Is God's Blessing: Rehabilitating Morality in Neoliberal Russia*. Berkeley: University of California Press.

———. 2013. "On Love: Remaking Moral Subjectivity in Postrehabilitation Russia." *American Ethnologist* 40 (1): 201-15. https://doi.org/10.1111/amet .12014.

———. 2014. "Attunement and Fidelity: Two Ontological Conditions for Morally Being-in-the-World." *Ethos* 42 (1): 16-30. https://doi.org/10.1111/etho.12036.

———. 2019. *A War on People: Drug User Politics and a New Ethics of Community*. Oakland: University of California Press.

Index

ritual oratory, 183–84
Robbins, Joel, 17, 115
Romanized script *(chữ quốc ngữ)*, 63
Rosaldo, Renato, 52
Rydstrøm, Helle, 13

Saigon, Vietnam. *See* Ho Chi Minh City, Vietnam (HCMC)
Samuels, Annemarie, 127
Schegloff, Emanuel, 17
Schieffelin, Bambi B., 213n33
Schneider, David, 115
Schutz, Alfred, 81, 84
Segal, Lotte Buch, 189
Shohet, Merav, 90, 194
sideshadowing logics and narratives
  and ambiguities and contradictions, 23, 109, 197, 198–99, 203, 208n23, 208n24
  and asymmetrically reciprocal love, 182–83, 185, 187–88
  and care narratives, 144–46, 146–47, 148–49, 181
  described, 18, 101–2
  and everyday ethics, 158
  in family narratives, 176–79
  and interpretation of family conflicts, 147, 149
  and interpretation of love narratives, 115
  and patriotic narratives, 60
  and scope and structure of study, 20, 33, 102
  and "thick" ethnography, 190
  and troubling dichotomies, 23, 190, 197
Sidnell, Jack, 90
Smith, William Robertson, 75
"social evils" discourse, 12, 108, 163, 179, 182
socialism, 62, 104, 170, 217n15. *See also* Communist Revolution
socialist autobiographical statements *(lý lịch)*, 46, 47, 57
sociocentric societies, 218n26
Sơn Mỹ (Mỹ Lai), 6
Sons and Lovers (Lawrence), 176
soothsayers, 106
Sophocles, 198
South Vietnam, 25
spirits and ghosts. *See* ancestor worship/veneration
Stevenson, Lisa, 184
Stonington, Scott, 134, 136
subjectivity

care as intersubjective practice, 128
  and empathy, 224n19
  and ethical/moral cultivation through bodily discipline, 69, 74, 91, 93, 96
  and intersectional moral selves, 201, 202, 216n5, 216n11
  and intersubjectivity in ritual, 82
  and linguistic anthropology, 19, 74
  and love as moral process, 100–101, 216n5
  and sacrifice, 74
  and scope and structure of study, 13, 30–31, 37
  and socialization of children, 91, 93, 95–96, 98
  subjectification, 19, 74, 95–98, 212n10
  and thick ethnography, 201–2
  and *tình cảm*, 211n2
  and Vietnam's political-economic transformations, 96
suffering
  and caregiving responsibilities, 123, 125–26, 129, 132, 137, 140–43, 144–45, 149–50, 157–59
  and history of Vietnam, 23–27
  and impact of Vietnamese development, 65–66
  and narratives of postwar progress in Vietnam, 41, 67–69
  and narrative structures, 46
  and production of cohesion and continuity, 10
  and retirement benefits under *đổi mới*, 39
  and Vietnamese pride, 62
  and wartime struggles, 47–52, 52–56, 56–61, 68, 209n3, 213n18
  See also *hy sinh* (sacrifice); inequality
superstition, 62, 103, 106, 114, 193, 195, 227n9
syncretism, 23, 25, 195–96, 209n47

taxation, 64
Tây Sơn rebellion, 24
teleological narratives, 18, 47, 60–61, 101, 109, 158, 179, 207n20
Thailand, 2, 61, 86
thick ethnography, 188–91
Thomas, Lynn, 178
Three Submissions *(Tam Tòng)*, 104
Throop, Jason, 187, 224n19, 225n29
tình cảm (loving sentiment)
  and asymmetrical reciprocity, 20–23, 95, 145, 193, 227n13

Founded in 1893,
UNIVERSITY OF CALIFORNIA PRESS
publishes bold, progressive books and journals
on topics in the arts, humanities, social sciences,
and natural sciences—with a focus on social
justice issues—that inspire thought and action
among readers worldwide.

The UC PRESS FOUNDATION
raises funds to uphold the press's vital role
as an independent, nonprofit publisher, and
receives philanthropic support from a wide
range of individuals and institutions—and from
committed readers like you. To learn more, visit
ucpress.edu/supportus.